Advance Praise for
*Wake 'em Up: How to Use Humor and Other Professional Techniques to Create **Alarmingly** Good Business Presentations*

"*Wake 'em Up* teaches you to be irresistible as a presenter."
Mark Victor Hansen,
Co-Author of the #1 New York Times
Best-selling series, *Chicken Soup for the Soul*

"Mastering the skills in Tom's book will virtually guarantee that you will always be in demand as a speaker."
Dottie Walters, President,
Walters International Speakers Bureau,
Co-Author *Speak and Grow Rich*

"At Hawaiian Tropic we believe that fun and excitement keep our corporate staff and distributors productive. Tom can teach you how to create this excitement every time you address a group."
Ron Rice, Owner and founder,
Hawaiian Tropic/Tanning Research Labs., Inc.

"Tom's materials will cut five years off a speaker's learning curve."
Cavett Robert, Founder and chairman emeritus,
National Speakers Association

"When I recruited Tom Antion to play for the West Virginia University Mountaineers in the early 70's, he was an exciting high school football player. It doesn't surprise me that he's turned into such an exciting professional speaker. His Book *Wake 'em Up* will teach you how to create excitement when you speak to any size group. I use some of his tips in my own speaking engagements."
Bobby Bowden, Head Football Coach
Florida State University

"In *Wake 'em Up,* Tom Antion teaches us how to get our message across, do it with humor, and keep the audience awake all at the same time. That's great, although I've learned through experience that when I'm not doing 1 and 2, I prefer that the audience doze off.—It makes my getaway easier."

Gene Perrett,
Author and head comedy writer for Bob Hope

"Tom Antion has mastered the art of communicating in an interesting and humorous fashion. His book *Wake 'em Up* is a "how to" and what "not to do" for speakers. It's a great read for presenters who have been in front of audiences for years as well as those folks just starting out. Hat's off to Tom for a job well done!"

David Kliman, President
Meeting Professionals International

"This book gives you advanced presentation skills and humor training that would otherwise take you years to learn. It's an absolute must-read for anyone who wants to be a fantastic presenter."

Patricia Fripp, CSP, CPAE, Past president & first
woman president of the National Speakers Association

"We live in a world of entertainment. If you have hard hitting business content and need a way to inject appropriate humor to keep people with you, this is the book that will teach you how to do it."

Robert W. Pike, CSP "The Trainer's Trainer"
Editor Creative Training Techniques Newsletter
President, Creative Training Techniques International, Inc.

"Anyone who has ever been in one of Tom Antion's audiences would attest that Tom clearly *practices what he preaches!* In this informative and enjoyable book, you'll find dozens of practical tips, tools, and techniques that will show you that *learning can be fun!* Enjoy *Wake 'em Up.* I know you will."

Edward E. Scannell, CMP, CSP
Co-Author *Games Trainers Play* series
Past National President, American Society of
Training and Development, Meeting Professionals
International, and the National Speakers Association

"Wake 'em Up provides solid tips for all those who want to perfect their presentation skills. Tom shares the secrets of top professionals on how to convey business information with maximum excitement and good humor. I've written 52 books. I wish I could say I wrote this one. It's a winner!"

Larry Wilde, Author, and motivational humorist
Director, The Carmel Institute of Humor

"In my 25 years with Marriott, I have seen countless presentations from all types of potential vendors, executives, and trainers. If these people had used Tom's book *Wake 'em Up* as their guide, their presentations would undoubtably have made a bigger impact on me."

Roger J. Dow, Vice President,
General Sales Manager, Marriott Lodging

"Wake 'em Up is a great book for the novice and old pro alike. I've been on the circuit for over 20 years and gleaned a number of valuable tips. More importantly, the book leaves "nothing to chance" for a presenter or speaker wishing to enhance their skills and deliver humor like it should be done. This book is a must."

Floyd Wickman, CSP, CPAE
Speaker and author of *Mentoring: A Guide for Mentors and Proteges,* Owner of the world-renowned *Sweathog* Real Estate Seminars

"Las Vegas, the *Community of the Future* was built on excitement. To help people in your community or organization create dreams and visions of a better tomorrow you must be able to instill the same kind of excitement in them. Tom's book teaches you the art AND science of doing just that. His tips have helped me enormously."

John O'Reilly, Chairman of the Board of Trustees, Greater Las Vegas Chamber of Commerce, Chairman/CEO, Keefer, O'Reilly, Ferrario & Lubbers, Attorneys. and O'Reilly Gaming Group providing consultation, development, and new product representation.

Other Educational Materials by Tom Antion

VIDEOTAPES
Make 'em Laugh: How To Use Humor in Presentations

AUDIOTAPES
Make 'em Laugh: How to Use Humor in Presentations
Business Lite For Human Resource Professionals
Business Lite For Women Only

Other Services From Antion & Associates
Keynote Speeches
Seminars
Video Tape Evaluation and Critique
Audio Tape Evaluation and Critique
Video Feedback Coaching

WAKE 'EM UP

How to Use Humor and Other Professional Techniques to Create Alarmingly Good Business Presentations

by

Tom Antion

Your A to Y Guide (No ZZZZZs Allowed) to More Interesting, Fun, and Memorable Programs

Anchor Publishing
Landover Hills, Maryland
and
Creative Training Techniques Press
Minneapolis, Minnesota

Anchor Publishing
Box 2630
Landover Hills, MD 20784
(301) 459-0738, Fax (301) 552-0225
tom@antion.com, www.antion.com
ISBN 0-926395-12-2

Creative Training Techniques Press
7620 West 78th St.
Minneapolis, MN 55439
(612) 829-1954, Fax (612) 829-0260
Training Version ISBN 0-926395-14-9

Electronic Clip art by Corel Corporation
Edited by Janet Novotny
Cover by Vicki Flores, Optima Design
Cover illustration by ChiD Studios
Printed in the United States of America
First Edition

Publisher's Cataloging in Publication
  (Prepared by Quality Books Inc.)

Antion, Tom.
    Wake 'em up: how to use humor and other professional techniques
to create alarmingly good business presentations / Tom Antion.
    p. cm.
    Includes bibliographical references and index.
    Preassigned LCCN: 96-86293
    ISBN 0-926395-12-2

      1. Business presentations.   2. Public Speaking.   3. Humor in
business.   I. Title.

HF5718.22.A68 1997   658.4'52
                                             QBI96-40371

Limits of Liability and Disclaimer of Warranty
The author and publisher shall not be liable in the event of incidental or consequential damages in connection with, or arising out of injury sustained as a result of excessive laughter caused by using the techniques described in this book. All business presenters, speakers, and audience members should consult their doctor before attempting to use or allowing themselves to be exposed to excessively interesting information.

    The author and publisher of this book have used their best efforts in preparing this book and the information contained herein. No warranties of any kind are expressed or implied other than Tom says, "If you use this stuff you won't bore your audience's to tears."

Dedicated to Mom, Dad and Freeway

About the Author

Tom Antion, "Mr. Business Lite," is an international-ly acclaimed expert in the field of high-impact and humorous communication techniques. He is a full time professional speaker and entertainer who has been featured on major news media worldwide in-cluding the Canadian Broadcast Network, The Aus-tralian Broadcast Network, Associated Press, The Tokyo Today Show, and many radio, television, and print outlets across the United States. His clients include, Kodak, Blue Cross/Blue Shield, John Wanamaker Department Stores, Hallmark Cards, Siemens Rolm, and The National Geographic Society.

A favorite at many corporate and association meetings, Tom was the fea-tured speaker at the All California Regional Conference for *Meeting Profes-sionals International* and also for their educational retreat in Ottawa, Canada. In addition to his busy corporate speaking schedule Tom has pre-sented to more than half the chapters of the prestigious *National Speakers Association* where he is the one called to teach other professional speakers how to make their audiences say WOW!

Tom was a starting offensive guard for West Virginia University where he earned his Bachelor's degree in psychology. Tom says he got his clinical experience in psychology in the six years after he graduated when he owned a nightclub just outside Morgantown, West Virginia. The ultimate entre-preneur, Tom has never had a job. Starting from scratch, he owned five apart-ment buildings and a hotel BEFORE he graduated from college. He currently owns four small businesses including Prankmasters, Inc.^{SM} a firm that has custom designed more than 4500 good-natured practical jokes.

Tom is the author of the only video seminar of its kind, *Make 'em Laugh: How to Use Humor in Presentations.* This 4½ hour training course is considered the standard of the humorous business speaking industry. By whom? Why Tom and his mother, of course!! Tom is also the creator of *Cuss Your Lunch,* the most outrageous and unique customer service presentation ever.

For a great speaker for your next convention, corporate or civic meeting call Tom at (800) 448-6280 or contact your favorite speakers bureau.

Acknowledgments
(OK. I know you won't read this, but they will.)

Thanks to: **Mom** and **Dad** who have supported me in everything I have ever done (except the time I ran away from home and tried to survive on grass soup and hot dogs—that lasted about three hours). **Janice Stevens** for her NO ZZZZZs idea at our brainstorming session and her tireless late night editing. **Bonnie Davies** for sticking with me through all the ups and downs. **Chris Davies** for keeping my computer running and being such a good friend. **Art Gliner** for his overall assistance especially on the international section and for always coming through whenever I needed a list of something. **Sheila Feigelson** for her wonderful name tag ideas, female presenter segment, and proofreading and editing. **Paul Radde, Ph.D.,** Director of the Audience Centered Seating™ Institute for being such a great mentor and teaching me all about *State of the Art Seating* and the trick to keep my tie straight. **Dottie Walters, Lilly Walters, Michael Walters,** and **the Cowboy** my "left coast" family, plus all their fine support staff. **Carol Krugman** for all around support for me, "the fence man," and for being such a great leader of all my MPI net buddies. **Janet Novotny** for being such a top-notch editor—or is it editriss? **Joan Eisenstodt** for sharing her precious time and vast experience with me and also for getting me on MPI network. **Cindy Butler** and **Andrea Scott** and the rest of my "MPI Net buddies" for their title suggestions. **Larry Tracy** for his section on hostile audiences. **Vicki Flores** at Optima Design for her excellent cover work (take another look at the beautiful work she does). **Wolfe Rinke, Ph.D.,** for being a great business mentor and for contributing to the involvement section. **Dave Voracek** "The Brochure Doctor," for his help on the back cover. **Sally Walton** for keeping me up on diversity issues. **Bob Lunsford** who was always there when I would get into some weird computer problem and who did such a fine job typesetting this book. **Dan Poynter** who got me started writing and publishing many years ago and who is always ready with a good joke. **Marie Betts-Johnson** and **Mary Murray Bosrock** two fine protocol experts that helped me on the international section. **Maggie Bedrosian** who keeps trying to teach me that *Life is More Than Your To Do List* (For those of you that don't know, that is the title of her latest book). **Steve Hardiman** for his WordPerfect tips. **Pat Carlyle** for her videoconferencing tips. **David Rich** for his sales and marketing tips and also for being a great roommate at Meeting World. **Gene Perret** and **Linda Perret** two famous and funny people for their manuscript review. **Bob Lucas** for his help on the body language section. **Lizz Curtis Higgs, Patricia Fripp, Hope Mihalap, Nance Rosen, Denise Koepke, Barbara Sanfillippo, Joyce Saltman, Marianna Nunes, Sue Hershkowitz** and **Lola Gillebaard,** for their contributions to Chapter 19. **Mike Rounds, Doug Fox,** and **Vern Hoven** for their contributions to Chapter 17.

and to my idol

Charlie Jarvis —folks there's not a funnier man on earth—for the countless hours he has spent on the phone with me talking about humor.

If I forgot anyone out there, it's only because it's three o'clock in the morning and I'm desperately trying to get the last words typed on this manuscript. Please forgive me and watch for your name in the next printing.

TABLE OF CONTENTS

Foreword xix
Backword xx
Preface xxi
Introduction xxiii

PART I—The Basics 1

Chapter 1—Why Use Humor? 3

Chapter 2—Audience 9
  Pre-Program Questionnaire...10
  All Male/All Female 15
  Size..16
  Outdoors..16
  Time of Day 16
  International 17
          Get the Facts First..18
          Know What NOT To Do 19
          Tips From *Put Your Best Foot Forward* 22
          Visuals...23
          Words..24
          A Few Other Tips From Around the World 24
          What To Do Before You Go 25
  In Fun..27
          Nametags..28
          Handouts 29
  Alcohol..35
  Connecting with the Audience 36

Chapter 3—Room Setup 37
  Equipment...37
  Atmosphere...38
  Seating...39
          Standard Arrangements...43
          Troubleshooting 46
          Additional Seating Tips 46
  Sound System 47

Music...47
    How To Get Licensing..48
Visuals..48
Climate...49
Distractions..49
    Doors...49
    Stage 50

Chapter 4—Introductions & Openings 51
By Another Person...51
Self-Introductions 54
Openings 54
    Starting Off 54
    Response To Introduction 55
    Localized/Personalized Comments....................56
    Additional Opening Tips 58
Bonus Material...59

Chapter 5—Body 61
Maintain Interest Level..61
    Use Attention-Gaining Devices.........................63
    Use as Much Humor as You Need 64
Making a Point With Humor 65
Learn Material Easily Using Bits 65
Make Bumper Car Transitions....................................68

Chapter 6—Closings...71
Bonus Material...72

Chapter 7—Selection of Material 75
Appropriate Targets 75
    People, Places & Things 76
Inappropriate Targets 76

Chapter 8—Delivery...79
Stage Fright is Good..79
    Symptoms 80
    Reducing Stage Fright 81
        Visualization 81
        Advance Strategies 81

Pre-program Strategies 82
Strategies During Program 83
I Can't Heeeeere You! 84
Joke Telling...85
The Punch Line 85
Rule of Three 87
Callbacks..88
To Laugh or Not to Laugh—That is the Question 88
Timing...89
Types of Pauses...89
Humor Placement 90
Dynamic Range..92
Dynamic Range Quick Fixes.........................96
The WOW Factor 96
Other Important Delivery Tips 96
Extra Special Genius Technique..........................97

Chapter 9—Bombproofing 99
Theory of Relevance...99
Humor Risk...100
Saver Lines 101
Pre-Planned Ad-Libs...102
I drop something or something falls.............103
Something is broken 104
Lights go out..105
Microphone squeals 105
Projector light burns out 106
Slide is upside down.....................................106
Highlighter runs out of ink 107
Can't find an important document or visual......107
You rush into the wrong meeting 108
Someone points out a misspelling 108
You trip going to the lectern........................108
You hear a loud crash 109
Emergency situations....................................109
Universal 110
My pre-planned one-liners............................110
Acknowledgments to Tough Situations 111
Watch Your Clock So They Don't Watch Theirs 112

Chapter 10—Movement and Appearance 115
    Stand Up and Be Counted 117
    Stage Positioning 117
    Bad Habits...118
    Clothing...119
    Is Anybody Out There? 120
    Bonus Tips 121

Chapter 11—Involvement and Interplay 123
    Axe the Lectern...124
    Standing Ovation 124
    I Won! I Won! 125
    May I Help You? 126
    Old Yeller..126
    Mental Involvement...126
    I Get So Emotional 128
    I Could Do Without Some Emotional Audiences 131
    Interplay 132

Chapter 12—How to Practice...135
    Practice Alone...136
    Use Your Friends . . . Carefully..................................137
    Record Your Presentations...137
    Get Coaching 140

PART II—Types of Humor...143

Chapter 13—Thirty-Four Ways to Be Funny.............................145
    Acronyms and Abbreviations 145
    Advertisements 147
    Alliteration 148
    Anachronisms 148
    Asides..149
    Audience Gags..150
        Ten Wanted Men...150
        Stone the Speaker 150
        Dr. Heckle & Mr. Sly..151
        What is He Talking About? 151
        He Tripped Me...152

Bloopers 152
Caricature 153
Cartoons and Comic Strips 153
Comic Verse 154
    Limericks 156
Costumes 156
Definitions 157
Exaggeration 158
Fake Facts and Statistics 159
Jokes 159
Juxtaposition 160
    Oxymorons 160
    Pleonasms 160
Letters 161
    Fake Surveys 162
Magic 163
Malaprops and Usage Blunders 164
One-Liners 166
Parody 166
Props 167
    Why Use Props? 167
    Types of Props 168
    Tips For Using Props 169
Proverbs and Fortune Cookie Humor 169
Question and Answer Sessions 170
    Plant Stooges 170
    Solicit Questions 171
Quotations 171
Roast Humor and Insults 172
Self-Effacing 174
Signs 176
Simile 178
Toasts 179
Words and Sounds, Places, Food, and Numbers 181

Chapter 14—Storytelling 183
Enthusiasm 184
What to Do After Identifying a Story 184
Do's 185
Don'ts 187

Tricks 189
Extra Special Bonus Genius Technique.........................190

PART III—Sources, Organization, A/V and Computers..191

Chapter 15—Sources and Organization of Material 193
   Sources of Material...193
     Daily Information 193
     Reference Material...195
     Other Speakers...197
     Old Humor is Good Humor..............................198
     Industry-Specific Humor 199
   Organizing Your Material 200
     The Computer 200
     Hard Copy..201
   Bonus Tips 201

Chapter 16—Audio/Visual Equipment and Computers...................203
   Why Visuals are Effective 203
   Overhead Projection 204
   Projection Setup..205
   Projection Screen 206
   Correct Overhead Projection 206
   Slide Projection...209
   Flip Charts...210
     Extra Flip Chart Tips 212
   Video 213
   Computers (Pre-Program)..214
     Internet 215
   Multimedia...216
   Computers (Post-Program) 217
   Five Tips to Be Funny with A/V 217
   Overhead/Slide Design Tips 218
   Bonus Tips 221

Bonus Chapters 223

Chapter 17—Technical and Financial Presentations 225
Creating a Favorable Learning Situation...................................226
Involving Your Participants..228
Characteristics of a Good Technical Program 228
Choosing the Appropriate Program Length 230
Using Team Presentations..231

Chapter 18—Sales Presentations 233
Getting the Sale..234
Following Up After the Sale...237
Use Product Related Stories 237
Tips Galore...238
One-on-One or Small Boardroom Presentations..............238
Larger Presentations 238
More Sales Tips 239

Chapter 19—Women, Humor and Business Presentations.............241
Nance Rosen—Senior Corporate Executive............................242
Denise Koepke—Trainer 244
Barbara Sanfillippo—Speaker 245
Lilly Walters—Speakers Bureau Owner 246
Hope Mihalap—Humorist 247
Sheila Feigelson—Speaker and Humor Consultant 248
Lola Gillebaard—Speaker 250
Patricia Fripp—Speaker...251
Joyce M. Saltman—Humorist, Professor, Therapist 252
Marianna Nunes—Speaker 253
Lizz Curtis Higgs—Encouraging Humorist 254
Sue Hershkowitz—Speaker 256

Closing Comments 257

Appendices..259
A: Action Plan to Improve Your Use of Humor 260
B: Addresses 261
Audio and Video Tapes...261
Books 261
Book Search Services 261

Comedy Writing/Stand-up Comedy Workshop 261
Computer Programs 262
Exercises, Brainteasers, Activities, Icebreakers 262
International Resources...262
Music Licensing...263
Newsletters..263
Professional Joke Services..263
Props 263
Speaker Services 264
Speaking Organizations 264
Speech Writing and Research Services 264
C: Tips for Television & Videotape and Videoconferencing.................265
D: Worldwide Video Color Systems 267
E: Room Setup Checklist 269
F: Tom's Banquet/Luncheon Tips 271
G: Selected Bibliography 273
H: Wake 'em Up Glossary 278
Index 289

FOREWORD

Humor carries your message on wings that go straight to a person's heart and funny bone which makes the message irresistible. *Wake 'em Up* teaches you how to be irresistible.

You'll laugh your way through this book as you learn the professional secrets of being funny and of creating interesting presentations. My friend Tom has created a step-by-step systematic approach that allows anyone to apply the advanced techniques that top professionals use to sugar coat their poignant, powerful and sometimes painful messages. Without this coating your audiences may not be willing to listen at all.

Humor is the shortest distance between somebody's head and heart so that their spirit is stabbed alive and is willing to come to work. You'll learn how to *Wake 'em Up, Make 'em Laugh*, and move your audiences to action whether your message is technical or painful; educational or motivational; delivered to an all-male, all-female, or mixed audience; or given to support staff, professionals, executives or international audiences.

Tom will get you to convulse with humor that has been invisible to you previously. He'll also manifest the ways you can use humor, stories, and little life incidents to make your message meaty, meaningful, and magnificently memorable. Once you tap into this new source of power for your presentations, you will realize the time you spent reading and implementing the techniques in this book was well worth it.

Mark Victor Hansen
Co-Author of the #1 New York Times Best-selling series,
Chicken Soup for the Soul

BACKWORD

Author's note: I wouldn't think of making you wait until the end of the book to hear a few words from one of the most influential people in the speaking business today.

When Tom Antion asked me to write the *Backword* for his new book, I thought he was kidding. As I thought about it more, I realized that much of the success he has enjoyed came from his willingness to push the limits of convention. As I've watched him grow into a polished and exciting keynote speaker, I'm reminded of other top speakers who have been so successful for Walters International Speakers Bureau over the years. One of the traits these speakers had in common was their ability to make their audiences laugh in the right amount, at the right times, and for the right purposes. Tom's book is an excellent resource for teaching executives, managers, speakers, trainers, and salespeople how to impart their valuable information with just the right amount of excitement, levity, and laughter. Mastering these skills will virtually guarantee that you will always be in demand.

Dottie Walters, President
Walters International Speakers Bureau, Glendora, CA
Co-Author of *Speak and Grow Rich*

PREFACE

by Robert W. Pike, CSP
President, Creative Training Techniques International, Inc.

If you let your hair down, you might be surprised what you find in it.
—Balki Bartokomous, *Perfect Strangers*

Yes, I know what you are thinking—A preface is supposed to be written by the author. Well this book is NOT about sticking to normal convention. This book is about maximum involvement and excitement. Tom asked me to write this preface because he knows I am a firm believer in the importance of impact in any kind of speaking assignment.

Your image is very important in today's business world. Every time you speak you are representing yourself and your business. If you are an effective and dynamic communicator, you will cast a favorable light on virtually all your business endeavors. This means you will be more valuable and less likely to be sacrificed if your company's business climate gets tough. If you are the leader of your organization, you will increase your power to create the entire image of your company and your power to motivate employees and clients to act. You must take it upon yourself to move them so you can sell more of your ideas, products, and services.

In the training arena, which is my specialty, we are faced with especially difficult challenges simply by virtue of the fact that we are with the same people for anywhere from one to several days. We must be able to gain and maintain the attention of our trainees in hectic work environments.

Whether you are a CEO, trainer, manager, or salesperson, to get your message across you must *Wake Up!* your audience. You must command their attention so that your message can get through. This book is dedicated to giving you the professional tools and specific techniques to command that attention. More than that, it will show you how to set the stage so the audience *desires* and *enjoys* listening to you. Imagine that!

This book slants heavily toward the use of appropriate humor as one of the most effective tools in waking up your audience. It also covers the entire range of skills needed to be a NO ZZZZZs presenter. For even if you focus exclusively on humor, you still need many other skills to make you a polished presenter. I know you might be apprehensive about using humor. Many people are, until they see the tremendous benefits that await them with relatively little risk—if the humor is done right. This book teaches you how to do it right. It will also give you many other tools and tricks of the trade that I am certain you will not see in your average presentation skills book. It will take you far past the beginners level, even if you are a beginner.

Being an effective communicator is a learned skill. Anyone—yes, I said any-one—can improve upon this skill. Tom believes in this so much he provides this personal guarantee: If you implement as little as 10 percent of what you learn here, you will double your effectiveness as a business presenter. Since he doesn't know how to measure this, he'll just refund your money if you swear to the fol-lowing: 1. You read the entire book; 2. You tried to use at least 10 of the hundreds of tips included; and 3. You don't feel this book helped you become a better busi-ness presenter.

I believe that one of the purposes of any presentation is to have the audience leave impressed with themselves, not intimidated by the presenter. Using Tom's techniques will help you to do this.

INTRODUCTION

Why in the world would people get up at an ungodly hour of the morning and drive hundreds of miles to attend a *Humor in Presentations* seminar? I'll tell you why. It's because the value of humor and excitement is now being recognized as a legitimate tool for making your business and personal life better. Numerous benefits are associated with the appropriate use of humor in both business and social settings. This book focuses on a specific use of humor; that is, humor used to make business presentations more effective.

You will also find in this book literally hundreds of advanced presentation techniques that professionals use to create highly polished programs. They are broken down into easy-to-understand segments that anyone (even a beginner) can learn. With a little practice you will be doing things in your presentations that will blow away your competition, amaze your colleagues, and get you the results you want.

What exactly is a presentation? One of Webster's many definitions is "to bring before the mind." So, a presentation can be delivered to an audience of one, assuming that person has a mind. It can be delivered to 5 people in an informal meeting, to 30 people in a small audience, to 250 people in a medium-sized audience, to 1600 in a large audience, or to 100,000 in a super large audience in a football stadium—or any number in between. The word presentation usually denotes a formal setting, but I want you to think of a presentation as anytime you try to bring your ideas before the mind of a listener.

Most people use the term audience only after their listeners reach more than a few in number. That is not really accurate, so for the rest of this book I will use the word audience even if you are presenting to only one person.

The main rule to keep in mind as you read this book is that there are no rules. All the principles you will learn are violated regularly by a top presenter somewhere. I'm going to give you generally accepted principles—and tell you about the exceptions. I want you to think about how these principles and the exceptions can be applied to your presentations.

Some of you may be apprehensive about your ability to use humor. You may have had one or more bad experiences in your attempts to use humor. I personally guarantee that anyone can use humor effectively and appropriately. You may not be a joke-a-minute presenter but, in most cases, you wouldn't want that reputation anyway. You don't have to be a nut to get your point across. That will cause you to lose credibility.

To make good use of humor in your presentations, all you have to do is choose appropriate humor from existing sources, make sure it is relevant to the points you are trying to make, and practice enough so your delivery is smooth. I'm going to show you how to do all that and more so that you create excitement and interest in your topic. You will truly be a NO ZZZZZs presenter.

To be a humorous and effective presenter it doesn't even matter if you can't tell a joke to save your dog's life. Actually, you will find very little mention of jokes in this entire book. You don't even have to worry about writing your own humor.

This book will teach you how you can adapt easily found generic humor to your presentation needs. Believe me, when you start looking around, you will find that humor literally surrounds you.

Also, you have a tremendous advantage if you are not a comedian or humorist. People will come to your presentations to get the information they need and won't expect to be entertained. They will expect to snooze through at least part of your presentation. Any humor you use will be considered to be

> *You could very likely be the hit of your next convention or meeting.*

a big bonus. You could very likely be the hit of the convention or meeting. You don't even need to elicit a big belly laugh to be a hit because you are using humor to make your points.

In addition to being a teaching instrument, this book is a source of some instantly usable humorous material even though it's not a joke book. Feel free to use or adapt the ideas and material in this book to suit your needs. Keep in mind though that when I say instantly usable, I mean instantly usable after you practice and test. I never encourage my clients to try out or test material in presentations that really count. That's plain risky.

You will see throughout this book a mixture of the serious and the humorous. I believe, and I have proven to many business people, that this is a winning combination. I also feel that rigid structure and absolute organization are counterproductive. That's why, when you least expect it, I'll change up on you and do something different.

I want you to push your limits, but don't do anything that is not you. You will look affected and probably do worse than if you just delivered your normal routine. I'm known for my sometimes outrageous style; if you tried to copy me, you would likely fall flat—just as I would if I tried to copy your style.

You will also notice a disdain I have for boring presenters. I call them all kinds of names like *breathing sleeping pills* and *hammock heads*. Don't worry. These names don't apply to you even if you know you are boring right now. The fact that you are trying to improve by reading this book makes you OK by me.

> *It amazes me that experts don't try to become better presenters.*
>
> Joan Eisenstodt
> 1991 Meeting Professionals International
> Meeting Planner of the Year

Many of the tips offered will help you improve your regular presentation skills in addition to your humor skills. This book will even change your nationality. After you apply the ideas and techniques in this book you will be an honorary citizen of NO Z Land. (I hate puns. Don't ever use them.)

To get you started on the path to effective, memorable, and NO ZZZZZs presentations you must have a firm grasp of the basics.

Part I The Basics

Chapter 1 will teach you, if you don't know, and remind you, if you do, of all the good reasons to use appropriate humor in presentations.

Chapter 2 will discuss all the audience information you should have to increase your chances of success. Emphasis will be placed on the audience rather than on you. To be successful, you must always think of your audience's needs.

Chapter 3 will teach you how to take control of the logistics of your presentation even if you don't think you have much control over seating arrangements, sound systems, and other room parameters.

Chapters 4, 5, and 6 will take you through a presentation, from your prepared introduction through your closing.

Chapter 7 will help you choose appropriate jokes, stories, and one-liners and tell you the types of humor you should absolutely avoid.

Chapter 8 will show you how to deliver your punchlines and teach you the importance of timing. The best, most highly targeted, and funniest humor will fall flat if you don't know how to deliver it and milk it for all it's worth.

Chapter 9 will teach you how to *bombproof* your humor and give you all the details on what to do when a humorous comment fails. You won't need to avoid humor because you are afraid of *bombing*.

Chapter 10 will teach you to make your gestures and body language add to your presentation. You will learn what to watch for.

Chapter 11 will give you eight ways to let the audience participate in your presentation. Modern audiences want to be involved.

Chapter 12 will show you how to practice, on whom to practice, and what to expect if you hire a speaking coach or attend small group practice sessions. Perfect practice makes perfect punchlines. The only way you can be assured of delivering humor effectively is by practicing.

Part II Types of Humor

Chapter 13 will give you 34 simple forms of humor you can easily add to any presentation.

Chapter 14 will help you learn how to tell stories. Because of their importance in making points, stories get their own chapter. A good storyteller is hard to find. You can become one by practicing the techniques in this chapter.

Part III Sources, Organization, Audio/Visual Equipment & Computers

Chapter 15 will tell you where to find and organize immediately usable humor. It also discusses why old humor is good humor.

Chapter 16 will show you how your computer can create humor and how to properly use slide projectors, overhead projectors, and flipcharts—and make them funny.

Bonus Chapters

In **Chapter 17** technical and financial presenters will get their *wake up call* on the hows and whys of adding spice to facts and figures.

Chapter 18 focuses specifically on the art of humor in sales. We all sell, but some folks are known as sales professionals. This chapter is for them.

Chapter 19 saves the best for last. It highlights women presenters. You'll hear from some of the most effective women presenters in the country and how they create *Wake 'em Up* programs.

In short, or long, whichever you prefer, I'm going to give you all you ever wanted to know about using humor and advanced presentation techniques. In addition, I'm going to give you insiders' tips and tricks that the pros use to create insomniacs out of their audiences; i.e., the audience is so excited they couldn't go to sleep if they wanted to. You must decide what fits *you* and add it to your presentations slowly. Start with one technique at a time. You will not become a humorous *Wake 'em Up* presenter overnight. With practice you will evolve into a more lively and fun presenter. If you already use humor effectively, take the information you learn here and use it to fine tune your technique and take yourself to the next level.

The ideas and techniques you will find in this book can be adapted and applied to one-on-one sales presentations or to major keynotes in front of thousands of people. You might ask, *Why should I know about large audiences if I only present to a few people at a time?* The reason is that when you become a NO ZZZZZs presenter, people will notice and you will be asked to present to larger groups. The same question might be asked in reverse by a major keynoter, executive, or political figure. *Why should I bother knowing about small audience settings? I already present to large groups.* You need to know that the humor and stories that are successful in large groups do not necessarily translate to small group settings. Without this knowledge you might fall flat when talking to five CEO's in a boardroom setting.

A bigger answer waits for both of these presenters. I know it's a cliché, but it doesn't matter how good you are now, there is always room for improvement. An old coal miner friend of mine who is one of the smartest men I know says, "The schoolhouse door is always open." I believe him, so let's go right in.

He is not only dull himself, but the cause of dullness in others.
—Samuel Foote

Illustration by: Tracy Collamore

Don't let this happen to you!

Part I
The Basics

The Sandman is your biggest competitor.
—Elmer Wheeler

Why use humor?

Why should I bother using humor in my presentations? Can't I just deliver my information and sit down? You sure can—and that's what most people do. The problem is that most people are not effective presenters. They are *nighty nite, snooze inducing, say-your-prayers, hit-the-sack, unlicensed hypnotists.* They are ZZZZZs presenters. They might be experts in their field and be able to recite hours and hours of information on their topic, but is that effective? No. An effective presentation is one that achieves its purpose, whatever that may be.

CHAPTER 1

I don't think that most presenters define their purpose clearly even to themselves. As part of being a NO ZZZZZs presenter you must ask yourself: Why am I here? What do I want to accomplish? Am I here to sell something? Am I here to motivate? Am I here to persuade? Am I here to get votes? What do I want the audience to take home with them when I'm done? Once you've answered these questions I can tell you how and why humor and many other professional techniques will help you achieve your goals. But if you don't even know why you are there, then I can't help you.

According to Bob Orben, Special Assistant to President Gerald Ford and Former Director of the White House Speech writing Department, "Business executives and political leaders have embraced humor because humor works. Humor has gone from being an admirable part of a leader's character—to a mandatory one." I know you are a leader because you picked up this book. You recognized there is a higher level waiting for you and developing outstanding presentation skills will help you reach it.

A survey of top executives who earned more than $250,000 per year conducted by a large executive search firm found that these executives believed their communication skills were the number one factor that carried them to the top. Mastering the use of humor and other high-explosion techniques puts a fine polish on those skills which can help propel you to the top more quickly. The ZZZZZs people may make their slow progression up the corporate ladder (nowadays only if they're lucky), but the NO ZZZZZs people shoot off the top of the ladder holding onto a rocket.

Like these NO ZZZZZs presenters, there are many benefits you can derive from using humor in your presentations. Keep in mind that these benefits only help you reach your ultimate purpose for making the presentation. They are not purposes themselves unless, of course, you are only interested in entertaining. Using humor does the following for you:

HELPS YOU CONNECT WITH THE AUDIENCE. What audience is going to listen to you if they don't feel you are one of them?

MAKES YOU MORE LIKEABLE. The more an audience likes you, the more they will be likely to agree with your ideas.

AROUSES INTEREST. Many of you speak to audiences that don't even want to be there. Humor can help you gain their interest.

KEEPS ATTENTION. Grabbing interest at the beginning of a presentation is not enough to carry you to the end. You must keep the attention of the audience all the way. Unfortunately our audience's attention spans are becoming shorter and shorter. They are becoming more of the MTV generation where the average time a shot is on the screen is just a few seconds. According to Ron Hoff in his presentation skills book, *I Can See You Naked,* "If corporate managers ever saw their own meetings on TV, they would pick up their remote controls and zap themselves into oblivion in the flick of an eyelash." We are competing with movies that have $100 million in special effects. We must be prepared to deliver

> *Hey, Alex—You know the really great thing about television? If something important happens, anywhere in the world, night or day . . . you can always change the channel.*
>
> Reverend Jim Ignatowski
> *Taxi*

a fast-paced program that surprises members of the audience. At times we need to knock them in the head to make sure they are present. Humor and other presentation devices placed appropriately will help you do this.

HELPS EMPHASIZE POINTS AND IDEAS. Anyone who has ever taken a simple speaking course knows that you must hit your audience on the head with your point over and over before they get it. Humor is one of the hammers you can use.

DISARMS HOSTILITY. Nonfrivolous humor can be used to take the edge off audiences that are clearly against you.

REDUCES RELATIVE STATUS. Many of you are what I call the "big-shots" of your organization. Your position as boss creates a big barrier to listening. Don't forget, "BOSS" spelled backwards is double-SOB and that's the way your audience will look at you if lord your status over them. Making a little fun of yourself (self-effacing humor) will do wonders for opening lines of communication.

OVERCOMES OVERLY FLATTERING INTRODUCTIONS. Introducers come in all quality levels. If you get one that makes you sound like God, it will create expectations in the audience that you couldn't possibly live up to. Humor can neutralize that problem instantly.

GETS YOUR POINT ACROSS WITHOUT CREATING HOSTILITY. Sometimes you have to deliver tough negative messages. The careful use of humor can help you do your dastardly deed without creating unnecessary anger.

HELPS RELATE FACTS AND FIGURES. A friend of mine says, "I don't want to bore you with sadistics" (see "Malaprops," Chapter 13). Technical and financial presenters must be especially careful to spice up long lists of numbers and generally dry material. You must keep in mind that most people in your audience are not as passionate about your subject as you are or they would be up in front of the group. Think from the audience's point of view and do whatever it takes to break up boring material so you don't lose your audience totally.

Joan Eisenstodt, from Eisenstodt Associates, and former MPI Meeting Planner of the Year says, "High content, informational speakers almost always fall flat if they don't use some humor. I equate appropriate humor with warmth and audiences respond to warmth." She also notes, "After 25 years watching audiences and presenters, I know that even subtle humor can help the audience respond positively to information that could be considered boring."

MAKES A POSITIVE IMPRESSION. Laughter and good humor create bonds. Even if the audience members don't like you, they will like you better if you can make them laugh or smile and they will leave with better thoughts of you.

SHOWS THAT YOU DON'T TAKE YOURSELF TOO SERIOUSLY. The old saying goes, "If you take yourself too seriously, no one else will." You don't want to be known as a stuffed shirt. If you can laugh a little bit at yourself at the right times, your audience can laugh *with* you and not *at* you.

HELPS PAINT PICTURES IN THE AUDIENCE'S MIND. The pictures humorous storytellers can paint are what people remember, not the words.

MAKES INFORMATION MORE MEMORABLE. Joyce Saltman, a college professor and well-known speaker in the health care field, did exhaustive research for her 1995 doctoral dissertation *Humor in Adult Learning*. She concluded that "Most researchers agreed that humor generally aided in the retention of materials as well as to the enjoyment of the presentation of the information."

LIGHTENS UP HEAVY MATERIAL. Appropriate humor added to heavy, serious material gives the audience a few seconds to relax. Even Shakespeare employed this device, called "comic relief," extensively to provide distraction or offer respite from the serious events of a tragedy.

Tom's List

YOU WILL BE ASKED BACK. If you succeed in your original purpose for making your presentation, you may be asked back. If you also make the audience feel really good by entertaining them at the same time, your chances of being asked back will be much higher.

YOU WILL GET HIGHER EVALUATIONS OR MORE SALES. If you make the audience feel good, they will like you better and reflect that in your evaluation scores or buy more *and* more often from you.

YOU WILL MAKE MORE MONEY. If you are a professional presenter, you will be booked more and your fees will rise. If you present as part of your job, then read the next item carefully.

YOU WILL BE MORE PROMOTABLE. Having and conveying a sense of humor is on virtually everyone's list of top leadership skills. A humorous and engaging presentation style will push you up the ladder where good communications skills are a must.

IF IT'S GOOD ENOUGH FOR POPES AND PRESIDENTS, IT'S GOOD ENOUGH FOR ME. I don't know about the pope, but I do know that all modern-day presidents are coached extensively on the use of appropriate humor for many of the reasons stated above.

YOU WILL MAKE PEOPLE HAPPY. This is my favorite benefit. I get great satisfaction from knowing that I have brightened someone else's life. I had an executive come up to me after one of my humor seminars and say, "You opened up a whole new world for me." I almost cried right on the spot. I'll never forget it.

When on earth, do as the earthlings.
—Mork

Audience

You can't catch many fish by using food *you* like for the bait. You must give them what *they* like. You must absolutely, positively know your audience.

You should know what the members of the audience have in common (interests, enemies, competitors, etc.). You should know what the hot topic of conversation is—and be sure they are joking about it themselves. It may be too hot. You should know the restaurants where they eat, the name of their newsletter, how much money they make, the name and record of the local sports teams, etc., etc., etc. The more you know about the audience, the better job you will do. Your goal should be to make that audience know that the presentation they are witnessing was created specifically for them.

CHAPTER 2

If you don't present to the same audience all the time, you must have a method for getting this information. Most NO ZZZZZs presenters use some form of pre-program questionnaire which is sent out well in advance of their program. I got the basis for mine from Dottie Walters at Walters International Speakers Bureau. I made some slight changes to suit my presentation style and I keep adding and deleting questions to tweak it to perfection.

Your conversations with the program coordinator will give you some of the information you need. You should fill in as many of the blanks as you can before you send out the questionnaire to save the program coordinator some work. This also proves you were paying attention to what he or she said.

PRE-PROGRAM QUESTIONNAIRE

This pre-program questionnaire is for Thomas Antion's presentation to
_____ on   /   /   .

    These questions are designed to help my staff and I prepare a program specifically suited to the needs of your group. Please take a moment to answer all the questions fully and return the form to my office. We have already answered some of the questions based on our initial conversation. Please double check these answers and make additions and corrections.

    We would also appreciate receiving any printed information on your group that may help us with background information (e.g., corporate reports, news items, in-house publications, products, services, employees, etc.). Thank you for your help!

Please return this questionnaire to: **THOMAS ANTION**
    Box 2630
    Landover Hills, MD 20784

No later than: /   /   . **E-mail— tom@antion.com**
    www.antion.com

If you have any questions please call: (800) 468-6280 (USA Only)
    (301) 459-0738
    FAX (301) 552-0225,

THE PRESENTATION

Presentation Title: _____

Time Frame? Start Time _____ End Time _____ Any breaks? Y N

What is on the program just before I speak?

_____

What happens on the program right after I speak?

_____

Appropriate dress for presentation?

_____

Conference title and theme?

_____

Specific purpose of this meeting/session (e.g., awards banquet, annual meeting, etc.)?

_____

Specific objectives for my presentation?

_____

Sensitive issues that should be avoided?

_____

Introducer's name? _____

Introducer's Phone Wk. _____ Hm. _____

Is there any publicity work I can help you with while I am at your event? Y N

Radio _____ Television _____ Other _____ Type _____

Who are the other speakers on the program?

Speaker_____ Topic _____

Speaker_____ Topic _____

What speakers have you used in the past that covered topics related to the material I will be presenting for you? _____

What did you like and/or dislike? Withhold their names if you like, but do comment on the material they used! _____

_____

Please share any "local color" you may know of relating to the location where my program will be held. _____

_____

Please share any "industry color" related to your organization or industry.

_____

What comments or suggestions do you have that will help me make this presentation the best your audience has ever had? _____

_____

THE AUDIENCE

Total number attending? _____ Spouses attending? Y N

Percentage male/female _____ Average age? _____

Average annual income _____

Educational background _____

Major job responsibilities of audience _____

Will there be any "special guests?" Please explain. _____

_____

Why is your group attending this meeting (voluntary, mandatory, etc.)?

_____

How will they be notified? _____

What is their overall opinion regarding the subject of my presentation, (favorable, hostile, etc.)?

_____

Please provide the names and positions of three main "movers and shakers" in your organization that will be in the audience, who are well known and well liked. I may joke with them or call on them if the need arises. My staff or I may also want to contact them for more research information on your group (with your permission, of course).

Name _____ phone _____

Name _____ phone _____

Name _____ phone _____

DETAILS ABOUT YOUR AUDIENCE

Problems? _____

Challenges? _____

Breakthroughs? _____

What separates your high-performance people from others?_____

_____

Are there any hearing or sight-impaired audience members? Y N

If yes, please provide names and contact information _____

_____

TELL ME ABOUT YOUR INDUSTRY/PROFESSION

Problems? _____

Challenges? _____

Breakthroughs? _____

TELL ME ABOUT YOUR ORGANIZATION

Problems? _____

Challenges? _____

Breakthroughs? _____

Significant events? Mergers? Relocations? _____

_____

TRAVEL INFORMATION

Location of presentation and venue name _____

_____

Address _____ Phone _____

Location at the site (room-name, etc.) _____

Airport to arrive at _____

How will I be transported from the airport to your site?

Taxi? _____ Rental Car? _____ Driver? _____

Driver's Name _____ Phone _____

If an emergency occurs on the way to the site, who would be an alternate contact if you are unavailable?

Name _____

Business phone _____ Home Phone _____

Thank you for taking the time to provide this information. I will use it to prepare an outstanding presentation for your group.

That's a lot of information, isn't it? Well, that is only the beginning for me. I call as many people in the company or association I can, to get to the heart of what is really going on in their organization. Sometimes these people will virtually write much of the humor used in a presentation. They know what is funny to them. Remember, you are there to give them what *they* want.

If you are addressing a general, unrelated audience with few common denominators, base your humor on general subjects or specifically relate it to the points you are trying to make. Many people are married. Many have kids. Almost everyone goes to a doctor. They have car problems, etc. There are plenty of general subjects to fit any audience.

Get acquainted with any regional differences. If you are speaking in a small town located in a rural area, you wouldn't crack cab driver jokes. They couldn't be expected to relate. If you are from a large metropolitan area and you are speaking in a rural area, you may comment on how you appreciate their calmer way of life and make fun of your rat race way of life. You certainly wouldn't want to say anything that insulted their way of life. The safest target to joke about is you (see "Self-effacing Humor," Chapter 13).

ALL MALE/ALL FEMALE

There is nothing I like better than an all female audience. All female audiences tend to laugh more easily and loudly than all male audiences. Audiences that consist of more than 50 percent women are good too. The presence of the females provides a good buffer and makes it OK for the men to laugh, since so many other people are laughing

All male audiences are the toughest because the male ego gets in the way of laughter. Males look around to see if anyone else is laughing before they laugh, and they won't laugh as loud because they think they will look less powerful.

If you present to an all male audience it is more critical to bond and be "one of the guys" especially if you are a female presenter. I'm not being sexist here. I don't believe in sexism. I'm just giving you the thoughts to keep in mind if you are a female presenter and you want to be successful in front of a general all male audience. You must realize: not all males out there in the business world are as sensitive as me (send all big hugs to me in care of the publisher). If your all male audience is a general audience not from the same company or field, stick to sports, business, and money to best connect with them.

One of the hardest audiences to deal with consists of a group of executives from the same company when the CEO is present. If you say something funny, the executives will start to laugh, but they choke it off until they check to see if the CEO is laughing. If he or she is laughing, then they go ahead and laugh. This kind of audience will create timing nightmares for you. If you are the CEO and you are in the audience for a presentation, it is your obligation to laugh and at least act like you're having a good time to "give permission" to everyone else to laugh. If you want to be a NO ZZZZZs presenter, you can sometimes take it upon yourself to gently explain to the CEO how everyone will look to him or her for approval.

SIZE

The size of your audience has a direct effect on the types of humor which are most appropriate, the expected audience response and the timing of the presentation.

Members of a small group of businesspeople tend to be too self-conscious to laugh much. Use short one-liners. Be brief and informal with your humor; don't use any long stories or jokes.

In small groups laughter will come more quickly. It's now OK to stretch to jokes and short stories. Such a presentation will take less time to deliver than to a large group.

A presentation to very large crowds in enormous rooms or venues such as stadiums will take longer to deliver because laughter comes in waves. The portion of the audience right in front of you will laugh first. Then most of the rest of the crowd will laugh. The third wave will come when those slower to get the joke finally do, and when those who laugh because everyone else is laughing kick in. You must allow time for this phenomenon to occur. In large crowds you must play to the back of the room. These people are hardest to reach.

OUTDOORS

Outdoor presentations are really tough because they are usually full of distractions. The sound systems are often inadequate. It is virtually impossible to use overheads or slides because you have no control over the lighting. Flip charts will blow over if you don't weight them down. If you are presenting outdoors, I recommend you cut down on the overall amount of humor. When you do use humor, be more animated and forceful and concentrate on hammering out the punch lines.

TIME OF DAY

The first speaker of the day for an early morning (7:00 a.m. to 9:00 a.m.) program should not expect hearty laughter. People are not conditioned to laugh a great deal in the early morning. Many won't even be awake yet. Use more information and less humor. I was asked by a sales speaker to open up an early morning seminar. He said, "I just want you to get them laughing before I go on." I told him that it was not a good idea, but he insisted. I opened up the seminar with some sure-fire humor to test their responsiveness and got little response. I cut my material and brought the speaker on stage. He couldn't get them laughing either. I sat in the audience and watched. By 10:15 a.m. they were laughing at just about anything.

It's important for you to know when NOT to expect hearty laughter so you don't waste your best material at a time when laughter normally wouldn't be expected. If you didn't know that early morning programs aren't the best for laughter, you might have your confidence shaken so badly that the rest of your presentation might slide into Z-land. Also, keep in mind that I am giving you general principles. You might run into a lively group sometime—just don't expect it.

Many consider brunch to be the best time of day to expect a responsive audience. It is late enough that the folks who sleep late are now awake, but not so late in the day that early risers are starting to get tired. Lunch is generally a time for good response for the same reasons as brunch.

In the afternoon people are starting to get tired. Audience members will retain less because they are not listening as closely as they did in the morning. You can use more humor and less hard information, but don't expect laughter to be as intense.

The last speaker of a long afternoon or evening program should not expect a great response, again because folks are too worn out. Keep your presentation short and crisp and acknowledge the lateness so that the audience knows you care about them. Once I was the last speaker on a long program in Baltimore, Maryland, for a food service management company. I was being introduced at 8:35 p.m. on a Monday night in the fall. What do you think the mostly male audience was thinking about at 8:35 p.m. on a Monday night in the Fall? Of course! MONDAY NIGHT FOOTBALL! I got up and said:

There are three things I would never want to be: 1. a javelin catcher; 2. the scoop man at a Donkey Basketball game; and 3. the last speaker on a long program. (I looked at my watch.) *It's now 8:40 p.m. I'm going to limit my remarks to 15 minutes. I guarantee you will be in the hospitality suite in time for the kickoff.* I kept my promise.

Do you think I had more of their attention than if I had not made the comment? You bet I did! Even though it had been a long day, they all had a good laugh during my talk. A little care for your audience will go a long way.

INTERNATIONAL

Audiences in the United States are becoming more and more diverse. It is your responsibility as a presenter to be aware of and acknowledge significant portions of the audience from differing backgrounds. If you are presenting in a different country, it is up to you to find out about local customs and types of humor that are appreciated. The response to humor is quite different and normally much more subdued for cultures outside the U.S. Paying close attention to this fact will give you a greater chance of connecting with international audiences in and out of the

> *Few audiences around the world are as obviously receptive as North American Audiences.*
>
> Marie Betts-Johnson

U.S. You will also be more aware of etiquette and customs that will make you a welcome NO ZZZZZs presenter anywhere you go.

Get the Facts First

If you are not familiar with your intended audience, you might ask in your pre-program research, *How diverse is your group? What are some of the characteristics of the members from each of the countries represented?* The answers to these questions will help you plan your strategy for connecting with a particular audience.

When I was doing my planning for a presentation in Washington, D.C., I found out that 25 percent of the audience was Asian Indian. I knew very little about the Indian culture and didn't have long to plan. What I did know was that the Dunkin' Donuts store located near my home was owned and operated by Indians. That was a good excuse to stop in, down a few eclairs, and do some research. I told the proprietor what I was trying to accomplish and he was glad to help. Out of all the information he gave me about humor in India, I only used one line. That was all it took to connect. The line was, *I want to tell all my new Indian friends I'm sorry Johnny Lever couldn't make it.* Johnny Lever was one of the top comedians in India. They lit up and I went on with the program.

If your local donut shop isn't run by the appropriate nationality for your next presentation, don't worry. There are other sure-fire methods to get the information you need. If you are presenting out of the country, get the opinion of local people before you attempt to use humor. If you are presenting in the U.S., seek out members of the nationality to whom you are presenting. If you don't happen to know any, you can always call their embassy. I've called our State Department, The World Bank and even Voice of America for information. Just tell the receptionist you want to speak to someone from the country of interest. Don't forget to tell them you want to converse in English.

KNOW WHAT NOT TO DO

When presenting to foreign audiences you must check all your comments, especially those intended to be humorous, carefully so you don't accidentally offend someone. Customs are quite different around the world. It is easy to make mistakes when you are in a totally new environment. In some countries you may hear open joking on television about subjects that would be taboo in the U.S. That doesn't mean you can attempt to joke about the same subjects in your presentation. You'll never get the audience to connect with you or laugh if you accidentally say or do something offensive. A good resource that gives you a fun look at customs in other countries is Roger Axtell's, *Gestures: The Do's and Taboos of Body Language Around the World.* I'll talk more about the science of gestures in Chapter 10, but Roger Axtell's book gives lots of useful information on things to do, as well as NOT to do, when in a foreign country.

Here are just a few serious mistakes that could easily be made during a presentation:

● In Colombia, if you wanted to show the height of an animal, you would hold your arm out palm down and raise it to the appropriate height. If you are trying to show the height of a person you do the same thing, but your palm is *vertical.* So, if you meant to show the height of a person, but you did it palm down as we normally would in the U.S., you would have either insulted the person by treating him or her like an animal, or you would have confused your audience because they would now think that you were actually talking about an animal that had the name of a person. See how crazy this can get?

● I've got another animal problem for you. In Hong Kong, Indonesia, and Australia you would never beckon someone by putting your hand out and curling your index finger back and forth (The way you might to coax someone on stage with you). This gesture is used to call animals and/or ladies-of-the-night and would be offensive to your audience.

● In Latin America and the Middle East, people stand much closer together when they converse. If you were interacting with a person from one of these cultures and maintained a distance considered to be a normal U.S. personal space, you would be sending a very unfriendly message. Asians, however, typically stand farther apart than North Americans. Your understanding of this will keep you from

> **What he meant to say:** *"Ich bin Berliner!"*
> **Translation:** *"I am a Berliner!"*
> **What he said:** *"Ich bin ein berliner!"*
> **Translation:** *"I am a jelly doughnut!"*
>
> John F. Kennedy during an impassioned speech at the Berlin Wall

chasing them all over the stage. Keep this in mind, too, if you go into the audience to interact with them. Since they are seated, you control the distance for interpersonal space. Also, **NEVER TOUCH AN ASIAN AND, ES-PECIALLY, NEVER TOUCH AN ASIAN CHILD ON THE HEAD.** The spirit is thought to reside there and it is considered sacred.

Fortunately, sometimes your mistakes will be considered funny. Hermine Hilton, the well-known memory expert, tells of a presentation in Nigeria where she tried to pronounce the names of members of the audience and innocently added a sexual innuendo. She said everyone was falling on the floor with laughter. Most foreign audiences do appreciate your effort to speak their language, even if innocent mistakes are committed.

So to be on the safe side, verify the meaning of foreign words or phrases that you are taught, prior to using them. Carol Krugman, veteran international meeting planner, told me of how some Hispanic friends taught her a toast in Spanish, many years before she actually learned the language. Early in her career, at a luncheon following a sales pitch, she thought she would impress the potential clients by offering the toast, which she thought meant, "Health, money and good luck in your life." After a split second of stunned silence, the Mexican gentlemen at the table burst out laughing, raised their glasses to her and downed their tequilas in one gulp. In fact, what Carol had wished them was "Health, money and power behind their zippers!" P.S. She got the job—and learned Spanish shortly afterward!

"TO HEALTH"
TOASTS AROUND THE WORLD

Esperanto	Je zia sano
Chinese	Kan bei
Danish	Skål
French	A votre santé
German	Prost
Hawaiian	Kamau
Portuguese	Saüde
Irish	Slainte
Italian	Salute
Japanese	Kampai
Russian	Na zdorovia
Scottish	Slainte
Swedish	Skål
Spanish	Salud

You can't go too far wrong by wishing good health to those you meet in other countries. Get local help for pronunciation (also see "Toasts," Chapter 13).

Here's a few more international tips I've run across:

- You might think you are putting your audience to sleep in Japan, don't worry. In Japan it is common to show one's concentration and attentiveness by closing the eyes and nodding the head up and down slightly. Then again, maybe you really are a speaking sleeping pill. Let's assume the former.

- You won't get questions from Asians because questions are considered a form of criticism. Asians believe it would be rude to ask you a question because it means that you didn't explain your subject well enough. Or, they may not wish to appear unintelligent because they didn't understand you (saving face). Use visuals and written materials liberally with these audiences.

- Applause is accepted as a form of approval in most areas of the world. In the United States the applause is sometimes accompanied by whistling. If you hear those whistles in many parts of Europe, you better run. It is a signal for disapproval.

- If you were finishing a presentation in Argentina, and you waved goodbye U.S. style, the members of the audience might all turn around and come back to sit down. To them the wave means, "Hey! Come back." In other parts of Latin American and in Europe, the same wave means "no."

Another handy and inexpensive source of international background information is the *Culturgram* published by the David M. Kennedy Center for International Studies, at Brigham Young University, Provo, Utah. Each *Culturgram* is a four-page newsletter, updated every August, that gives you an easy-to-understand overview of the country of your choice. It includes customs and common courtesies, along with information about the people and their lifestyle. References are also included for additional resources. Currently *Culturgrams* are available for 142 countries (see Appendix B).

By far the most comprehensive source of international customs I know of, other than taking live protocol training, is the *Put Your Best Foot Forward Series* by Mary Murray Bosrock. This four-volume series covering Asia, Europe, Mexico/Canada, and Russia is an indispensable tool for anyone with an interest in the global community. It is a must for presenters who want to put that "fine polish" on their international presentations and actions when visiting a foreign land. I especially liked the "Letters" from the people of the individual regions. These personal letters give a great insight into how to act when dealing with the inhabitants of the region. Make this a must purchase when you are leaving the country (see Appendix B).

A Few Tips From Among the Hundreds Included in Each Volume:

Put Your Best Foot Forward—Russia

Do not expect a lively reaction after you have made a presentation at a seminar or a conference. If nobody approached you, it is not a sign that the audience was not impressed.

To a Russian, joviality and cheerfulness may be interpreted as light-mindedness and might even be seen as impolite. After a meeting, however, joviality and relaxed interaction go a long way toward developing trust.

Never refer to a Russian as "Comrade."

Put Your Best Foot Forward—Mexico/Canada

Do not call Mexicans by their first name until invited to do so.

- Mexicans hold a handshake, squeeze of the arm, or a hug longer than people from the United States and Canada do.

- Do not give a knife or a letter opener as a gift. This symbolizes the severing of friendship.

- In Canada, do not take sides in debates about contentious national issues such as the place of English and French languages in Canadian society.

If going to Quebec, have business cards printed on one side in English and the other side in French.

Realize that Canadians get down to business quickly. Meetings are well organized and extraneous discussion is kept to a minimum.

Put Your Best Foot Forward—Europe

- Humor is ever present in English life. It is normally self-effacing, sarcastic, and sexist. (This doesn't mean that you, as an outsider, can joke about what they joke about.)

In France, never violate the French sense of privacy! Never ask personal questions such as income, address, job, etc.

In Germany, men rise when a woman enters the room, except at a business meeting.

Put Your Best Foot Forward—Asia

● Never wink at anyone in Hong Kong. This is considered a very rude gesture.

● In Singapore, do not chew gum.

● In Taiwan, pace yourself. Drinking and toasting can go on for hours.

Until I studied this series of books, I never realized how much positive impact you can create for yourself just by knowing simple tips about the culture you are addressing.

Another really handy resource when doing business globally is *The International Business Communications Desk Reference* by Susan H. Munger. This concise manual covers all the things you need to know about currencies, exchange rates, time zones, business holidays, metric conversions, postal stuff, customs regulations, and lots more. It also has a section on how to handle written and spoken translations, which will help you avoid miscommunication.

Visuals

Regardless of one's nationality and culture, cartoons and comic strips (see "Cartoons" Chapter 13) are the most universally accepted format for humor. These pieces of visual humor are seen in newspapers and magazines in most areas of the world. They may be found in newsstands in large cities or in large libraries. It might be fun to collect cartoons and comic strips when you travel so you have a ready supply when you need one for a presentation. Be careful to avoid cartoons that have political overtones. If you are presenting to a small group, you can show the periodical or pass it around. If you want to use the cartoon or comic strip in a visual, you may need permission from the artist or copyright owner. Always read the caption for a foreign audience and give them time to mentally translate what you say. It may take what seems to be forever (4-6 seconds) for the idea to sink in. Another good resource for cartoons is *Witty World International Cartoon Magazine* by Creators Syndicate (see Appendix B).

Other forms of visual humor that transcend most cultural barriers are juggling and magic. Good resource materials are available on both topics. *Speaking With Magic* is a book by Michael Jeffreys that not only teaches you simple tricks, but gives you the points you can relate to the trick. Two good magic videos for speakers by master magician Tom Ogden are *Teaching and Training with Magic* and *The Magic of Creativity*. I got Michael's book and the two videos from Royal Publishing (see Appendix B). For juggling and other magic books, call or write for a Morris Costume's Catalog (also see Appendix B). There is a small charge for the catalog, but it's worth it.

Words

Terminology is different in most areas of the world even if the language is English. Highly tested humor that would work anywhere in the U.S. may fall flat in another country simply because the audience doesn't understand one of the words. For example, in Australia, "breakout sessions" are called "syndicates." If you were making a joke in Australia that used the word syndicate, you might totally confuse the audience and they wouldn't laugh. People from most other countries will not relate easily if you mention measurement units such as miles per gallon or miles per hour. You should avoid talking about seasons of the year, which may not be the same as in the United States, sports figures, or celebrities that don't have worldwide name recognition. Rethink all the humor you normally use and try to identify problematic words. This is difficult to do by yourself. Try to find a person familiar with the local culture to help you.

When using translators, humor is tougher because timing and word play don't translate well. You might have to slow down considerably because of interpretation. Some speakers use half sentences to keep up the pace. This is very difficult and requires practice.

Speakers have been known to have fun with interpreters (of course, I would never do this). An unnamed speaker I know purposely mumbled to his interpreter to see what would happen. The interpreter mumbled back. Then the speaker mumbled again. It was hilarious.

Even when the audience speaks English, they may not be able to understand your accent. Avoid idioms and slang and check with local residents to see if you can be easily understood. You may have to adjust your normal rate of delivery and style.

Art Gliner, a longtime humor trainer, gave me this tip: He learns how to say "Happy New Year" in the different languages represented in his audience. That technique always gets a laugh and the further it is from New Years, the better it works. Art also tells me a word of welcome given in the native language works well too.

Difficulties may also arise in question and answer sessions if the presenter cannot understand the questioner. Try to speak with as many local residents as possible before the program so you can get a feel for *their* accent.

A Few Other Tips From Around the World:

● In general, Asians do NOT tend to show excitement. This is rapidly changing. In Malaysia, Singapore, and Indonesia, humor has recently been introduced in business seminars and was well-received by standing room only crowds. Humor is well accepted in Thailand. Thais really want to have fun when they learn. Take lots of small gifts when you travel to Asia to give out and be prepared to receive some too. Research the perfect gift, the appropriate wrapping, the timing of the presentation, the value of the gift, presentation etiquette, and any taboos that might be involved.

- Do not expect standing ovations in Australia. It doesn't seem to be part of their culture.

- Many logistical parameters can be different in foreign countries and you should be prepared. Many countries have different standard paper sizes and use two hole punches instead of three. Any video you plan to use must be converted to the appropriate standard for that country (see Appendix D). You may need an electrical converter to operate equipment you bring with you.

- Outside U.S. borders don't refer to yourself as an American. We must remember that we are not the only Americans. There are North Americans, Central Americans, and South Americans.

- In Japan you should never use self-effacing humor that is normally well received in North American culture. Actually, the Japanese don't like humor in seminars at all. They do appreciate a high degree of humility, so feel free to apologize profusely for your lack of linguistic capability and anything else you can think of to show you are not arrogant.

- Unlike the Japanese, Australians love humor. Plan to use it liberally. But, as always, do your research.

WHAT TO DO BEFORE YOU GO INTERNATIONAL
by international protocol expert Marie Betts-Johnson

- Do your homework. When researching your potential audience, inquire about the age of the attendees. Many Asians, Latin Americans, and Middle Easterners have been educated in the U.S. Such audiences will feel perfectly comfortable with U.S. humor and communication styles. On the other hand, if your audience members are a mix of all ages, it is best to err on the safe side and use well-researched humor, avoiding political statements and, in some instances, such as in Japan, avoid humor altogether.

- In the U.S., speakers connect with their audience through eye contact. This is not the case in many other parts of the world. Asians will not wish to make eye contact with you as a sign of respect. Middle Easterners and Latin Americans may indulge in a penetrating stare toward male presenters that may make you want to run for cover. Like the Asians, these people may not make eye contact with a woman out of respect for her.

- To North Americans, eye contact is the connection from your heart to the hearts of your audience members. Be prepared to feel a sense of isolation when addressing an international audience. I once felt as if I was stranded on a desert island when speaking to an international group of doctors. The Northern Europeans, who are unaccustomed to showing emotion, maintained very stiff countenances. The Koreans had deadpan expressions. The Middle Eastern contingent did not look at me. But, I kept on going, determined to do the best job possible. At the end, the applause was controlled and I ended my presentation feeling as if I had not done a good job. The president of the organization approached me and told me that my luncheon speech was the highlight of the entire event and the information they received warranted an editorial in their international professional publication.

- As a speaker in a foreign land, your actions before and after your speech could determine your ultimate success. Understand greeting rituals and the order of introductions, handshaking, and bowing. Bow to your audience in front of the lectern in Japan before you begin your speech. Always apologize for your lack of linguistic ability and, whenever possible, learn some phrases in their language. Do not be afraid to make mistakes. Use the effort to add to your audience's enjoyment! Your attempt to please them will be greatly appreciated.

- Before or after your speech, you may be invited to dine with your hosts. Understand their dining rituals and be prepared with an eloquent toast in their language. Be prepared to be a good conversationalist. Watch your voice volume in Asia: the lower the tone, the higher the rank. It is best to ask many questions and show your respect by discussing their culture and rich history. Their style of dining may be very different from what you are accustomed to, such as the use of chopsticks, continental style (using both knife and fork), or using the right hand only (not the left one) in the Middle East.

  If you have a sensitive constitution, do not ask about the food. You may not like the answer. For instance, in Baghdad, I was once served sheep's testicles, which are considered a delicacy. I realized I would have felt better had I not asked. Take something to soothe your stomach and try everything that is offered. Eat slowly in Asia. You do not want to finish before your hosts. In the Middle East, accept seconds if possible to demonstrate how much you are enjoying yourself.

- Bring many small gifts that are wrapped appropriately. If you are going to China, wrap your gifts after clearing customs, as they will wish to inspect them. There is a myriad of gift giving rituals for each country you visit. In Asia, the manner in which a gift is presented adds to the overall significance of your gift.

● Dress well and be conservative. This is especially true for women. There are many precautions a woman should take in Asia, Latin America, and the Middle East. Women in the U.S., in general, tend to be outgoing and friendly. These traits may be misconstrued in many other parts of the world. Be careful not to damage your credibility.

In summary, every culture has unique likes and dislikes when it comes to humor. They also have customs that can be very different from our own. Your knowledge of these differences will help you create a connection with your international audience. You must do your homework, but it is worth it since a laugh sounds the same and produces the same good feelings in any language.

IN FUN

Sigmund Freud wrote:

> The most favorable condition for comic pleasure is a generally happy disposition in which one is in the mood for laughter. In happy toxic states almost everything seems comic. We laugh at the expectation of laughing, at the appearance of one who is presenting the comic material (sometimes even before he [she] attempts to make us laugh), and finally, we laugh at the recollection of having laughed.

This concept has been termed *in fun* by people that study humor. If you want your audience to laugh, they must be *in fun*. You, the speaker, must be *in fun*. The emcee or program coordinator must be *in fun*. The whole program should be designed *in fun*.

Don't do anything to take them out of *in fun*. Don't discuss controversial subjects like religion or politics and don't make unfriendly comments to audience members. If a problem occurs which must be dealt with, find an *in fun* way of doing so. For instance, if I'm at a presentation and someone asks me who I voted for I say, "I voted for the USA." That's a cute way to say that I really don't want to talk about it.

Dr. Charles Jarvis, one of the greatest humorists of all time, told me about a friend of his who was an excellent speaker, but lost his audience when he forced someone to turn off a tape recorder. He was so nasty about the way he said it that the *in fun* audience totally turned against him.

An *in fun* audience is more critical for the speaker who is there to entertain, but the concept should be in the back of every NO ZZZZZs presenter's mind. Your material may be controversial by nature, but that doesn't mean that you should go out of your way to do or say things that will take the audience further out of *in fun*.

Also, pay close attention to the total program. One friend of mine had to present comical material just after a passionate plea went out to the audience to collect funds for starving babies. He came on stage just after the teary-eyed audience had seen slides of emaciated children. If you ever get caught in this situation, DON'T start right in with your humorous material. Start out gently with a sincere reference to what the audience has just seen. Cut most of your early humor and get to your subject to ease the audience's transition to your more lighthearted topic.

> *In London, theatregoers expect to laugh; in Paris, they wait grimly for proof that they should.*
>
> Robert Dhery

How do you put *in fun* into practice? You could pass out fun snacks to the audience or put balloons on their chairs. Meeting announcements and agendas can be decorated with cartoon characters. Funny props (see "Props," Chapter 13) are great for putting people *in fun*. Do anything you can to be sure your audience knows that it's OK to laugh. One time I had a ventriloquist introduce me at an early morning meeting to wake up everyone and get them *in fun*.

NAMETAGS

According to Sheila Feigelson from Happy Associates, Ann Arbor, Michigan, there are many ways to encourage people to laugh with each other and get them *in fun* WITHOUT being an entertainer. Sheila says,

There is always a certain amount of tension when people get together. They're thinking about things like: Who's here? How long will the meeting last? What's this going to obligate me to? Is it going to be any fun? How will my opinions and ideas be accepted? Some lighthearted humor and shared laughter help to reduce the natural tension and put people at ease. It can have an energizing effect, and perhaps most important, it can create the kind of climate that invites participation. Sheila makes creative use of nametags to help get her audiences *in fun*. She says when nametags are being used, they can serve as a wonderful icebreaker by including more than the participant's name and title. At one meeting, Sheila got tired of the old standby nametag "Hello, my name is . . ." so she instructed participants as they arrived to write their own name and the name of someone they are NOT. People looked quizzical at first, and then they got into the spirit and started laughing. Since there are so many people that each of us are not, our choices are almost limitless. During the introductions, people told who they were and who they *weren't*! It was fascinating. One person said, "My name is not Mary. She's my sister, and everyone gets us mixed up." And that led to another person volunteering, "I'm not Robert Redford . . . but no one ever confuses us!!!"

Another nametag idea is to have people write their name and three significant numbers. After all, what do people say after they read your name? It's hardly an invitation to conversation, let alone smiles and laughter. So, on one occasion, Sheila wrote down three numbers that just came into her head: 3, 1, and 10. As she greeted old friends and new acquaintances, they looked at her nametag and asked about the numbers. She replied, "I have three sons, one husband, and ten years ago is when I think I last cleaned out my kitchen junk drawer!" She noticed that several people returned to the registration table and added numbers to THEIR nametags as well! The conversations became more animated and personalized.

Another great conversation stimulator is to write your name and something that people in the room probably don't know about you. One of Sheila's reluctant participants insisted, "No one here knows me at all. I don't know what to write." "Perfect!" She said. "It's wide open for you!" This also works well for groups where people DO know each other pretty well. After all, no one knows everything about everyone else!

Other additions to nametags include the name of someone who makes you laugh, a childhood toy or game, a favorite funny TV show, or old radio program. It's hard to think about funny things without smiling and laughing out loud! This affects the tone of the meeting and helps people connect in positive ways immediately even as they are creating their nametags. Sheila once asked a large group who work in the same company to think about their job title. Since many job titles tell little about what a person actually does, she suggested that they rename their jobs to reflect their daily tasks and to put that on their nametag. People were delighted with this and they laughed uproariously!

I sometimes use colored nametags or hang specially printed ribbons from nametags. I've even had participants put their nametags in the middle of their backs or wear them upside down.

From a simply practical standpoint, nametags allow you to call the audience members by name, which helps build rapport. Your audience members love it when you call them by name.

Office supply stores sell several different types of badge kits. Some have alligator clips and some have safety pins to hold the nametag to the participant's clothing. Some people don't like the safety pin method because it puts a hole in their clothes. The cheapest way is to buy the ones that stick on like labels. Also, laser printers and software make it easy to create professional looking nametags.

HANDOUTS

Handouts are multipurpose tools that enhance most presentations. They are also another way to get audience members *in fun*.

I provide handouts for virtually every presentation I do. One of the reasons is that audience members really enjoy being able to take something home with them. For me, it is also a way to make sure they have easy access to my name and phone number in case they have questions or if they want to hire me.

Computer programs make it very easy to create totally customized handouts for your presentations. These are valued by the participants and meeting planners much more than generic ones. I always make a customized cover that is printed on colored paper and that uses some type of graphic that pertains to the group. For instance, if I am speaking to the printing industry, I go to my electronic clipart

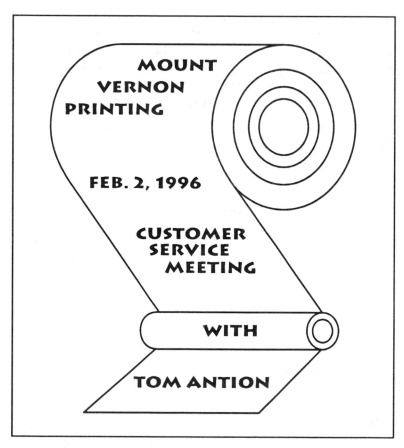

Illustration 2-1 Customized handout cover

collection and find something that pertains to printing. In this case I located a large roll of printing paper (Illustration 2-1). If I don't have any clipart that pertains to the industry, I'll put a cartoon of myself standing on a map of their state (Illustration 2-2). Don't be afraid to be creative. If it is customized to them, they will love it.

Most of the time I customize the inside of the handout too. I only use modules that I know will pertain to their group and many times I include quotes that I got from the actual attendees during my pre-program interviews (Illustration 2-3).

I always try to put something fun in the handout. In Illustration 2-4, I simply pulled out on-file humor that pertained to the group and gave it to them. This vir-

Illustration 2-2 Handout cover customized to area of presentation
(I'm originally from Western Pennsylvania.)

tually insured that the handout would not be thrown away. In Illustration 2-5, I gave the attendees a reason for using the handout when they got back to their offices. The stress reducer exercise is lots of fun and again gives my handout a

Cause: Expectations are too high
Fix: Rule of Two

Cause: Many of us didn't grow up with computers[1]
Fix: Team High tech generation with chronologically gifted generation

Cause: Limited and expensive access to experts
Fix: "Computer Translator"[2]

Cause: Belief that computers are our savior

Paper less Society[3]

More Leisure Time[4]

Fix: Understand that computers are just another business tool

Thanks to:
1. Chuck, for WSJ article.
2. Thelma, for this term.
3. John, example.
4. Jim, for his quotes.

Illustration 2-3 Customized handout interior
Audience members who helped me prepare are named in the handout.

longer life. For space reasons I didn't put my name and address on each page in these examples. But when I am actually preparing handouts all my information goes at the bottom of each page.

Some presenters believe that you should not give out handouts until the end of

---

TAKE HOME FUNNIES FROM TOM'S HUMOR LIBRARY

COMPUTERS:

It's great because now I'm perfect. Anything that is wrong I can blame on my computer.

The computer has revolutionized business. It used to take months to figure out you were broke.

To err is human. To really screw up requires a computer.

Go ahead put it on the computer. At least you'll know where it is, even though you can't find it.

Kids used to forget their homework. Now they claim it's lost in the computer.

You get your kids a new computer and they bring home the same old report cards.

Computers perform complex calculations in 1/100,000 second, and send out invoices ten days late.

ACCOUNTANTS:

My CPA is shy and retiring. He's $250,000 shy. That's why he's retiring.

Old accountants never die. They just lose their balance.

How is your daughter doing in accounting class?
Great! Now instead of asking us for her allowance, she bills us for it.

Remember the bookkeeper
Perched on the stool,
Green eye-shade tilted,
Quill for a tool.
It wasn't too fast,
But nowhere in town
Did you hear the excuse
"Our computer is down."
        R. S. Sullivan

Illustration 2-4 Jokes and one-liners for the audience

NO COST STRESS REDUCER FOR YOUR ORGANIZATION

Instructions: When times get tough, take a few minutes and think up captions for these cartoons or copy this page and hold an organization wide contest.

Illustration 2-5 *In fun* exercise for the audience

your presentation. They think the attendees will read ahead and not pay attention to you. That could be a valid concern if you could not give them out very far in advance of the presentation. I give mine out early enough so the attendees can look through them to satisfy their curiosity before I start. Plus, I have built in elements like the stress reducer, take home funnies, and sometimes a custom crossword puzzle to encourage them to get *in fun* before I start.

I also use my handout as an involvement technique and memory jogger for me. I recruit audience members to follow along with the handout to make sure I'm on track. It gives them something to do and it substitutes for my notes. As soon as the audience member tells me the next topic, I start talking without notes because I've practiced each section thoroughly (see "Bits—Chunks, Series," Chapter 5).

Another way to use the handout for involvement is to make an outline, but leave blank spaces for key words. The audience members must fill in the blanks. Example: It takes only __4__ seconds for a telephone customer to decide whether they like you or not.

ALCOHOL

If an audience has been at a cocktail event of one hour or longer, you usually will have some boisterous audience members to deal with. You could be faced with hecklers, disruptive and loud people, loud snoring sleepers, etc. Unless you are a comic who is very good at mild insult humor, you SHOULD NOT use heckler lines like: *Hey, buddy. There's only one Mic and I've got it.* Or, *If I'm going to make an ass of myself up here, I want to do it myself.*

When you suspect you may have a problem because of a long cocktail hour, let the meeting planner know in advance that he or she should be prepared to tell the heckler that there is a phone call waiting. This gets the person out of the room where the meeting planner can try to calm them.

Request in advance that the bar be shut down when you are speaking, or people who really like to drink will be getting up and down during your presentation distracting everyone.

Many professional speakers guarantee their work EXCEPT when the audience is drunk or too tired. Patricia Fripp, told me about a time she was booked to speak to a vegetable company. They had the meeting in a winery. The entire group including the president were pickled. The meeting planner forced her to go on. Patricia said, "Half the crowd missed me completely and the other half saw two of me. I guess it evened out."

> *An ounce of prevention is worth a pound of bandages and adhesive tape.*
>
> Groucho Marx

Remember, you are the one standing up there looking foolish. Take every precaution you can when alcohol is flowing.

CONNECTING WITH THE AUDIENCE

Audience members assimilate information in three different ways. Some people hear the information, some see the information, and some feel the information. Although most individuals switch their emphasis frequently, one style usually predominates for a given individual. The styles of information transfer are called respectively auditory, visual, and kinesthetic.

For you to connect with the most audience members, you should include information throughout your program that appeals to all three of these styles. People that are primarily visual assimilators may be daydreaming throughout the portions of your presentation where you are using only words to convey your information. They will perk-up when you use a visual aid such as an overhead, flipchart, or prop.

People that are kinesthetically oriented are looking for those words that describe feelings and that evoke emotions. They will also wake up and come to attention if you have them come up on stage with you and you shake hands with them or put your hand on their shoulder (not in Asia). Auditory assimilators might just love to hear you talk or they might like to hear a recording of JFK or some type of music

When you plan your program so that auditory, kinesthetic, and visual elements are interspersed throughout, you will increase your chances of connecting with all the audience members and decrease the chance that old Mr. Sandman will come knocking on their heads.

Always enter a strange hotel room with extreme caution.
—Magnum, P.I.

Room setup

The arrangement of chairs, the sound system, the lighting, and the overall climate of the room can make a big difference in the way a presentation is received. You may not think you have much control over these items; but think again, because you do.

EQUIPMENT

If you have prior access to the room where your presentation will be held, you should always get there as early as possible. I have never had a presentation where everything about the room setup was perfect. There is ALWAYS something amiss. Expect minor problems to be the norm.

CHAPTER 3

The first time I gave the full day seminar associated with this book I had a few MINOR problems. The sound man who had the mixing board, wireless microphone, and tape deck didn't show up. The videographer was delayed with a speeding ticket and showed up 10 minutes before the program was to start. That caused a 40-minute delay.

So what did I do? I dug into my NO ZZZZZs bag of tricks. I had a back-up, hand-held microphone with a long cord with me so I plugged it into the meeting room's sound system. One of the other presenters had a portable cassette player so we played the opening music on the cassette player and put the microphone in front of the speaker. It wasn't the best sound, but it got the job done. I had a good quality home-grade video camera there that was supposed to shoot secondary footage. It was just being moved to the main camera position when the video technician showed up.

Fifteen minutes into the program the video projector, an integral part of the program, conked-out. Since the projector was to be used throughout the day, something had to be done and done quickly. So what did I do this time? I did just as any really polished, unshakable, NO ZZZZZs presenter would do—I told the audience to take a break and started scrambling to check out the projector. I determined that it was nothing that I could fix fast, so I made plans to bring in several monitors arranged as back-up. This was not as good as an 8-foot by 8-foot screen, but it would have to do. While I was checking out the video projector, one of the seminar participants was watching and overheard my decision to bring in the monitors. He said, "Listen, I've got a video projector at my office. I can go get it and have it set up in 20 minutes." He did, and I gave him a $90 audio tape album for his thoughtfulness.

These were obviously more than minor problems, but being prepared with backup equipment and being in the room early enough to do something about the problems saved the day. A little help from a friendly participant didn't hurt either.

ATMOSPHERE

Unless you are using slides or video projection, you want the room lights at maximum intensity for normal business presentations. This could change if you want a comedy club atmosphere where the presenter is extremely well lit and the audience is in relative darkness. Darkened seating allows the audience members to laugh as loud as they want without feeling like everyone is looking at them.

Half of your effectiveness with humor is realized because the audience can see you. The audience wants to see your face. They want to see your expressions. They want to see your body language. It is easier to establish a bond when the speaker and the audience can see each other, which is one good reason to avoid reading your presentation from behind a lectern. I attended a presentation in Washington, D.C., by a "big name" author. I'll call him Mr. Sleeping Bag or SB for short. Before the presentation Mr. SB was in the room with 300 people with a bored, nasty look on his face. I tried to make eye contact with him when he walked by me and he stared right through me. He conducted a three-hour slide

> **Frank Burns:** Why does everyone take an instant dislike to me?
> **Trapper John McIntyre:** It saves time, Frank.
>
> M*A*S*H

show with no breaks. Oh, no!! Better start handing out the kerchiefs and caps because the audience was just settling down for a long winter's nap. He was totally "in the dark" behind a lectern. I am an audience watcher, so I know he never connected with the audience. Besides being in the dark, the man made several other inexcusable mistakes that indicated little regard for his audience. Three hours is too long to go without a break. Starting at the one-and-one-half hour mark people were constantly getting up to go to the restroom or getting refreshments.

What could this sleepy time presenter have done to dramatically increase the effectiveness of his presentation? Since I'm supposed to be talking about lighting right now, I will. All he had to do was place a soft light on himself that lit him or at least lit his face. A low intensity light placed properly would not have affected the visibility of the projection screen at all, but would have helped him connect with the audience. They would have been able to see his face. As it was, all they heard was a voice coming from the darkness.

The other problems I mentioned were not lighting related, but I'll tell you how to fix them now anyway. TAKE CARE OF YOUR AUDIENCE'S BASIC NEEDS. Three hours with no break is ridiculous. Schedule a short break and you won't have audience members interrupting the presentation every few minutes. I never go more than one hour and fifteen minutes between breaks. Tell them exactly when to return so people aren't wandering around wondering when 10 minutes is up. A good trick to get them back is to build anticipation of what they will get when they return. You could say something like, *When you return from the break I'm going to show you never-before-seen video footage of our newest super improved widget.*

If you are nervous or scared or bored before a presentation, don't let the audience know. Old SB would have been better off hiding from the audience than alienating them with his sourpuss face. If you're nervous or scared, go out and greet audience members. It will make both of you feel better. If you can't do that, stay hidden until it is time to start.

It was a shame this guy had no basic presentation skills because his content was excellent. I'm sure his book sales suffered at that event.

SEATING

Seating arrangements are a critical part of any successful presentation and are especially important for humorous presentations. The best situation is when you have total control over the seating style and setup of the room. As a professional NO ZZZZZs presenter, you must consider not only interaction, but safety and comfort as well. (For this discussion I'll be using laughter and interaction synonymously.)

By far the best seating arrangement for laughter is semicircular. When audience members are seated close together on a curve, they can look to their left or right and see the faces of each person in the row. This togetherness allows laughter to pass immediately from one person to the other. You will even see audience members elbowing and slapping their immediate neighbor on the knee.

Illustration 3-1 Semicircular seating.
Each chair faces directly toward the presenter.

In a straight row theater style, when an audience member looks left or right, all he or she sees is the ear of the next person in the row. If that next person is not laughing, the other audience member is less likely to laugh. According to researchers A.M. Rankin and P.J. Philip, laughter is contagious. They suggest that one of the most prominent aspects of laughter is its ability to cause imitation in other individuals, i.e., many people will laugh just because they see others laughing. Another researcher, Antony Chapman, reported an experiment that supports the findings of Rankin and Philip. He found that laughter can be a "socially facilitated" phenomena. Under the right conditions, the person(s) laughing don't even have to understand the humor. If you use a semicircular seating arrangement where each audience member can see everyone's face in the row, you will create a much greater likelihood of people seeing someone else laughing. You, the presenter, will have a much better chance of having your audience enjoying laughter using the semicircular setup.

Illustration 3-2 Shifted semicircular seating.
Chairs are faced toward the screen when the bulk of
the presentation uses visuals.

There are several other advantages to semicircular (Illustration 3-1) over straight row seating for the humorous presentation, notes Paul O. Radde, Ph.D, Director of the Audience Centered Seating™ Institute. Most notable is *comfort* and *line of sight*, accomplished when each chair is set facing the presenter directly. In straight row setups, audience members seated toward the outside of the rows must turn their heads sharply just to see the presentation. This creates great discomfort in the neck and lower back. In addition, a sharply turned neck reduces blood flow to the brain. So, those on the outside of a seating section are less able to think clearly and participate wholeheartedly. An uncomfortable audience member is less likely to laugh and more likely to tune out all together. You may as well turn out the lights 'cause the party's over—at least for them. In consideration of the comfort of your entire audience, circle the seating.

Line of sight is essential for humor, Dr. Radde says, "If they can't see you, they can't hear you." Many audience members who can't see very well read lips to understand what is said, yet don't know that they rely on lip reading. When the audience is at a distance from the presentation, the presenter is not visible or is poorly lighted, or when visibility is poor, the audience finds that they cannot understand what is being said. For the humorist who relies heavily on gestures and facial expressions, it is essential that he or she be well-lighted to the audience.

If the bulk of the presentation consists of looking at a screen, you could point all the chairs at the screen instead of where the presenter will be standing (Illustration 3-2). Do whatever it takes to keep your audience comfortable.

Always attempt to be as close as you can to the first row in whatever seating arrangement you have. Distance between you and the audience is a definite barrier to interaction. Don't use a riser unless it is absolutely necessary for you to be seen.

You may get some resistance from room setup personnel who are not used to semicircular seating arrangements, but don't give up. If you get to the presentation site early, you can usually make changes yourself. Remember—you are the one who will look bad if the presentation doesn't go well. No one will ever blame the setup crew if the audience goes off to dreamland.

However, sometimes it will not be possible to change seating arrangements. Other presentations may be scheduled before yours or union restrictions could prevent your from moving the seats yourself. Shoot for the best when you can and be persistent. On the other hand, don't be distracted if you end up with a poor seating arrangement. If you are prepared and have a powerful message, you can still do a good job.

If you have to present in a situation where the seats are fixed, don't despair. If the seats can't move, you can (Illustration 3-3). Be more animated and move around! This will cause the audience to move their heads to see you, thus creating more interaction and increasing the chance they will see another face that is laughing. It will also give them a chance to relieve some of the tension in their necks.

Another trick you can use if you're stuck with fixed seating is to ask the audience to choose a new seat after they come back from a break. Anytime you use this technique you must tell the audience why you are doing it and you must give the instructions *before* they take a break. American audiences have a "homing

Illustration 3-3 Fixed theater style seating.
You must move, if the seats cannot be adjusted.

instinct" for the same seat they started with and they will be upset if you snatch it away for no reason.

For example, tell them that part of the reason to come to a presentation is to meet and interact with new people and changing seats will help accomplish this goal. In addition to making the audience more comfortable, this is a good technique to add networking value to your presentations.

Do watch out for a situation where seating arrangements in an organization have been established over a long period of time. If you come in as the "new kid on the block" and try to make drastic changes, you may upset many "old timers." Make changes slowly and always tell your audience why.

Still, it's best to be able to arrange the seating optimally. Let's take a look at standard seating arrangements and see how effective they are and what you can do to make them better if necessary.

Standard Seating Arrangements
Board Room Rectangular Table (Illustration 3-4)
Disadvantage: Participants can't see the faces of people seated on the same side of the table.

Possible Changes: 1. Ask people seated on the long sides to bow their chairs back away from the table (helpful if chairs have rollers). Since this makes extensive writing difficult, you must give them hardback tablets. **2.** Present from a corner of the table (X^1). **3.** Present from the middle of the long side of the table (those next to you will naturally fan out so they can see you).

Board Room Oval Table
This setup is good because seats are already bowed and people can still be close to the table to take notes.

Classroom Rectangular
Tables (Illustration 3-5)
Disadvantage: Participants can't see faces of people seated on the same side of the table.

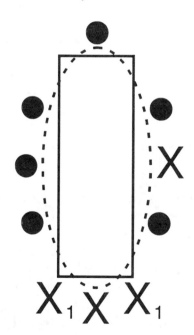

Illustration 3-4 Rectangular Boardroom table.
Present from the various X positions and MOVE.

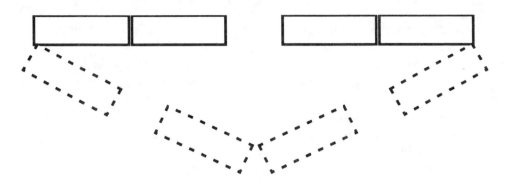

Illustration 3-5 Classroom rectangular seating.
Shift tables to a chevron pattern so each participant can see more faces.

Possible Change: Create two aisles and chevron the tables to approximate a semicircle.

Classroom U-shaped (Illustration 3-6)
Disadvantage: Participants can't see faces of people seated on the same side of the table.
Possible Change: Move tables slightly to create a horseshoe.

Straight Theater Style with Movable Seats
Advantage: Audience members close.
Disadvantages: 1. Audience members cannot see the faces of other audience members in the same row. **2.** Audience members near ends of rows must turn heads sharply to see presentation.
Possible Change: Move chairs into a semicircular pattern.

Straight Theater Style with Fixed Seats
Advantage: Closeness of audience members
Disadvantages: 1. Audience members cannot see the faces of other audience members in the same row. **2.** Audience members near the end of rows must turn heads sharply to see presentation.
Possible Change: The presenter should move more than usual.

Banquet Round Tables (see "Tom's Banquet/Luncheon Tips" Appendix F)
Disadvantages: 1. Audience members are spaced far apart. 2. Audience members must turn chairs in all different directions with relation to the table to see the presentation.
Possible Changes: Leave the setup alone. Ask program coordinator or introducer to invite participants to turn their chairs toward the front and get comfortable

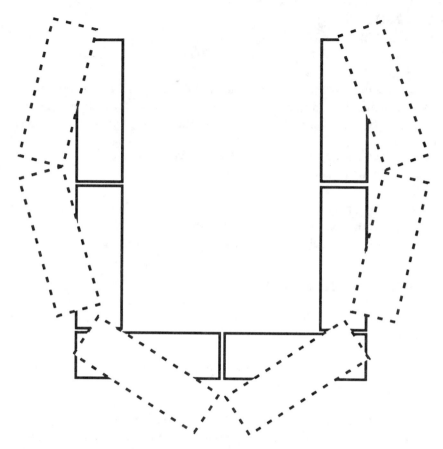

Illustration 3-6 Classroom U-shaped seating.
Bow out tables to resemble a horseshoe.

before the presentation begins. If program coordinator or introducer forgets to do this, you do it. Another option would be to seat only five or six people at the half of the round table facing the presentation.

Also, try to make sure the area where you are speaking does not have service doors near it. If possible have the room set so the service doors are behind the audience as they look toward you. You don't want any extra competition from busboys and waitresses.

Troubleshooting

Set or troubleshoot any meeting room setup using one or more of these Audience Centered Seating™ practices advocated by Dr. Radde.

● When possible set the presentation toward the long wall of the room to draw all audience members closer to the presenter and A/V surfaces. Long narrow bowling alley-type sets place the back row as much as 135 feet from the presenter.

● Circle the seating and face each chair directly toward the presentation and audio visual surfaces.

● Set for ease of access and exit—no row more than 13 seats, so no one crosses over more than six to get seated. Cut single chair access lanes in large seating sections to provide more aisle seats and easier access.

Additional Seating Tips

● People prefer to sit by aisles. Avoid chairs next to walls. Audience members will feel trapped.

● Aisles should get bigger as they get nearer the exits because they must accommodate more people.

● Seat for least distraction and best focus on presentation. Turn off wall sconces behind the presentation. Set away from open windows, clocks, and entry doors.

● Even after you have pre-set the seats perfectly, suggest to audience members that they adjust their seating slightly for comfort.

● Encourage seating in the front of the room by cordoning off back rows with masking tape, rope, or string, or placing reserved signs on back tables.

● Avoid reserving seats through tipping chairs up against tables. The jutting legs tend to bruise shin bones and trip audience members.

Trick: Only put out 50-75 percent of the chairs for the expected number of participants and you will almost always have a packed house. Stack the rest of the chairs in the back corner of the room for easy access if needed.

Trick: When you have a choice, opt for a smaller room. This again gives you a better chance for a packed house.

SOUND SYSTEM

If it is hard to hear, people won't listen. As a humorous NO ZZZZZs presenter you must have an excellent sound system because some of the time you will be talking while your audience is laughing. Stand-up comics need good sound too, but they are a little different because they tell a joke, then people laugh (they hope). They tell another joke, then people laugh. A humorous presenter will be rolling right along making points, showing product features, telling stories, and dropping one-liners and must be heard all the while.

A humorous presentation demands a better sound system than a serious talk. In a serious talk, words can be missed and the main message can still be very clear. In humor it doesn't work that way. If key words are missed in a joke or story, it will ruin the humor. No one will laugh and you will look like a giant goober (it will, however, give you a good chance to use a saver line from Chapter 9 that they won't hear either).

This need for a thorough sound check is another good reason to be in the room early. You need to check the microphone to make sure it works. You need to check to see how far your mouth should be from the microphone. You need to know how loudly you should talk. Realize that during your check the audio level should be very loud. People will absorb the sound once they get into the room.

Make sure the sound system is carrying to all parts of the room. If someone speaks prior to you, try to go to the back of the room to see how he or she is coming across. If you have someone at the presentation with you, have them signal from the back of the room if changes are needed after you have started.

If the amplifier controls aren't handy after you have started, you can adjust the sound by changing the distance between your mouth and the microphone and/or increasing or decreasing the loudness of your voice. Try not to use the latter method too often so you don't strain your vocal mechanism.

Music

Background music playing when participants enter a room is a great way to set the mood for a NO ZZZZZs meeting or event. It also makes you look like a more polished presenter. The proper selection of music gets people in the right mood and adds a touch of drama to the presentation. You can also use music when the participants are leaving to give them a pleasant atmosphere as they exit. Avoid turning music on or off suddenly. It should always fade in and fade out slowly.

When selecting music, generally you would pick upbeat music for upbeat presentations and slower music for more serious ones. This is very subjective, but not usually too critical unless you're the type who would play loud rock music at a retirement home. If you have no clue how to pick music, get some expert help or buy music designed for presentations from a training supply company that has labels that tell you when to use it.

If you are on a tight budget and can't arrange for professional sound equipment, don't worry. In small rooms a decent boom box will suffice. If you are in a larger room, you can put the microphone that will be used for the presentation in front of the speaker of the boom box. This will send the music through the room's sound system.

BIG WARNING: DO NOT PLAY COPYRIGHTED MUSIC WITHOUT THE PROPER LICENSING OR YOU WILL BE SORRY. THE MUSIC POLICE WILL GET YOU. Don't worry though, I'll explain below how you can still use music without the threat of a lawsuit.

As this book is being written, lawsuits abound between meeting planners and Broadcast Music Incorporated (BMI) and The American Society of Composers, Authors, and Publishers (ASCAP). If you want to use copyrighted music, make sure you tell your meeting planner. At the time of this writing, the sponsoring organization is ultimately responsible for the proper licensing of music played at an event. However, the real life story says that you should clear your use of music with the sponsoring organization well in advance of the program. If you don't, you may be the one responsible for a lawsuit against the organization that hired you. Better hang up your laser pointer because you won't last long as a speaker pulling those kinds of stunts.

How to Get Licensing

If you are doing your own public seminars and you want to use copyrighted music, you must obtain your own license. Call BMI or ASCAP (see Appendix B) for details.

The way to get around this hassle is to play copyright-free music which, for use as background music, is just as good. This music is available through production music houses or you can get prepackaged music for meetings from a company called Resources for Organizations (see Appendix A).

I say again, if you are going to use music, don't forget to tell your meeting planner (if you have one) so he or she will not be surprised. You don't want the meeting planner or chair of the meeting getting all upset because of the threat of a lawsuit.

Visuals

Some type of visual in the room as the participants enter is a good way to signal them that your presentation will be different. It could be an interesting picture or funny quotation on the overhead screen or a nicely done color flip chart page. It could be anything that makes the participants take notice. It will build their anticipation of your presentation.

Climate

Uncomfortable people will not listen to you. The unwritten rule is that meeting rooms are always too hot or too cold, so you'll have to do your best.

When setting air-conditioning levels, the room should be cooler than you think it should be. The body heat of the audience will bring the room to the comfort level. Make sure it does, and be ready to make adjustments as you go. If you can't get the right temperature, make sure you acknowledge the audience's discomfort and encourage them to make the best of it. Your care for them will automatically make things a little better.

Distractions

It is up to you to keep room distractions to a minimum. The meeting planner and everyone else are usually too busy to think about all the little details that can make your presentation a success.

Doors

One of the biggest sources of distraction has to do with something every meeting room has and that is a door. Doors squeak, they slam shut, and they allow people to walk in the audience's line of sight. According to Tom's Law of Presentations, these three things are only allowed to happen at the exact moment of your best punch line or most dramatic statement.

However, doors are very easy to deal with if you can gain access to the room early. The first thing I do is check to see if the doors squeak. If they do, I call maintenance or find a little oil can and oil the hinges. If it's an old hotel, this probably hasn't been done in 30 or 40 years. Then I let the door swing shut on its own. This tests the closing mechanism. If it is hopelessly weak and allows the door to slam shut, I either ask for it to be adjusted (which no one ever knows how to do) or I have someone stand at the door to open and close it for latecomers. The latch of the door can make lots of noise to, so you simply tape the catch mechanism shut.

Door location can also be a pesky problem. Sometimes the room is set so there is a door behind or very close to the stage area. If someone would enter this door during your presentation, it would be very distracting. You can usually tape up a "Please Use Other Door" sign to help with this. When you know you have any kind of door problem, try to alert the planner or recruit people from the organization to police the doors for you.

Stage

The stage background can be a distraction. If possible, I try to find out what my background will be so I don't blend right in. If I have a blue curtain and I wear a blue suit, it will be harder for the audience to separate me from the background. Wall sconces directly behind the stage can also be a distraction. I try to have these sconces turned off or I remove the bulbs because such unplanned backlighting causes the front of a speaker to darken considerably. However, planned backlighting from above is OK because it creates a halo effect which makes the speaker stand out from the background. I beg for this all the time because it's the only way a guy like me is ever going to get a halo.

Also check to see that any risers and stairs to the risers don't squeak and are sturdy. You may fall down on purpose some time for fun, but you don't want to accidentally fall if you can help it. If you do fall, use a pre-planned ad-lib from Chapter 9 such as *Give me an inch and I'll take a fall.*

A good beginning makes a good ending
—English Proverb

Introductions and Openings

Many speakers pay little or no attention to their introduction. They think it has little or no effect on their overall performance but, in fact, it does. Introductions are a time to bring a speaker and audience together so that the speaker can deliver a message to an audience which has been made receptive. You must take control of your introductions if at all possible!

CHAPTER 4

INTRODUCTIONS BY ANOTHER PERSON

One way to do it is to let your introducer know well in advance how important the role is and why it is important. The following sample letter shows you how to do this.

Dear (Introducer's Name),

   Introductions are important not only for my benefit, but
for yours too. A well-done introduction can make a big difference in how a talk is received. It sets the proper tone for
the audience and gets the program off to a great start.
   I have included a sample introduction for you to use. Feel
free to personalize it in any way you see fit. Since there will
be food service during this function, it would be helpful if
you would make an additional announcement about 10 minutes before I start. This announcement should urge your
members to get their coffee refills now because the program
will start shortly.
   Call if you have any questions or if you need help.

                    Thanks,

                    Tom

   Paragraph one tells the introducer the importance of a good introduction. Paragraph two makes mention of personalization. If the introducer can handle it
without getting carried away, a personalized comment or two helps to connect the
speaker with the group. Hopefully the introducer has gotten to know you a little
personally. A comment that reveals that helps the audience accept you. Use
paragraph three to give any tips that will help the presentation go smoothly.
   Short introductions are always best for several reasons: 1. An introduction that
is too flowery builds resistance in the audience which you will have to overcome;
2. If the introduction keeps expectations low, the audience will be pleasantly
surprised that you are dynamic and funny and they will laugh more easily; 3.
When your introducer is terrible, less damage will be done.
   Always write your own introduction, double space it, and print it in a large,
easily readable type style. Send it to your introducer well in advance and bring
extra copies with you to the presentation.
   When preparing an introduction, use your name several times and also name
your subject. Give a reason for you being chosen as the speaker and a few things
about you that will cause the audience to feel you are qualified to speak. Make
sure benefits to the audience are apparent so they know there is something to be
gained from listening. Don't build resistance by telling them how great you are.
Limit your qualifications to two or three items and use only the ones that pertain
to that group. I always like to insert a simple joke for the introducer that teases me

a little and gets the audience primed to laugh. If possible, I use the same "test" humor each time I am introduced. The amount of laughter I hear in response to this joke acts as a gauge to tell me the degree to which the audience is in fun. Here's a sample of a typical introduction I use.

INTRODUCTION

Tom Antion

Here with us today to talk about a lighter way to do business is **1**{Tom Antion}. Tom is the **2**{author} of six books and is now working on his seventh which is titled *Business Lite: Humor, Effectiveness & The Bottom Line.*

Tom brings to us a **3**{great depth of small business experience. He owned an apartment rental business and a hotel <u>before he graduated from college.</u> He currently owns four small businesses}. **4,5**{His consulting firm Antion & Associates helps companies & individuals realize the great benefits associated with enthusiasm and lightheartedness in the workplace}.

6{Tom is a frequent keynote speaker before all types of business & civic groups}. **7**{The last time he spoke, the audience was glued to their seats. . . . Tom did this to make sure no one left}.

8,9{Here to help us discover a lighter and more profitable way to manage our businesses} is Tom Antion **10**{(lead enthusiastic applause)}

1. Name mentioned several times.
2. The word *author* means credibility.
3. Business experience means credibility.
4. Mentions availability to consult, plus establishes in the audience's mind that you help other companies.
5. Benefits to audience.
6. Shows availability for other talks.
7. Easily delivered joke (test humor).
8. Subject.
9. Benefits to audience.
10. Reminds them to applaud.

Nothing in this introduction underscores the fact that I'm going to be really funny. Had I put in the introduction that this will be the funniest presentation you have ever heard, I would have built an instant resistance. The audience would dig in and say to themselves, "Yeah, let's see how funny this guy really is." It makes it much easier on you to sneak up on them. Here's another benefit for you. If you don't turn out to be all that funny, you will not have bombed because you still delivered your serious message. If you advance bill yourself as funny, the exact same presentation could be considered a bomb.

SELF INTRODUCTIONS

If you have no introducer, you'll have to do it yourself. Then you have no excuse for a bad introduction. Keep it extra short and be careful to eliminate most of your "big brag" items. It's OK if someone else reads or tells about how great you are, but it sounds really bad if you do it.

You can slip in your brag items later as the talk progresses. For example, if you wanted the audience to know you are a consultant, you might say something about it during the body of your talk like, *A couple weeks ago I was doing some consulting for . . . and I found blah, blah, blah.* Always make a point when you throw in brag lines and don't do too many or you'll sound like a name-dropper.

To make my self-introduction funny I might say, *A couple months ago I was consulting with Saddam Hussein on customer service techniques for the nineties.*

OPENINGS

Eventually, after all the hoopla of pre-program questionnaires, room setups, and introductions, you will go on. Here are three major parts to an effective opening.

1. Small talk or unique/challenging statement
2. Response to introduction
3. Localized/personalized comments

Starting Off

You would think that starting off would be a critical time in the presentation wouldn't you? In fact, it's not at all. You can say virtually anything in the opening moments because no one will absorb what you are saying. You can recall your last visit to the city. You can compliment the group. You can talk about the weather. It really doesn't matter.

If we take our example from the theater, you will note that nothing of significance happens until the audience is ready to settle down to the *business of listening*. When you go to a play, the curtain rises and the maid is dusting or the butler is picking lint off a pair of pants. Nothing really important happens until the audience has had a chance to focus on the stage.

You can say anything to use up time, but don't use up too much time. Some speakers think that fooling around too long makes the audience become restless. However, this approach starts a nice slow relationship with the audience where you don't come on strong until they get to know you a little. This might be a good time to show some concern for the audience's comfort. You could ask, *Is it too hot for you, or can everyone see OK?* If it is too hot or they can't see, do something about it or call someone who can. Show them how concerned you are.

If it is too hot and you can't do anything about it, you have an opportunity to make light of that fact. If you don't, everyone will be thinking about it anyway and not listening to you. You could walk over to the air conditioner and pretend to read a notice, *Maintained by the Devil-May-Care Air Conditioner Company.* This lighthearted attitude will demonstrate the fact that you can be flexible enough to handle any adverse situations that may arise. If you can handle it, then your audience will likely follow.

If you want to take a more hard-hitting approach, you can use a unique humorous opening, or a challenging or electrifying statement that will speed the normal focusing process. These openings command attention.

I opened an employee appreciation luncheon once with the statement, *I'm here to talk to you today about Quality Improvement.* I thought the audience members were going to cry until I started laughing and said, *You've heard enough about that lately, haven't you?* In fact, they had it up to their ears with Quality Improvement training.

At a sales training seminar the first words out of my mouth were, *I want you to fail! I want you to fail because in order for you to succeed you must fail! To succeed to high levels you must fail a great deal!* This was a serious NO ZZZZZs opening that commanded immediate attention.

Response to Introduction

The first *important* part of an opening is your response to your introduction. From here on, what you say is very important because it characterizes you to the audience. If you typically introduce yourself, you can skip this part for now and review it when you do a presentation where you are introduced. A response to an introduction is what you say to or about your introducer or what you say about what your introducer said. Can I make that less clear for you?

For instance, if your introduction was too flattering and syrupy you could say:

● *After that, I can't wait to hear what I have to say.*

● *Now I know what it feels like to be a pancake with too much syrup on it.*

● *My mother would have been proud because you read that just like she wrote it.*

If your introduction was too long you could say:

● *This is not the second coming.*

● *I have been feeling a little sick lately. I thought I had the flu, but I guess it must be my eminence.*

- *If you had gone on about me much longer, I might have started to believe some of it.*

For an introduction that is too short you could say:

- *That was the shortest introduction I have ever had. My life just passed before my eyes and I haven't even been up here long enough to die.*

- *Hey! What happened to all that good stuff I paid you to say?*

- *I know I don't deserve all the nice things that WEREN'T said about me in that introduction.*

If you're doing a funny talk and the introducer is a GOOD friend you could say:

- *I normally don't allow a long introduction and in the short amount of time I gave you, Joe, you were starting to screw that up.*

If you're on a program with several big-name speakers you could say:

- *Most of the speakers you've heard here today are like a <u>Who's Who</u> of speaking. I'm more like a Who's He/She?*

Sometimes you will get an introduction that is just bad. Say:

- *Thank you very much for that INTERESTING introduction.*

- *If I'm going to bomb, I want to do it myself. I don't need your help.* (Be careful when, how, and to whom you say this one. You don't want to take the audience out of *in fun.*)

A safe approach when you get a bad introduction is to just skip the response and make general comments to the audience. You don't want to embarrass the introducer.

Localized/Personalized Comments

If you plan on making any comments to specific people in the audience or about the location of the presentation, now is the time to do it. Anything you say at this point should be personalized and/or localized and broadly understood.

One of the things I enthusiastically and sincerely say somewhere in the beginning of a talk is, *I am so happy to be here.* However, that can mean uh-oh, it's pillow time to the audience because everyone says that. What I do is find a reason specific to that group and tell them *why* I am so happy to be with them. This shows the group that I am thrilled to be with them at that very moment. They can't help but like you a little more because of this simple statement. And you know what? I really am thrilled to be with them. If you really aren't happy, it will show, so don't say this unless you mean it.

Another thing I let the audience know even before the talk starts is that I am a giving and helpful person. There is nothing hidden. I do this as I'm walking around talking to people before the program. I'll say to most everyone, *Let me know if there is anything I can do to help you.* Saying this sincerely to a person in your audience is a quick way to build rapport. You will have instant friends in the audience who are less likely to nod off.

If you have a head table, a joke on one of the persons up there with you will work. Audiences like to be able to see the reaction of that person. Make sure you clear it with your target first. If you tell a joke on someone at the head table and he or she doesn't laugh, the audience will not laugh either. This will put a damper on the rest of your talk. Also, if you have four vice-presidents of a company at the head table and you only tease two, the other two may be offended. If the CEO, owner, or highest ranking officer is there, joke about that person because BIG targets are the best. I say again, make sure you clear the joke with Mr./Ms. Big first.

You can also research your introducer and/or the emcee. This will give you ready material if you want to have some fun with them. You may get opportunities for quick retorts to the emcee's jovial barbs (ad-libs).

One of the best ways to comment is to relate to something that happened at the event. This makes you look like a quick wit and a NO ZZZZZs presenter who is highly in tune with the function. You should always be on the lookout for these items before it's time for you to present.

Not too long ago, I was the last speaker at an awards banquet. Prior to my talk, an award was given to a person named Bonnie who had been on the road for 467 days. When I took the microphone I said, *Bonnie, I know how you feel. I've been on the road so long, my roommate sold the house and I can't find him anywhere.*

If you're willing to put in a little effort, you can pre-plan potential comments by visiting the room before the program to determine if it has any quirks that could be mentioned, or you might work up some jokes about the food. All you have to do is find out what is on the menu. A luncheon program I did was to have *Tuna Temptation* as the main course. During the lunch I could tell everyone was commenting about the name of the main dish. I quipped, *I generally don't like seafood, but the Catfish Convulsion was superb* (see "Alliteration," Chapter 13).

Keep in mind that you are not required to start with a funny joke or story. This is the method that everyone expects. You can do the unexpected sometimes and really surprise the audience.

The reason that everyone expects something funny at the beginning of a talk is because that's been the norm for a long time. Robert Skovard, Editor of the *Executive Speaker Newsletter* (see Appendix A) and compiler of the book *Openings*, says, "Among the most frequently used attention-getting devices in the more than 130 examples in *Openings*, is humor." He goes on to say, "Significantly, very few involve the telling of jokes. Rather, they employ a quick observation, a self-put-down, a one-liner, an aside, an aphorism, or a brief personal anecdote." Skovard's book is a tremendous resource and it is completely cross-referenced under many topics.

Some additional opening tips

Make points that folks agree on first. Never create controversy early, unless you are doing it for dramatic effect.

Never tell a long involved story. If it bombs, you will have a tough fight to win back the audience.

Never tell (in your opening) any story or joke that has a remote chance of offending someone. After you warm up the audience, you may be bolder.

Somewhere in your opening you must tell the audience why you are there. They need some selfish reason to listen to you.

Using humor in your opening tells the audience that yours is going to be a fun presentation. It tells them that they might actually enjoy it. Don't disappoint them!

Here are some other ideas for No ZZZZZs openings

Ask a funny or outrageous question like, *How many of you have ever swung from a tree like Tarzan?* Then go on with comments about it being a jungle out there.

Make an outrageous statement like this, *Since 1989 there have been 250 water buffalos collecting social security in this district.*
Note to reader: After that last statement you are seriously wondering why you purchased this book aren't you? To make this work in real life you would follow up with the following statement, *Of course, there aren't 250 water buffalos collecting social security in our district, but ABC is happening and we must do XYQ (no ZZZZZs allowed) about it.*

Mention something in the local newspaper that is outrageous, funny, or an example of what your presentation is about.

- Use a funny quotation that relates to your subject. *Mark Twain said, "I don't mind what the opposition says of me, so long as they don't tell the truth." The truth is . . .*

Trick: Use some highly tested humor in the beginning of a presentation to gauge the responsiveness of the audience.

BONUS MATERIAL

- *Thank you for that wonderful introduction that I so richly deserve and so seldom get.*

- *I won't speak too long today because of my throat. . . . Actually [substitute name of chairperson] threatened to cut it if I went too long.*

- *I asked your chairperson what I should speak about. He said, "About 20 minutes."*

- *I'm always a little intimidated by a microphone. Of course, a microphone never made a fool of anyone. It only shows them up.*

- *Groucho Marx said, "Before I speak, I have something important to say."*

- *Many of you may be wondering why I'm here. . . . I'm wondering about that myself.*

- *I feel like I felt on my wedding night. As I said to my wife/husband, "I am very warm and very nervous . . . but I'm glad to be here."*

- *[Insert name of someone you want to tease] called me three times to do this banquet. On the third time . . . I accepted the charges.*

- *Mark Twain said, "A man can live a month on one compliment." [Insert name of introducer] has just assured my immortality.*

- *Adlai Stevenson said, "Praise is like perfume . . . it's all right to smell as long as you don't swallow it."*

- *I'm here free of charge tonight and by the time I'm done I think you'll agree I was worth every penny of it.*

Men perish because they cannot join the beginning with the end.

—Alcmaeon, (Circa 500 B.C.)

Body

The four questions I'm asked most often about using humor are 1. When should I use humor in my presentation?, 2. How much humor should I use?, 3. How do I make my point with humor?, and 4. How can I remember all that humor? The first, third, and fourth questions I can answer easily, but the second you must answer for yourself. Don't worry though, it is easy to determine and I will tell you how.

CHAPTER 5

MAINTAIN INTEREST LEVEL

To answer question number one, you must first understand the listening pattern of an audience in a typical boring presentation.

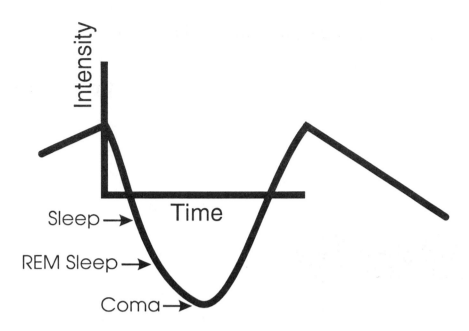

Graph 5-1 Typical listening pattern of audience during snoozer presentation.

In Graph 5-1 the vertical axis represents intensity or interest level of the audience and the horizontal axis represents time. A typical "goodnight kiss" presentation starts out with a hopeful audience at or before the introduction of the presenter. If the introduction is halfway good, the interest level will stay up or rise slightly. Then the boring presenter gets up and tells a dumb and/or irrelevant story or joke and the interest level begins to fall rapidly. As the presenter gets deep into the subject matter, the audience passes through sleep (ZZZZZs), rapid eye movement sleep (New Improved ZZZZZs) and soon into a comatose state (Extra Heavy Duty, Industrial Strength ZZZZZs).

At a critical moment in the presentation, the interest level of the audience rises sharply. This is usually the moment Mr. or Ms. Hammock Head says, "In conclusion." This sharp rise in intensity is primarily due to the audience members putting on their shoes and gathering their briefcases. After droning on for another 15 minutes, the on-stage anesthesiologist figures enough is enough and immediately drops dead, but no one in the audience notices.

Even if you are a really good presenter, it is still tough to keep an audience's interest level up. Every person in an audience daydreams to a certain extent. He or she can't help it. The human mind can listen far faster than you can talk. The mind of each audience member is naturally bored. For those of you that like numbers, the average rate of speech is 140-180 words per minute. The mind is capable of listening at 700 wpm. It's no wonder audience members get bored.

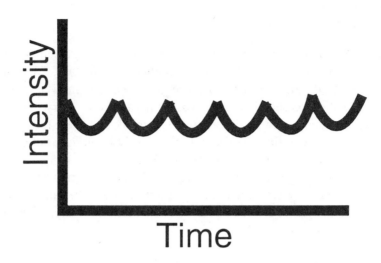

Graph 5-2 Ideal listening pattern of audience.

I'm going to assume that you are not satisfied with letting an audience get bored with you. If you were, you probably would not be reading this book. You want an audience listening pattern as depicted in the graph above.

In Graph 5-2, the interest level of the audience is kept high above the zero level for the entire length of the presentation. Each little wave is an intensity curve that takes the audience up and down, but still at a high level of interest. If you want to deliver effective NO ZZZZZs presentations, it is your responsibility to keep the interest level up.

The peak of each small wave occurs during the presentation when the good presenter has used an attention-getting device or a series of them to grab the audience. There are many tools available.

ATTENTION-GAINING DEVICES

Humor, of course
Props
Stories
Voice inflection
Stage movement
Asking questions of the audience
Showing visuals
Playing music

- Gesturing
- Using quotations
- Reading or reciting poetry

Effective NO ZZZZZs presenters use attention-getting techniques spaced throughout their presentation to keep the audience's interest up. Each of these is discussed in detail throughout this book. The great sales and motivational speaker, Zig Ziglar, hits the audience like clockwork with a joke or story every seven to nine minutes. I even shorten that more to between six and eight minutes for high content talks and several times per minute for mostly humorous talks.

So, my response to the original question "When should I use humor in a presentation?" is at the beginning, the middle and the end, or anywhere you want a peak on your intensity wave. Use humor throughout your presentation and space it at intervals to provide a change of pace and to reemphasize your message in a new and interesting way.

USE AS MUCH HUMOR AS YOU NEED

How much humor should I put in a serious talk? That's my second most frequently asked question. I can't give you the exact answer on that one, so I'll give you the answer everyone hates. It depends. You must ask yourself a series of questions. The answers to these questions will lead you to the final percentage that is right for you.

- Why am I here? Am I here to entertain, inform, motivate, answer questions, etc.?

- What is the nature of my subject? Am I here to congratulate the audience on breaking last year's sales record or am I here to inform the audience there will be massive layoffs?

- What is the nature of my audience? Are they fun-loving and laid-back or do they normally want the information fast and dirty?

- What about me? Have I developed appropriate humor that helps make my point or hold attention? Have I practiced one-liners until I'm comfortable telling them?

The answers to these questions will clearly direct you in the appropriate amount of humor to use.

MAKING A POINT WITH HUMOR

One of the old saws of public speaking says that you should "Tell 'em what you're gonna tell 'em. Tell 'em. Then tell 'em what you told 'em." When you want to make a point during your presentation, you can use a similar formula. You tell 'em the point, illustrate the point, then tell 'em the point again. This formula, however, can seem boring and redundant if you don't spice it up a little. One way to do it is to use humor. Here's the formula:

1. Make your point.

2. Illustrate your point (in our case with a humorous two-liner, but you could use props, humorous props, funny stories, serious stories, case studies, etc.)

3. Restate your point.

Here's an example where your point is "The Importance of Communication." You say:

1. First make your point by saying, *Accurate and clear communication is an important part of our everyday lives.*

2. Then illustrate your point. In this case use a humorous two-liner. *It's like the student pilot who was asked over the radio to state his altitude and location. He said, "I'm five feet nine and I'm in the left seat."*

3. Then restate your point in a slightly different manner by saying, *You can see how what we may think is clear communication could be interpreted incorrectly especially when people are under pressure.*

LEARN MATERIAL EASILY USING BITS—
(AKA CHUNKS OR SERIES)

A bit is a section of material that is so related that it makes it easy for you to memorize. Each point flows naturally from one to the next so you can deliver the information without notes (if you know your material).

Until I learned about bits, I never thought I could be a professional presenter because I'm not great at memorizing long talks. I discovered that no one memorizes long talks. They have a mental or written outline consisting of key words that trigger the individual bit in their minds. Pros use this concept to be able to deliver long presentations without the use of notes.

Becoming less dependent on notes has several advantages. When you stand before a group and deliver information without using notes your credibility automatically rises. The audience thinks, "Wow! This person really knows the material." Since you won't be tied to a lectern or forced to hold notes, you can get physically closer to the audience or actually enter the audience on occasion. The closer you are to them, the better you will connect. When you leave the script at home you can talk naturally to the audience rather than read to them. You will also be more confident because you no longer have to worry about your notes getting lost. If you do feel the desperate need to have some notes with you, all you need is a cheat sheet with the first three to five words of the bit.

Using bits has another big advantage. We are busy people. It's tough to find a spare hour or day to practice a full presentation. Bits can be practiced when you have a few minutes here and there. You will be more likely to practice your material (and we all need practice) if you can practice a three or five-minute chunk rather than the whole presentation.

When it comes to humor, bits are an important tool to make your work easier. Laughter is cumulative. The synergy effect applies. Two funny stories or comments back-to-back will be funnier than the sum of each individual piece of humor. Three pieces will be even better. To see how intensity is built with humor, refer to Graph 5-2. You will see the miniature intensity curves that look like ocean waves. Graph 5-3 is an expanded version of just one of these waves.

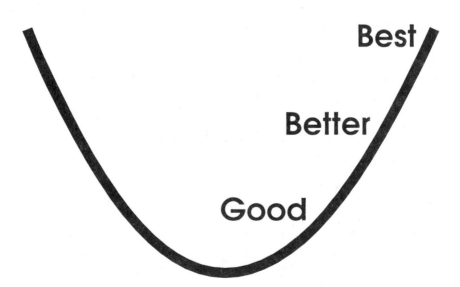

Graph 5-3 Expanded view of intensity curve.

Before using a humorous bit in a presentation, you should try to rate each piece of humor you intend to use on any particular subject. Anything you use should be good, but some pieces will be obviously better than others. Test them out in as many situations as possible before you add them to your presentation. The best joke or story will go at the peak of the intensity curve. Each joke, story or one-liner will be placed in the presentation in order of expected laughter. Start out with the "worst" of the best and build the intensity as you ascend the curve.

Here's an example of a simple three joke bit I use when I'm presenting to professional speakers.

> *I wasn't very good when I first started speaking. I think it was my first paid presentation. I was up on stage for about two minutes and the whole audience asked for a glass of water. Then another time I was at a banquet and the meeting planner came running up to me and started tugging on my sleeve. She said, "Will you shut up! You're interrupting the busboys." I was too dumb to have stage fright. I should have known something was wrong when the audience got up and started doing the wave. I think they were singing "Happy Trails to You."*

In this example, the line *I wasn't very good when I first started speaking* is the set up to the upcoming bit. It gave them the subject I would be addressing. The next two lines *I think it was my first paid presentation* and *I was up on stage for about two minutes and the whole audience asked for a glass of water* was the first joke of the bit. It gets a mild chuckle from speakers. The next joke about *interrupting the busboys* is a little better and the synergy effect kicks in because the speakers are now thinking about the subject of doing poorly in front of a crowd. The last joke about the audience *doing the wave* takes full advantage of the synergy effect because everyone is now fully engrossed in laughing at my troubles and the mental picture of a football stadium activity being put in a professional presentation setting is ludicrous. *I think they were singing "Happy Trails to You"* is an *extender line* to drag out additional laughter at the end of the bit. I actually sing the words "Happy trails to you."

This bit is only about one minute long. I have some that are five or six minutes long. The technique, however, is the same. I introduce the bit, then present my jokes, stories, or one-liners in increasing intensity.

To prepare, I practice the bit over and over until I can do it in my sleep. When the presentation comes, all I have to do is remember the setup line *I wasn't very good* and those key words trigger the bit. If I were using notes, all I would have to put on my cheat sheet would be the words "no good" and I could talk for the next minute with full eye contact. By using bits in a humorous presentation you might be able to do the whole talk without letting the audience know you are using notes. You look at the notes while they are laughing. Determine the key words that set you off and then practice, PRACTICE, **PRACTICE** those bits!

MAKE BUMPER CAR TRANSITIONS

Most presentation skills books will tell you to be a polished presenter you have to tie all your information together so it flows smoothly. You must lead your audience and alert them that slightly different, but related information is coming. This is called transition or segue (pronounced *seg-way*). LET ME STATE RIGHT NOW THAT I FULLY BELIEVE SMOOTH TRANSITIONS ARE NECESSARY IF YOU WANT TO HAVE YOUR AUDIENCE MEMBERS SO BORED THEY FALL RIGHT OUT OF THEIR SEATS AND SMASH THEIR HEADS ON THE FLOOR.

Come with me to the amusement park. Look around a little bit and tell me where the excitement is. Of course, it's over on the roller coaster where transitions are sharp. They are sharp and exciting even though you can see them coming. The excitement isn't over at the kiddie choo choo train (notwithstanding, the excitement you might feel watching your little munchkin on there for the very first time) where turns and motion are mild so the little ones don't get too upset. The excitement is also at the bumper cars where you can get blind-sided because cars are coming at you from all directions. The excitement isn't at the baby boat ride where a 2cm wave would flip your little bundle of joy out of the boat.

OK. I'll admit, some thought should be given to transition, especially with older, more traditional audiences, and when you have a very high content presentation. But you don't have to be a trite, snoozer by saying things like, . . . *speaking of bananas. I'm now going to talk about bananas.* You could, however, do a segue like that and then make fun of yourself for doing it by saying something like, *Don't you think that transition was really smooth?* Transitions are one of the places where you could plan to use some humor. This works well with technical audiences because they won't feel you are wasting their time. Since, in their minds, you are REQUIRED to do a transition anyway, it's OK if it's funny.

Segues aren't important at all for 85 percent or higher humor content presenters or stand-up comics. You can just bang away and as long as they are laughing, no one much cares about transitions. If you are not in this category, then you can begin paying a little attention to bridging the gaps between your points and topics. Just don't be trite and don't think you have to say something to make the transition.

You can make transitions by changing stage position, pausing, using visual aids, giving out a handout, or picking up a prop. Do anything that breaks the pattern of what you were doing in the previous segment and introduces what you plan to do.

For verbal transitions, one-liners, anecdotes, and questions work well. Also, people seem to like and need recaps, so I am in favor of saying things like, *To recap this section . . .*

Whatever you do, think in terms of roller coasters and bumper cars so you keep your audience excited and alert all the time.

To recap this section (am I getting too predictable?):

● Determine the appropriate percentage of humor and attention getting devices to use during your talk.

● Make sure you use at least one attention-getting device every six to eight minutes for high content talks; several times per minute for humorous talks.

● Find appropriate humor to support your points.

● Arrange your material in bits.

● Create *cheat sheets* if necessary with the first three to five words of each bit.

● Prepare roller coaster & bumper car transitions.

*Great is the art of beginning, but greater
is the art of ending.*
—Longfellow

Closings

One of the worst mistakes you can make as a presenter is talking too long. Not only will you send some folks to never, never land, you will make some of them downright mad. It doesn't matter if your entire talk was brilliant and the audience came away with information that will change their lives. If you talk too long, they will leave saying, "That speaker just wouldn't quit." Don't let this happen to you! Say what you have to say and sit down. Before you do, give them a well thought out closing.

The last thing you say may be the most remembered. You must put as much time into selecting and practicing your closing as you put into any other part of your presentation. Just like your opening, your closing does not have to be humorous. It could be motivational, challenging, thoughtful, respectful of the

CHAPTER 6

length of the presentation, or it could restate your point in a different way. This ending segment will have a strong influence on what the audience takes home with them when you are done. Please, at sometime during your talk ask the audience to do something. Many a great NO ZZZZZs talk went no further than the walls of the meeting room because the audience wasn't moved to action. If you haven't ask them to do something by now, the closing is your last chance.

If the subject is appropriate, I happen to be fond of humorous closings for several reasons. If you leave them laughing and applauding, you will exit, but an extremely positive impression about you will remain. Another good reason to leave them laughing is that the room will not be deadly silent as you are walking back to your seat. I hate when that happens. I do love laughter and feeling good; finishing a talk humorously gives me and the audience an opportunity to feel great. Talks that are for entertainment purposes only should generally leave the audience laughing.

Finally, if the subject is not appropriate to end with laughter, you could end with a touching story or quotation that leaves the audience thoughtful and quiet. Even the most serious subjects can benefit from humor, but the humor should be sprinkled throughout the body of the presentation. Don't put it at the end because closings are powerful and the audience will think your overall attitude toward the subject is flippant.

> *It's hard to believe a half hour has gone by when it feels like only thirty minutes.*
>
> Kelly Monteith
> *The Hit Squad*

This same technique can be very effective in ending a mostly humorous presentation. Have them laughing all along while you make your points. Then finish seriously. This contrast will create a great impact. It will convey the fact that you believe in a lighthearted approach to the subject, but the results are very serious to you.

A great resource for closings and lots of other good material is the book, *How to Be the Life of the Podium: Openers, Closers & Everything in Between to Keep Them Listening* by Sylvia Simmons.

BONUS MATERIAL

Here are some exit lines you may wish to use:

- *P.T. Barnum would have trouble getting people to leave his museum so he put up a sign that said, "This way to the Egress." When people went through the door, they found themselves on the street. I don't want to find myself there, so I'll finish up now . . .*

- *You've heard that "All's well that ends well." Well in my case it's All's well that ends. Goodnight.*

- *When all is said and done, there is usually more said than done. I think I've said enough. Good Luck.*

- *When a speaker says, "Well, to make a long story short," it's usually too late. I don't want you to feel that way about me. Thanks for having me.*

If you have a Question and Answer period:

● *Now let's open it up for questions. Ask me anything. If I know the answer, I'll give it to you. If I don't, I'll make something up.*

Complimentary and funny:

● *Secretaries are the backbone of an organization. They are the structure that holds everything together [start to get emotional and cry. Take out a hand- kerchief and hidden noisemaker. Blow your nose really loudly]. I'm sorry. I get so emotional. You're the greatest. Good bye.*

Paraphrase a quotation:

● *The next time you're feeling down, and you look in the mirror and see a few extra wrinkles, just remember what my old buddy Mark Twain used to say. "Those wrinkles are where smiles have been all these years." I'm Tom Antion. I love you.*

● *Now I'm going to say something in the public interest. Goodnight.*

● *George Eliot said, "Blessed is the man [I would substitute the word person for the word man to avoid sexist language], who having nothing to say refrains from giving us wordy evidence of the fact."*

● *An old-timer is one who can remember when time was marching on instead of running out. My time is running out, so in conclusion . . .*

● *My great, great, granddaddy always told me, "When you're holding a con- versation, be sure to let go of it once in awhile." I'm letting go of ours right now. Are there any questions?*

● *My talks usually have a happy ending. That's because everyone is glad they are over.*

Here's a guaranteed (but cheap and sleazy) way to get a standing ovation. All you have to do is have the audience stand and applaud themselves. It goes like this:

> *I don't want any applause, not that I was going to get any any- way, but what I would like is for everyone to stand up [have everyone stand up and wait until they are standing before you continue]. Now give me a really great round of applause for the folks who made this meeting possible and for yourselves, the members of this great organization. Thank you. I'm Tom Antion.*
(This doesn't mean I'm cheap and sleazy does it?)

Three things matter in a speech: Who says it, how it's said and what is said—and of the three, the last matters the least.

—John Morley

(Hey! This guy doesn't think this chapter is very important. Let's just see about that.)

Selection of material

I'm sure you take great care in selecting the educational material you present to your audience. The same care should be taken in selecting your humor. You must decide who and what to joke about while avoiding being offensive and/or inappropriate.

CHAPTER 7

APPROPRIATE TARGETS

You must constantly remember to base your humorous material on an important target shared with your intended audience. You get this information from your pre-program questionnaire and other pre-program research.

People—Use people they know in your jokes and stories.
Talk about their CEO or supervisor (get permission from these people first). Joke about or insult the CEO of a major competitor, but be careful here. You may want to work for the competitor some day. Always pick BIG targets to tease. Never pick secretaries, receptionists, or janitors as targets of humor.

Places—Quip about the places they go.
Their cafeteria, the bar across the street from their plant, or the crowded highway leading to where they work are all good targets for humor. In Washington, D.C., where I live, everyone jokes about troubles on the Beltway.

Things—Joke about the things that mean something to them.
Joke about their new marketing plan, company picnic, new voice-mail system, etc. Just be sure that they are joking about it themselves. The topic might be too hot to tease about.

As I mentioned in Chapter 2, if you have a general audience and you cannot get specific information, use general humor. Most people are married and have children and experience family conflict. They go to the doctor and dentist. They stand in line at the motor vehicle administration. They deal with financial problems. Joke about any universal problem which your audience can relate to.

Remember, always pick BIG targets. Joke about celebrities, media stars, and athletes that everyone knows. Keep in mind that there is a genuine sports interest in virtually every audience.

The best and safest target to use is the one that's reading this book (see "Self-effacing Humor," Chapter 13). You can joke about your physical appearance, clothing, weight, etc., without much worry of offending someone else.

INAPPROPRIATE TARGETS

The overriding principle is that you should not tease the audience about beliefs that are important to them or about any topic that is currently upsetting them. In addition, never use the following types of humor: racist, sexist, religious, puns, any type of off-color humor, or humor about physical or mental disability.

I was preparing a presentation for a large hotel chain and from my pre-program work I uncovered a topic that was ripe for humor. The hotel chain and the franchisees were having some clearly ludicrous contract negotiation problems. When I approached the meeting planner about the topic, he told me that the franchisees were pretty upset about the way things were going. My comments, even though they were funny, might make them think about a painful situation. I chose to cut them. Why should I take the chance? It was also another good lesson in clearing humor before use.

When it comes to the *nevers* mentioned above, there are established pros who get away with ignoring them. Dr. Jarvis has been doing a hilarious bit on religion for 20 years without a problem. But, he has done the bit thousands of times and knows exactly what he is doing during the rest of the presentation to be sure the audience is receptive. I've talked to him recently and he tells me that people are so sensitive now he uses extreme caution when using the bit.

Ethnic expressions are funny—Only if you are ethnic

Another well-known humorist, Doc Blakely, does a dialect bit that has been very successful, but he is extremely good at it. If you are not good at a particular dialect, it appears you are mocking the ethnic group to which it belongs.

There are lots of funny ethnic sayings and words. Try to resist using them unless you are making fun of your own background. In a business setting, it is much too risky to joke about another person's race, religion, or dialect.

If you are Polish, it may be OK to tell a Polish joke now and then. If you are Jewish, you are the only one who really knows about matzo balls, schmatas and schnooks. Remember—both Secretary of Agriculture Earl Butts and Secretary of the Interior James Watt were forced to resign because of "jokes that were deemed insensitive and insulting to minorities." If you want to use ethnic humor, use *Outer Slobovia* or some other OBVIOUSLY comic, nonexistent country in your jokes.

Disability and Blue Humor

You certainly cannot get away with any profanity or off-color (blue) jokes in a professional presentation. The most serious consequence I ever heard of with regard to using off-color humor was reported in the July 7, 1996, issue of the *Washington Post.* It seems that Captain Ernie Blanchard, a career military man with a virtually perfect record and no apparent emotional problems, committed suicide after telling a dozen or so dirty jokes at a Coast Guard Academy dinner in 1995. The initial investigation, which apparently drove him to his death, concluded that telling those jokes to 117 people constituted willful sexual harassment. This is obviously an extreme case, but it is representative of a politically correct atmosphere that must never be forgotten when you are the one at the microphone.

Along the same lines, you will never be invited back to speak if you use any jokes that make fun of a person's disability. Jokes on the subjects of stuttering, lisping, or amputees will no longer be tolerated and can be devastating your career.

Sexist Language

Avoiding sexist language is necessary in order to be in tune with today's society. There is an excellent section about this topic in the book *Speak Like a Pro* by Margaret Bedrosian. A *salesman* is now a *salesperson*. A *fireman* is now a *firefighter*. You don't look for a *chairman* for a meeting, you look for someone to *chair* the meeting or a *chairperson*.

You must be very careful in your use of humor in these sensitive times. People may fixate on one wrong word and tune you out and/or be offended. You may personally feel that using a little off-color joke once in awhile is OK, or you may think that no harm is done in using sexist language whenever you feel like it. I can assure you that you are wrong when it comes to professional presentations. Do whatever you want with your friends, but if you persist in any of these behaviors you will be labeled as "out-of-touch" and largely unpromotable in virtually every major corporation.

Other Touchy Subjects

It is simply not worth the chance of taking the audience out of *in fun* by bringing up controversial issues like AIDS, sex, abortion, politics, etc. The old adage holds true: If in doubt, leave it out.

Puns

Although there is controversy on this issue, puns are usually avoided by most NO ZZZZZs presenters. Puns tend to show how smart you are, which doesn't endear you to the audience. They also elicit groans rather than laughs. I don't know about you, but I don't want the audience groaning at me. Most of the time puns are better and more understandable when they are written.

Here's an example:

> The first orchestra was formed in Massachusetts, but it was *band* in Boston.

The words *band* and *banned* have the exact same pronunciation. If you deliver this line from the platform, the word *banned* will be heard and the joke, using the word *band*, will be lost. Better give them all pillows because their heads are about to hit the floor. Also, try not to use *fancy* language that is inappropriate for the educational level of your audience.

Neighbor: George, your office has that certain je ne sais quoi.

George Jefferson: Not anymore—I just had it exterminated.

My way of joking is to tell the truth; it's the funniest joke in the world.

—George Bernard Shaw

Delivery

STAGE FRIGHT
Stage Fright Is Good and Makes You Better Looking Too!

Before you learn *how* to deliver your lines, it is important to be *ready* to deliver your lines. Stage fright is a phenomenon that you must learn to control. Actually, stage fright isn't the most accurate term for the nervousness that occurs when considering a speaking engagement. In fact, most of the fear occurs before you step on-stage. Once you're up there, it usually goes away. Try to think of stage fright in a positive way. Fear is your friend. It makes your reflexes sharper. It heightens your energy, adds a sparkle to your eye, and color to your cheeks. When you are nervous about speaking you are more conscious of your posture and breathing. With all those good side effects you will actually look healthier and more physically attractive.

CHAPTER 8

Many of the top performers in the world get stage fright so you are in good company. Stage fright may come and go or diminish, but it usually does not vanish permanently. You must concentrate on getting the feeling out in the open, into perspective, and under control.

What Humans Fear the Most

1. Speaking in front of a group
2. Heights
3. Insects and bugs
4. Financial troubles
5. Deep water
6. Sickness
7. Death
8. Flying
9. Loneliness
10. Dogs
11. Speaking to dogs (just kidding)

Source: *The Book of Lists*

Remember—Nobody ever died from stage fright. But, according to surveys, many people would rather die than give a speech. If that applies to you, try out some of the strategies in this section to help get yourself under control. Realize that you may never overcome stage fright, but you can learn to control it, and use it to your advantage.

Symptoms of Stage Fright

● Dry mouth.

● Tight throat.

● Sweaty hands.

● Cold hands.

- Shaky hands.

- Give me a hand (Oops, I couldn't resist).

- Nausea.

- Fast pulse.

- Shaky knees.

- Trembling lips.

- Any out-of-the-ordinary outward or inward feeling or manifestation of a feeling occurring before, or during, the beginning of a presentation (Wow! What a dry mouthful!).

Reducing Stage Fright

Here are some easy to implement strategies for reducing your stage fright. Not everyone reacts the same and there is no universal fix. Don't try to use all these fixes at once. Pick out items from this list and try them out until you find the right combination for you.

Visualization strategies that can be used anytime

- Concentrate on how good you are.

- Pretend you are just chatting with a group of friends.

- Close your eyes and imagine the audience listening, laughing, and applauding.

- Remember happy moments from your past.

- Think about your love for and desire to help the audience.

- Picture the audience in their underwear.

Strategies in advance of program

- Be extremely well prepared.

- Join or start a Toastmasters club for extra practice (see Appendix B).

- Get individual or group presentation skills coaching.

Listen to music.

Read a poem.

Anticipate hard and easy questions.

Organize.

Absolutely memorize your opening statement so you can recite it on auto-pilot if you have to.

Practice, practice, practice! Especially practice bits so you can spit out a few minutes of your program no matter how nervous you are.

Get in shape. I don't know why it helps stage fright, but it does.

Strategies just before the program

Remember—Stage fright usually goes away after you start. The tricky time is before you start.

Be in the room at least an hour early if possible to triple check everything. You can also schmooze with participants arriving early.

Notice and think about things around you.

Concentrate on searching for current and immediate things that are happening at the event that you can mention during your talk (especially in the opening).

Get into conversation with people near you. Be very intent on what they are saying.

Yawn to relax your throat.

Doodle.

Draw sketches of a new car you would like to have.

Look at your notes.

Put pictures of your kids/grandkids, dog, etc., in your notes.

Build a cushion of time in the day so you are not rushed—but not too much time. You don't want to have extra time to worry.

If your legs are trembling, lean on a table, sit down, or shift your legs.

Take a quick walk.

Take quick drinks of tepid water.

Double check your A/V equipment.

Don't drink alcohol or coffee or tea with caffeine.

Concentrate on your ideas.

Hide notes around the stage area so you know you have a backup if you happen to draw a blank.

Concentrate on your audience.

Listen to music.

Read a poem.

Do isometrics that tighten and release muscles.

Shake hands and smile with attendees before the program.

Say something to someone to make sure your voice is ready to go.

Go somewhere private and warm up your voice, muscles, etc.

Use eye contact.

Go to a mirror and check out how you look.

Breathe deeply, evenly, and slowly for several minutes.

Don't eat if you don't want to and never take tranquilizers or other such drugs. You may think you will do better, but you will probably do worse and not know it.

Strategies when the program begins

If legs are trembling, lean on lectern /table or shift legs or move.

Try not to hold the microphone by hand in the first minute.

● Don't hold notes. The audience can see them shake. Use three-by-five cards instead.

Take quick drinks of tepid water.

- Use eye contact. It will make you feel less isolated.

- Look at the friendliest faces in the audience.

- Joke about your nervousness. *What's the right wine to go with fingernails?*

Remember—nervousness doesn't show one-tenth as much as it feels.

Before each presentation make a short list of the items you think will make you feel better. Don't be afraid to experiment with different combinations. You never know which ones will work best until you try. Rewrite them on a separate sheet and keep the sheet with you at all times so you can refer to it quickly when the need arises.

Use these steps to control stage fright so it doesn't control you.

I CAN'T HEEEEERE YOU!

Although this may seem obvious, make sure the audience can clearly hear every word you say. Most jokes and stories depend on key words. If you slur a word, the audience may miss the whole idea of the story (remember you need a good sound system too). Besides enunciating clearly, you must use the microphone properly. Hand held microphones must stay with you when you turn your head from side to side and must be directed toward the mouth of anyone you are conversing with during the presentation.

Larry Wilde, the author of more than 50 humor books, tells the story of the time he was auditioning to take over the television show *Let's Make a Deal* when Monte Hall retired. In the opening of the show he was supposed to engage in small talk with an audience member. He went up to someone in the first row and said, "Hi! What's your name?" Although the audience member answered him, there was dead silence in the sound booth. The sound men were actually laughing at Larry because he neglected to hold the microphone near the mouth of the audience member for the response. You might think this is common sense, but try it out and you will see that it is not as easy as it looks. It takes practice to do it smoothly.

If you are at a lectern, you should know how far your lips need to be from the microphone. Hopefully you checked this out before the presentation started. If that was not possible, you can watch the introducer or speakers that are on before you to get a feel for the proper distance.

When using a handheld or lectern microphone be very careful in pronouncing words that have the letter "p" in them. This letter tends to make a popping sound that is very distracting. If you are using a handheld microphone, you usually can significantly reduce the "p" sound problem if you hold the microphone at a slight angle. If the microphone is fixed on the lectern, you can de-emphasize the word with the "p" or turn your head slightly away from the microphone.

JOKE TELLING

Jokes! Jokes! Jokes! Everyone tells me they can't tell jokes. The good news is that it doesn't matter one bit if you can tell a joke or not. The better news is that if you really want to tell jokes, you can. I'm going to give you some simple techniques that will improve your joke and storytelling capabilities.

Being a humorous NO ZZZZZs presenter is quite different from being a stand-up comedian. Most stand-up comedians must be experts at telling jokes. Their only purpose is to entertain. If they do not skillfully make the audience laugh, they bomb. Laughter is their only desired result. You, as a NO ZZZZZs presenter, however, are using humor as a tool to convey your message or information. You should want the audience to have a good time, but it doesn't matter so much if the audience laughs as long as they get the message. Laughter is a bonus. Realizing this fact should take away much of the anxiety you may feel about using humor.

Let's get back to jokes. I really get tired of hearing people in my seminars tell me they *can't* tell a joke. I can't iron a shirt either, but I could if someone showed me how and I practiced enough (Note: As long as there is one dry cleaner store left on the face of the earth this will never happen). I might never be as good at it as my mother, but I could become competent if I really tried. It's the same with jokes. If you apply the delivery techniques discussed in this chapter, if you select appropriate and relevant jokes, and if you practice diligently, you will become competent at telling jokes and successful in your main goal of enhancing your presentations. As stated above, when it comes to professional presentations, being able to tell a joke does not matter. So, don't let it bother you if you have a little trouble at first. Just keep practicing. You will get more positive results out of storytelling, one-liners, and many of the simple humor techniques discussed in Chapter 13. The delivery techniques you'll learn in this chapter will also apply to these other forms of humor.

The Punch Line

Most jokes are designed to end with a humorous climactic word or phrase. Here's an example from Larry Wilde's book *Library of Laughter*:

> I can't understand why you failed in business.
> Too much advertising.
> You never spent a cent in your life on advertising.
> That's true, but my competitor did.

Everything in the joke up to the comma after "That's true" is the setup of the joke. "But my competitor did" is the punch line. The punch line gets its name from the delivery technique used. You must punch the line out a little harder and with a slightly different voice than the rest of the joke. Lean into the microphone and say it louder and more clearly than you said the setup lines. If the audience does not hear the punch line, they are not going to laugh.

Just before the punch line you should pause slightly (see "Timing," later in this chapter) to emphasize and draw special attention to the line. After you deliver the line, don't utter another sound. Give the audience a chance to laugh. Words or phrases appended to the climax tend to delay or impede laughter. Until you get some experience, it is really tough to wait. Beginners tend to be afraid that no laughter will come, so they keep going. If you keep talking during this period, you will easily squelch the laughter. As your confidence builds, pausing will become easier and easier. Sometimes waiting the audience out will actually give them a cue to laugh even if the joke wasn't that great.

When you deliver your punch line, deliver it to one person and one person only. It doesn't matter how large the crowd is, you can look one person right in the eye and deliver your line.

The person to whom you deliver the punch line is NOT randomly chosen. I deliver punch lines to a person I know is going to laugh. How do I know? I pay attention. That's how I know. It all starts with

> *If one talks to more than four people, it is an audience; and one cannot really think or exchange thoughts with an audience.*
>
> Anne Morrow Lindbergh

my pre-program research. If I have spoken to any of the audience members and they were laughing with me on the phone, I'll seek them out before the program so I know where they are sitting. That way I can look directly at them during the program. Before the program starts, I mingle with the participants, not only to meet them, but to see who is and who is not *in fun* (mingling with them helps to put them *in fun*). In addition, I watch the audience when the emcee or program coordinator is talking. This gives me a mental note of the people who are not only having fun, but also paying close attention to the person speaking. Don't be fooled by an audience that appears to be having great fun. It could very likely have been induced by alcohol at their social hour. They may be oblivious to what's happening on-stage.

After you have begun your presentation, another way to tell who to deliver to is by closely watching the audience. Some audience members who are really in tune with what you are saying will nod their head gently in approval. You should have great success delivering to these people.

There are two reasons for delivering your punch line to someone you know will laugh. The most important is that you want that person to be a good example for the rest of the audience. If you direct a punch line or comment to a person in the audience, the other members of the audience will naturally look in that direction. If they see someone laughing, there is a high probability they will laugh too. If you deliver your line to some sourpuss that hasn't laughed for 20 years, the rest of the audience will see an example of someone NOT laughing and they will be negatively influenced. A 1976 study by Antony Chapman and D.S. Wright supports the notion that the lack of laughter or inappropriate laughter (the kind of laughter you would get if you pick on someone or some group inappropriately and they laugh to save face) are inhibitors of laughter.

The second reason for delivering your punch line to someone you know will laugh has to do with confidence. There is little chance that you will get old sourpuss to laugh no matter what you do. If you kill yourself trying and fail, as you probably will, it will knock your confidence level and affect the rest of your performance. Combine this with the fact that you will be ignoring the rest of the audience, who will be watching this person not laugh, and you'll be quickly swinging in the wind. Deliver to the ones that appreciate you!

Rule of Three

One of the most pervasive principles in the construction of humorous situations is the Rule of Three. You will see it used over and over because it is simple, it is powerful, and it works (see—I just used it there in a non-funny situation). Most of the time in humor the Rule of Three is used in the following fashion:
The first comment names the topic, the second sets a pattern, and the third unexpectedly switches the pattern—which is funny. Here's a few examples from brochures advertising my seminars:

In the "How to Get There" section—
>   From Washington, D.C., take Rt. 50 . . .
>   From Baltimore, MD, take Rt. 95 . . .
>   From Bangkok, Thailand, board Asian Air . . .

>   By Metro take the Red line . . .
>   By car take New York Ave. . . . .
>   By steamship take the Chesapeake Bay . . .

While in front of a group I might point to an audience member and say
>   *You can make a difference in your company.*
>   [Pointing to the next person]
>   *You can make a difference in your department.*
>   [Pointing to third *fun* person]
>   *You can [pause]—Well not everyone can do this.*

The Rule of Three is also used in constructing bits as we saw in Chapter 5. Three jokes or one-liners on one topic is enough to create a rise in the audience, but not enough to tire them about that subject.

Don't forget that the Rule of Three is good in non-funny situations too. Even honest Abe Lincoln used it twice in the powerful, but short, Gettysburg Address: "We cannot dedicate. We cannot consecrate. We cannot hallow this ground"; "government of the people, by the people, for the people shall not perish from the earth."

Callbacks

If you refer to a word or phrase you mentioned earlier in your presentation, that's a *callback*. It works well if the previous piece of material got a good laugh—or if it was a groaner. If the previous material was good, mentioning it again will get more laughter and will make you look polished for being able to tie the previous material to the present material. If the previous material was poor, the callback will show your willingness to tease yourself, which is an admirable quality the audience appreciates.

Here's how it works: Let's say you used a successful two-liner in your *presentation—Don't rely on health books too much. You could die of a misprint.* Later in your presentation someone might notice a misspelling in one of your handouts or visuals. You could then call back and say, *See, that's one of those misprints I was telling you about earlier.* Another thing that might happen, that is just as good, is that one or more of the audience members might make the connection and do the callback for you. One of them may blurt out something about your health book line. That's great if they do. You are getting them involved and allowing them to feel superior to you, which makes them the stars. You could then comeback with, *See, I put that there to test you.* When you really get confident, you might actually make the misprint on purpose to set up this whole scenario.

To Laugh or Not to Laugh—That is the Question

Some humor "experts" say that you should not laugh at your own jokes and stories. This may work for some, but it is definitely not my style. When I'm in front of an audience, I'm having a great time. I'm there because I love humor and laughter and I love sharing it with the audience. I can't help laughing sometimes. I laugh at what I say. I laugh at what they say. I laugh at unexpected occurrences during the presentation. That's my style. I believe that to fully connect with an audience, you must be accepted as one of them. If I expect them to laugh, then I should laugh too.

Sometimes you can laugh to tell the audience it's time to laugh. Within a matter of minutes your stage persona will be evident to the audience. As soon as they catch onto your style and rhythm, they will pick up on the cues you give them.

When you laugh they know it is time for them to laugh. It's almost like holding up an applause sign. Some NO ZZZZZs presenters use facial expressions or gestures or a combination of many cues that tell the audience it's OK to laugh.

The opposite of a laughter cue is a *deadpan expression*. This is a serious expression that is contrasted with funny lines. The contrast evokes a larger laugh than the line could get by itself. I use this to set the audience up for some fun questions (see "Question & Answer," Chapter 13). I look completely earnest when I say, *I'm the foremost expert in the world [pause] on dumb questions.* It always gets a good laugh.

Timing

Timing is one of the most important aspects of humor and NO ZZZZZs presenting. Not only is timing involved in an individual piece of humor, it is also involved in the placement of that piece of humor in the overall presentation. Timing is also involved in spontaneous reactions to "expected" unexpected developments during the presentation.

Jack Benny said, "Timing is not so much knowing when to speak, but knowing when to pause." He should know, because he delivered one of the funniest and most famous lines in the history of comedy after an extremely long pause. He was being held up by a robber at gunpoint. The robber said, "Your money or your life!" Jack didn't say a word for an extended period of time. The robber became impatient and said, "YOUR MONEY OR YOUR LIFE!!" Jack finally replied, "I'm thinking." His persona as a cheapskate, coupled with a long pause indicating he was having trouble deciding whether to give up his money—or die—was hilarious. A pause lets the audience catch up and draw pictures in their mind. It is the audience's signal to imagine.

As we talked about in joke telling, a pause just before and just after your punch line gives the audience a chance to laugh. Absolutely do not continue to talk when laughter is expected. Laughter is hard to get and easy to discourage. Hold eye contact a little bit longer than you think you should when delivering punch lines because time is hard to judge when you are pumped up for a presentation.

As I mentioned in Chapter 2, the size of your audience will affect your timing. Your presentation will take less time to deliver to smaller audiences. Smaller audiences should mean quicker laughter. Conversely, presentations will take longer for extremely large crowds. Your pauses will be longer to compensate for the wave effect. Don't forget to watch for timing problems with a room full of executives from the same company when the CEO is present.

Types of Pauses

A true NO ZZZZZs presenter doesn't feel that he or she must jabber away constantly to keep the audience awake. Skilled presenters use silence to add to the effectiveness and polish of a program. Theatrical folks have identified a whole bunch of neat pauses which I'm sure they have a ball playing with. I'm only going to address some of the most obvious and important ones here.

Short
The shortest pauses, which last anywhere from one-half to two seconds, are for the simple purpose of separating your thoughts. All you have to remember is to slow down. Give the audience a fighting chance to absorb what you are saying. Change your voice inflection slightly at the end of each thought to cue the audience the next thought is coming. Also, use a short pause before and after any phrase (punch line) or word you want to emphasize.

Spontaneity
Another neat pause is known as a spontaneity pause. This is a planned "unplanned" pause so that you don't look too rehearsed. You might apply this pause when you want to pretend to search for a word or phrase that you already know.

Long
Long pauses of more than three seconds are very powerful. They command the audience to think about what you just said—that is if what you just said was worth thinking about.

Please[pause][pause][pause]—don't be afraid to be quiet once in a while. It can dramatically increase your impact.

HUMOR PLACEMENT
You are probably wondering how you decide where to put the humor you have so carefully selected to use in your presentation. You weren't wondering? Well, I'm going to tell you anyway. Do you remember the listening patterns we talked about in Chapter 5. That's a good place to start.

First of all, starting with a funny story or joke is expected and trite. You may want to postpone your story until the audience is resolved that you will be bestowing a rare case of sleeping sickness on them and then you surprise them with the humor. Don't be afraid to do the unexpected.

Humor is one of the attention-getting devices that can take your audience to the peaks of the intensity curves. To get started in figuring the placement of your humor, first find out or decide how much time you are expected to talk. Divide this time into equal segments (intensity curves). The time length of each curve will depend on the total percentage of humor you plan to use (Remember you figured this percentage by asking yourself questions like "Why am I here?" etc.). If the percentage of humor is to be low, you might make each curve six to eight minutes long. If the percentage of humor is very high, you might be making a humorous comment every minute. Going through this process tells you roughly how much humor or other attention gaining devices you need to accomplish your goals.

I'm assuming at this point that all the humor you have selected is relevant to your audience and your topic. We'll talk more about that in the next chapter. If it is not, throw it out now and search for something to replace it that is relevant to your program.

Next, you should be ready to place the humor in your program. Don't make the mistake of forcing humor and other material to fit the intensity curves. The intensity curves should be shifted to fit your material. They are only there as guidelines to remind you to keep the audience from booking the first flight to Z-land. It makes no difference if one segment goes several minutes longer than another.

All you have to do now is decide if you want humor in your opening and/or closing. Use the guidelines in Chapters 4 and 6 to make your decision.

Finally, the third aspect of timing has to do with "planned spontaneity." This term seems like an oxymoron, or contradiction in terms, doesn't it (see "Oxymoron," Chapter 13)? When it comes to professional presentations, preparation will be a big factor in your ultimate success. We'll talk more about *canned ad-libs* in the next chapter, but prepared remarks that *appear* spontaneous deserve a mention when talking about timing.

During the course of a presentation, windows of opportunity for witty remarks open and close. They are usually related to "expected/unexpected" happenings during the presentation or questions from the audience.

Let's say you are writing on the flip chart and your marker runs out of ink. Your window of opportunity is now open. You might jump through the window and say, *I guess I've come to the dry part of my presentation.* Window slams shut. Everything is fine. You look like a quick wit and a pretty cool NO ZZZZZs presenter.

What if you waited until you searched out a new marker to say the same line? The window had already slammed shut 30 seconds ago and now you are trying to jump through. You lose. The spontaneity is gone and so is the impact (except for smashing your head into the glass).

What do you have to do to be sure you will be ready when a window opens? Many problems can be anticipated. If you are using a slide projector, the bulb might blow. You may be interrupted by a loud noise. Your microphone might squeal, etc. Prepare comments in advance so you can recall them immediately when needed. If you let too much time pass between the incident and your comment, you're better off foregoing the comment. It's too late to make it funny.

Questions from the audience can be treated the same way. If you've been presenting your material long enough, you can probably anticipate most of the questions that come up. Prepare a witty answer to each question and use it when the question arises. Then go on and give your serious answer. Be careful when using this technique your witty answer doesn't make the person asking the question feel stupid.

DYNAMIC RANGE

This section is especially devoted to those of you who like charts and graphs. Those of you that don't like these things should read the following intro material and then skip to "Quick Fix" at the end of the section.

I invented the concept of Dynamic Range to help you improve your versatility as a business presenter, and to help you pick appropriate audiences for your skill and interest level (Did he say "pick" my audiences?). Yes, I did say pick your audiences. Some of you may not have this luxury because you must present as part of your job, but those of you that do, will move up faster in the speaking world. When you are a beginning speaker it is important for you to experience different types of audiences just FOR the experience. You will find that you enjoy certain types of audiences more than others, and certain types of audiences enjoy you more too. (If you follow the guidelines in this book, you should not have to experience a total bomb even if you are clearly in front of the wrong audience.) As you climb the speaking ladder where the audiences are bigger, or more important to your career, and the stakes are higher, you must learn to *just say "no."*

Most top speakers don't accept every request to speak even if they are available and the money is right. They pick their engagements to put themselves in front of audiences whose profiles indicate the greatest chance of success. If you are a highly technical presenter, you would not want to be speaking to a widget sales group at their annual retreat. Conversely, as a really fun retreat facilitator, you would not want to be speaking to a group of radar technicians who are only interested in performance data of the latest missile protection system.

The Dynamic Range charts in this section will help you learn to pick your audiences and learn how to expand your abilities so you are capable of handling a wider range of audiences.

I based the concept of Dynamic Range in speaking on the same concept that is used to rate stereo equipment. Dynamic range in the electronics world means the ability to reproduce soft sounds as well as loud ones. I have expanded on this to include several other parameters that are important to a speaker. These include: Serious/Outrageous Content, Slow/Fast Speed of Delivery, Slurred/Articulate Diction, Stationary/Animated Movement, Audience Needs and the WOW factor.

The first step to use this system is to evaluate yourself on each parameter. Many people have trouble with this, so it might be time to call in an objective third party like a coach or other accomplished presenter to watch you present or to review several of your tapes. Try to avoid using friends for this initial evaluation because they will be reluctant to tell you the truth. Here are some examples of how this works.

Parameter: Your Material
Maximum Range: Totally Serious to Totally Outrageous
Zero Point: Arbitrarily set for you
Goal: Have the widest range possible and always cross the zero point.

Example A: Fairly Serious Presenter

Let's say you are a fairly serious presenter, but you do try to lighten things up once in a while with a few one-liners. You get a mark deep on the serious side of zero and another mark just on the outrageous side. Congratulations, you crossed the zero point. Your one-liners helped you become a NO ZZZZZs presenter.

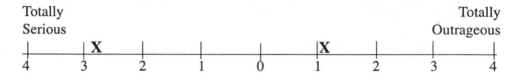

Example B: Really Serious Presenter

Now, let's say you are a really serious presenter. Your range of material is from totally serious to pretty darn serious. You have not crossed the zero point. You could be considered a ZZZZZs presenter. You will have a very high likelihood of your audience "spacing out" on you because your material is too heavy with no relief.

Example C: Outrageously Funny Presenter

Let's flop the last example over. You have outrageously funny material so you get a mark well to the right of the zero point. In fact, all your material is pretty funny with little or no content, so you get another mark still to the right side of zero. Same rules apply. You also end up with a poor range, not because you put them to sleep, but because we are talking about business presentations here. Unless you are a stand-up comic, you are expected to give some serious information, supported and enhanced with humor. It's not as obvious, but it is likely that you have failed because you did not provide the content that is demanded by most business presentations.

Have yourself rated on the other parameters. Can you speak softly to just one audience member and then boom out your message to the whole crowd? Can you slow your speed of delivery and add appropriate long pauses and then machine gun your words? Can you change your diction to better connect with a less educated crowd and can you be fully articulate when the crowd is well-educated and proper? Can you stand still to emphasize key points and then run around the stage to create excitement?

Use these graphs to have yourself rated:

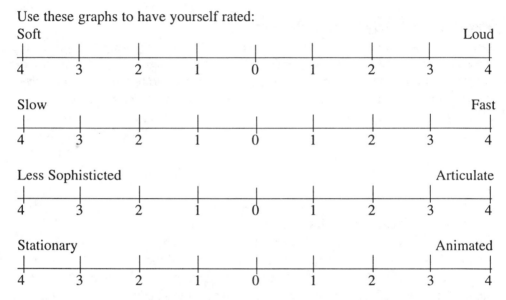

Soft   Loud

4   3   2   1   0   1   2   3   4

Slow   Fast

4   3   2   1   0   1   2   3   4

Less Sophisticted   Articulate

4   3   2   1   0   1   2   3   4

Stationary   Animated

4   3   2   1   0   1   2   3   4

It should be your goal to expand your range on these parameters. The wider your range, the more interest and attention you will be able to gain from any audience. You will also be able to connect better with a wider range of audiences.

I always pick audiences where my range on all parameters is larger than that required by them. If my range is bigger than what the audience requires, I say "yes" to the engagement. If my range is smaller or skewed in a different direction, I say "no" to the engagement. I always want to have somewhere to go if my audience surprises me a little once I'm on site. If they need more humor, I've got a reserve. If they need more content, I can go in that direction too. Maybe something happened at the event that brought the audience down, like someone getting sick or receiving some really bad news. If that's the case, you have got to be able to cut the wild stuff out of respect and still go on. What if they ask you at the last minute if it is OK to videotape? If you say yes, you have to be less animated so the cameras can follow you.

Avoid accepting engagements where the audience's needs are clearly out of sync with your abilities, likes, and dislikes. Don't get me wrong. I want you to

keep pushing your limits, but if your audience needs more than you can give—
that's right, you bombed. Although it will be a lesson learned, do yourself and
everyone else a favor. Learn to just say "no."

When it comes time to make a decision on whether you are right for a particular audience, you can chart them too. Never accept an engagement until you ask
enough questions and get enough reliable answers for you to make your decision.

Many of the questions you saw on the pre-program questionnaire in Chapter 2
should be asked before you even accept the engagement. I always ask the following questions of the meeting planner because I know what audience profile I'm
looking for. You will have to pick the questions for the parameters that are most
important for you.

What topic do you want?

How many people do you expect?

What are their responsibilities?

Are their spouses invited?

What is the average age? What is the range of ages?

What percentage is non-U.S.?

Why are they there? Mandatory _____ Voluntary _____

What is the male/female ratio?

What is happening before I speak and after I speak? (You might get a great
audience profile, but be doomed to failure because of the program schedule)

If I decide to accept the engagement, these questions are repeated on the pre-
program questionnaire. I want as many levels of verification as I can get, so that
I know what I am getting into. Chart the answers along a continuum to see if the
engagement appears to be a good one for you. If all the answers fall to the right
of zero, it's a no-brainer. Go ahead and accept the engagement. If some land to the
left you have to seriously evaluate their weight compared to the weight you have
attributed to the factors that would make you accept. This is obviously not an
exact science. When you get to the event some audiences will end up being better
than you expected and some worse. At least you now have a way of eliminating
the audiences that are clearly wrong for you.

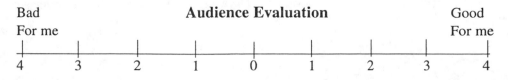

Bad For me					**Audience Evaluation**				Good For me
4	3	2	1	0	1	2	3	4	

Dynamic Range Quick Fixes

For those of you who hate charts and numbers and for those of you who didn't have a clue what the last section was about, I have included this bonus quick fix section.

● If your material is all serious, add some that is lighthearted and vice versa.

● If you always speak softly, speak loudly sometimes and vice versa.

● Work to improve your diction and level of vocabulary, but keep it at a less formal level in front of less articulate audiences.

● If you always stand still, move sometimes and vice versa.

● If you have the option, pick audiences that give you the greatest chance of success.

THE WOW FACTOR

What do you do during your presentations that cause the audience to say WOW? Dewitt Jones, a former photographer for National Geographic, uses slides that literally give you goose pimples. Tom Ogden, an award-winning magician from the Magic Castle in Los Angeles uses, what else, magic. Dave Gorden tells a story about Walt Disney. I use a special freeze frame video segment and shoot fire in the air.

In fact, there are many things that you can use or do to make your audience say WOW! You may have great voice quality like my friend, author, and former radio announcer, Rick Ott. You may use your appearance like professional speaker Larry Winget who wears funny glasses and ties. You might sing or play a musical instrument or juggle or use props.

If you want to push your name up the memorability chart, put something unique in your presentations that causes the audience members to go WOW!

OTHER IMPORTANT DELIVERY TIPS (IGNORE THESE AND YOU CAN START PASSING OUT BLANKETS)

● Don't signal your punch line. If the humor in your punch line depends upon the words *ruptured camel,* don't say *Did you hear the one about the ruptured camel?*

- NEVER repeat a punch line! Once the surprise is revealed, the joke is history. I'll repeat this, but I don't want to hear you repeating any punch lines. Let me repeat. **NEVER** repeat a punch line. **NEVER** repeat a punch line. **NEVER** repeat a punch line. You'll be shot by the humor firing squad if you repeat a punch line. OK. I'll let you repeat one, but only under certain circumstances. Here's the exception. If you had a joke or punch line that bombed miserably, you can *call it back* later to make fun of yourself.

- You must absolutely, positively memorize your punch line. You should be able to awaken out of a deep sleep in an earthquake and, without hesitation, deliver your punch line accurately.

- Give all the facts necessary for the joke to make sense. The humor is lost if you leave out the necessary details.

- **NEVER, EVER** explain your joke. If they don't understand, it's your fault for telling the wrong joke to the wrong audience. The hypnotist says, "You're getting sleeeepy."

- Use the fewest words possible to get to the punch line. Brevity is truly the soul of wit (never use a worn out cliché either). The longer the joke, the funnier it must be.

- Don't walk around too much when telling a joke or story. I walk, but I stop when important points are being made and when I'm delivering a punch line.

- If you use notes, highlight or mark upcoming jokes or stories so they don't sneak up on you. They will need special emphasis.

- **Practice! Practice! Practice!** I tell a joke or story 30 to 50 times in practice before I use it in a presentation (see more tips in Chapter 14).

EXTRA SPECIAL BONUS GENIUS TECHNIQUE

Would you like the audience to think you have a photographic memory? Would you like them to look at you in awe? Here's the technique. Refer to an article in a magazine or passage in a book, but do it in a special way. Pause and look up in the air as if you are thinking and picturing the publication in your mind. Then refer to the article by page number, left or right-hand page, passage's position on the page, etc. The audience will think you are some kind of genius. However, we know that you are just a savvy presenter who memorized the information and delivered it with that special WOW factor.

*Mr. Bill's Law: "If anything bad can happen to you,
then stay away from me, because
I'll probably get it too."*
—Mr. Bill, *Saturday Night Live*

Bombproofing

THEORY OF RELEVANCE

Are you afraid of bombing when you get up in front of a group? You don't have to be. With proper material selection, a few prepared comments in case of unexpected problems, and attention to time, worries about bombing can be virtually eliminated. Also remember one key point that Mike McKinley, past president of the National Speakers Association, told me: "The audience doesn't know your script. If you make a minor mistake, so what. Just keep on talking."

CHAPTER 9

When you want to get a message across using humor, there is one overriding principle that will give you the greatest chance of success along with the least chance of failure. If you make all your attempts at humor relevant to your presentation, you get an automatic excuse from your mother if your humor is not all that funny. If your humor is received as funny, so much the better; but if it isn't, at least you made your point. Audiences will be much more tolerant if the humor ties into the subject at hand.

At social functions, relevance is not as critical as it is in serious business settings. If you stray off the main topic just for fun, it's no big deal. However, if you are still a little apprehensive about your humor skills in a presentation, the theory of relevance will always keep you safe.

Even if your delivery is not great at this point, the proper selection of material will carry you a long way. You must consider the nature of the audience, your personality and style, and the nature of the subject.

If you keep the above principle of relevance in mind, you should never have to suffer the embarrassment of your humor bombing out.

HUMOR RISK

I'll be the first to admit that using humor carries a certain amount of risk. Most people believe, however, that the benefits of humor far exceed the risk. The risk comes in two forms. The first is in using inappropriate humor that offends. The second is using humor that is not funny.

If you follow the guidelines in Chapter 7, you should be able to minimize any risk of offending. I say minimize, because you can never please everyone. Most old timers in the humor field claim that 2 percent of any audience is there to be offended. Even if you don't use humor at all, you are likely to say something that will not sit well with someone. Some people get up in the morning and they are not happy unless they get offended. Poor souls. Don't let these people worry you. It's their problem, not yours.

Now, when it comes to the risk involved in not being funny, that *is* your problem. You need to understand that your risk changes depending on your position relative the group you are addressing. Such risk is in indirect proportion to your relative status.

Let's say you are the CEO of XYA Corporation and you are addressing your employees. You can tell just about any dumb joke (as long as it's not offensive) and get away with it. In the short run, it probably won't affect your career too much either way. I say *in the short run* because being a dork in front of your employees over a long period of time could affect their perception of you as a competent leader.

Now, let's play *Star Trek* and beam you to the lectern of a national conference where the audience is comprised of other CEOs and board members in your industry. The humor risk dynamics change quickly. If you make the same dumb mistakes that you did in front of your employees, you may be jeopardizing the image of your company. At the very least, you are making yourself look foolish. This could affect your future employability should you be forced back on the job market. It could also affect your negotiating power should you be involved in some type of merger or co-venture.

If you are an employee of a company and you are presenting to your superiors, your humor risk is naturally higher than when presenting to subordinates. Your promotability is now on the line. I'm certainly not trying to discourage you from using humor. You just need to know when you can be bolder and when you must be more conservative.

When presenting to a group of your peers, your risk is relatively low, but be prepared for the possibility of audience members giving you a hard time. Make an extra effort to make them feel superior. You could say, *I'm not sure why I was picked to make this presentation because I know many of you have much more expertise in this topic, but there are certain things I discovered that I thought you might like to know about . . .*

To reduce risk, regardless of your status, use humor only to make or reinforce a point. Also keep in mind what you learned about delivery in Chapter 8. Use the fewest words and least amount of time to get to the punch line.

SAVER LINES

Saver Lines are what you say when your supposedly humorous statement does not get a laugh. You shouldn't be ashamed to have to use saver lines. The top comedians in the world need them and some purposely make mistakes so they can get a laugh from the saver line. Johnny Carson was an expert at this. After a poor response to a joke he would say a comically insulting line like, "May an aroused herd of Yaks make an everlasting commitment to your sister" or "This is the kind of crowd that would watch *Bambi* through a sniper scope."

When it comes to saver lines there are two schools of thought:

The First School of Thought is used more by comics and speakers who use a very high percentage of humor. This method is most effective when a speaker shows a high confidence level and is fairly experienced. Say a witty, mildly attacking line to force them to laugh after they didn't laugh at your joke or one-liner.

- *Do any of you out there speak English?*

- *I've got a book for sale outside that explains these jokes. You may want to pick up a copy.*

- (If one person is laughing) *Will you be kind enough to run around the room so it looks like everyone is having fun?*

- *You have marvelous self-control.*

- *I've got 20 more bad jokes just like that one and no one gets out until you start laughing.*

- [Pick out a well-known person in the crowd] *Joe that's the last time I'm using one of your jokes.*

- *I know you're out there, I can hear you breathing.*

- *I'm not going to wait forever for you.*

- *I was waiting on you a little on that one.*

- *That was a Polaroid joke. It takes one minute to get it.*

- *Everyone doesn't have to be funny all the time—and I just proved it.*

The Second School of Thought is used by less experienced speakers and speakers who don't use much humor anyway.

If you don't use a high percentage of humor, the audience may not realize what you said was meant to be funny. All you have to do is keep right on talking and delivering your message (do give them that short pause we talked about to give them a chance to laugh). As long as your humor is making a point, you will be forgiven if it is not tremendously funny.

Trick (advanced technique): Purposely set up a mistake or marginally funny joke so you can use a saver line.

Trick: If no one laughs, you laugh. Then they think they are stupid because they didn't laugh. Then they laugh.

PRE-PLANNED AD-LIBS

Another way to keep from bombing is to always "expect the unexpected." I touched on this briefly in the section on timing. Canned or pre-planned ad-libs are pre-written responses to unexpected happenings or mistakes that occur during a presentation, i.e., microphone squeals, projection bulb burns out, you say the wrong thing, etc. Prepared ad-libs keep you mentally ready so you won't fumble for words when problems come up in a presentation. Prepared ad-libs actually do more than just save you. They make you look tremendously polished.

Here's the continuum: A bad presenter will stammer around when a problem occurs. A ZZZZZs person will say nothing and try to ignore the problem. A great NO ZZZZZs presenter will make a witty comment that appears to be spontaneous.

When you make a mistake admit it. If you don't,
you only make matters worse.

Ward Cleaver
Leave it to Beaver

This is especially important when you make a big mistake during a presentation. You should be the first one to joke about it. If you do, the chances are that your mistake will immediately become a nonissue, or a source of good-natured teasing later. If you don't joke about or at least acknowledge your gaffe, the audience will think poorly of you. There is a good chance they will be joking about you later behind your back or someone could start to heckle you and hold your feet to the fire over the mistake. At this point, you are going to have an uphill battle explaining away the mistake.

In truth, most of the problems that come up during presentations can be expected. All you have to do is write or search out a witty comment for each type of problem you think may occur. Go over your list before each presentation and soon you will have many of these lines ready to go instantly when needed.

NO ZZZZZs presenters are just waiting for a loud noise or for someone to yawn, or cough, or go to the bathroom, or write something down—or for anything to happen so one of these lines can be used.

The audience believes you are originating humor on the spot. You are just quickly re-calling pre-planned respons-es. Ad-libs impress listeners more than prepared jokes and they do not have to be as funny to get good laughter.

Only work on one or two responses from each category until your experience level in-creases. If you try to remem-ber too many, you will hesi-tate when the time comes to ad-lib and ruin the effect. I've included several common problems along with their possible responses. I've also included space for you to jot down some problems that you typically encounter. You can create some of your own *canned ad-libs* to deal with them.

I DROP SOMETHING OR SOMETHING FALLS
(substitute name of actual item)

- *That item must have been nervous.*

- *I must be so boring that item tried to commit suicide.*

I guess that item disagreed with my last point.

Is that the signal that I have talked too long?

I hope my point hits as hard as that item just did.

[Look upwards and hold your hands as if you were praying] *I swear I didn't make up that last point.*

If it wasn't for gravity, that would never have happened.

I'm going to pretend that didn't happen.

(Like Clint Eastwood) *Go ahead. BREAK my day.*

I was just trying to wake you up.

SOMETHING IS BROKEN

Humor can't fix everything.

I would fix this, but the only thing I learned in shop class was how to call for estimates.

That's what I get for buying this at a flea market.

I'll fix this right up. Just give me a hammer.

Does anyone have some SuperGlue?

Does anyone have a dollar bill on them? [If possible, go into the audience in search of a dollar bill apparently to fix the broken item.] *It won't fix this, but maybe I can bribe someone to get me another one.*

● *We really didn't need that* [with sarcasm] *MAJOR PORTION OF MY PRESENTATION did we?—All great speakers have a plan. Unfortunately, I don't. No. I'm just kidding* [go to alternate plan—and you had better have one!]

● *I know it's time for a BREAK, but this is ridiculous.*

This item just took a break so why don't we take one too. Let's resume at . . .

Just when I was smokin', this darn thing gets broken. Let's [take a break, alternate plan, etc.]

LIGHTS GO OUT

- *I guess I'll have to donate a portion of my fee to the electric company.*

- *The caterer will be here shortly with carrots for everyone.*

- *I guess God tried to hit me with a lightning bolt, but hit your electric box instead.*

- *I hope my talk hasn't left you in the dark.*

- *It appears that I need to shed some more light on this subject.*

- *Since you're all sleeping anyway, I decided to turn off the lights.*

- *This is carrying energy conservation too far.*

MICROPHONE SQUEALS

- *This is the portion of my presentation where I do my elephant impression.*

- *That is a result of many years of inhaling helium.*

- *I'll bet you never heard anyone clear their throat like that before.*

- *Don't be alarmed. This is only a test.*

- *Don't worry. I pass out earplugs at all my talks. —If I don't, someone else will.*

- *If you think that's bad, wait until I start singing.*

- *Is there an ear, nose, and throat specialist in the crowd? You'll have plenty of business tonight if this keeps up.*

- *The microphone and I are squealing with delight because we are both happy to be here.*

- *For those of you who can still hear, welcome.*

- *"Squeal" comes from the Latin word "Squel-en" which means: You will look like a big dummy before you start your talk.*

PROJECTOR LIGHT BURNS OUT

Overriding principle according to Nathan Hale—I will only regret it, if I have but one bulb to lose for my audience (always have a spare).

○ *This is the first time I have been brighter than my equipment.*

○ *I don't understand. I left this thing on day and night for six days to make sure the bulb worked.*

● [Talk to projector lovingly while patting it] *Now, don't be shy. These nice people really want to see you.* [Sternly] *And so do I.*

○ [Wave hand in front of the lens] *Wake up in there! Yoo Hoo. Wake up!*

○ *I have a joke. How many projectors does it take to mess up one presentation?*

○ *Patrick Henry said, "Give me liberty or give me a light bulb."*

○ *Does anyone happen to have a* [long description, recited quickly] *quartz, two-prong, Model 921 EYB, 125-Volt, 250-watt overhead projector lamp on them?*

○ *These overheads/slides are a little darker than I expected.*

○ [Refer to blank screen] *Can anyone see this in the back—or front—or anywhere?*

○ [Refer to blank screen] *Don't you enjoy the vivid colors of my visuals?*

○ [Pretend to read a service tag] *Last serviced by Thomas Edison.*

SLIDE IS UPSIDE DOWN

○ *This slide looks good no matter how you look at it.*

○ *You may want to stand on your heads for this one.*

● *I'll get another one; this one must be defective.*

○ *I have reversed my position on this issue.*

○ *I really want you to try to understand my position on this.*

○ *Maybe if I turn the screen over, you'll be able to see this one better.*

It was really difficult to take this picture.

If this slide doesn't confuse you, then you'll love the rest of my presentation.

This is my favorite slide and I didn't want anyone else to see it.

This slide holds a very special position in my carousel.

HIGHLIGHTER RUNS OUT OF INK

This is the dry part of my presentation.

I'm out of ink. I'll be back in a wink. ("K" words are funny.)

● *I wish I'd bought the extended warranty on this.*

Does anyone know where I can get this serviced?

Old speakers never die. Their highlighter just fades off into the sunset.

● *No comment.*

CAN'T FIND IMPORTANT DOCUMENT OR VISUAL
[Make one of these comments then go smoothly to your next document or visual. If you have a break coming up, tell the audience you will find it then.]

My dog ate my visual/paper, etc.

I had it here just a month ago.

Just give me a few hours. I'll find it.

[Pull out any piece of paper. Pretend it is a note to you.] *Dear* (your name) *I borrowed that* (visual/paper etc.). *I knew you wouldn't mind. Signed—* (college roommate or the name of an individual, not in attendance, who is significant to the group).

Is there a magician in the house that can make my (visual/paper etc.) *reappear?*

YOU RUSH INTO THE WRONG MEETING

○ *I guess you are all wondering why I called you here?*

○ *Surprise!*

● *I hope you like my presentation, but you'll have to come to another room to hear it.*

○ [Directed toward the speaker in the room as an apology for interrupting] *Let's have a big hand for your speaker.*

○ *I think everyone here except me is in the wrong room.*

● *I hope I didn't keep you waiting long.*

● *Is this where I sign up for squash lessons?*

○ *I just stopped in to let you know that, if you need me, I'll be in the* (conference room/Jefferson Room etc.)

● *I just thought I'd drop in to say "Hi!"*

○ *Did someone here order a pizza?*

SOMEONE POINTS OUT A MISSPELLING

● *As Mark Twain once said, "I don't give a damn for a man that can spell a word only one way."*

● *Oh! I apologize. My word processor had a virus.*

○ *That is the Swahili/pig Latin spelling.*

○ *That was put in there to test you.*

● *I knew I shouldn't have had my dog proofread this.*

YOU TRIP GOING TO THE LECTERN

○ *I also do magic tricks.*

○ *It took years of finishing school to learn to do that.*

- *I had a good trip. See you next fall.*

- *I'm the only speaker who can fall UP a set of steps.*

- *Is there a doctor in the house?* [Say this in a playful manner so you don't alarm the audience.]

- *All that money I spent at Arthur Murray's was a waste.*

- *OK. Who planted the banana peel?*

- *I used to be too humble to stumble.*

- *Give me an inch and I'll take a fall.*

- [Sing] *Blow the man down matey, blow the man down.*

YOU HEAR A LOUD CRASH

- *God must be throwing lightning bolts at me.*

- *I always like to start off with a bang.*

- *I'm flattered. You ordered fireworks for me.*

- *Was that a real noise or was it Memorex?*

ALARM GOES OFF

This is a special category because there is a real physical danger involved. Whether you like it or not, you are in charge of the calm evacuation of the room. You should already know where the exits are located, and have a plan in mind for an orderly exit. You must stay absolutely calm. The audience will take their cues from you. If you sprint off the stage screaming, you will be morally responsible for someone getting crushed in the ensuing stampede.

I keep the following comments in mind at all times:

> [Calmly] *Well it looks like it's time to take a break whether we need one or not. Please stay seated. It's probably a false alarm, but as a precaution we will go outside and see what is happening. Are there any disabled persons who may have a difficult time moving toward the exit* (you should know this already in smaller crowds)? *One person on either side should assist them.* [Now direct the crowd, by rows if necessary, to calmly move toward the emergency exits].

To recite the above directions calmly takes about 30 well-spent seconds.

After returning to the presentation room, and if nothing really serious occurred, you can use humorous ad-libs to regain the group's attention.

● *I knew I had a hot topic but this is ridiculous.*

● *I must really be a hot speaker to set off the fire alarm.*

UNIVERSAL

● *"I feel like the javelin thrower who won the toss and elected to receive."* —George Bush

● *This* (broken or malfunctioning item) *must have been made by* (competing company). <u>Note</u>: Be careful with this one. You might want to work for this competing company someday.

● *For an encore ladies and gentlemen I will now juggle chain saws.—I think it would be easier than being up here right now.*

Think up some problems that are specific to the presentations you do and list them below. Then try to think up witty responses to go with them.

My prepared one-liners:

Problem:

My One-Liner:

Problem:

My One-Liner:

Problem:

My One-Liner:

Problem:

My One-Liner:

Problem:

My One-Liner:

The overriding principle here is never ignore that which is obvious to the audience. This shows the audience that you are aware and interested in them and that you are strong and secure enough to mention the problem.

Sometimes you can even take advantage of a situation without doing any fancy ad-libbing. A few years back I was introducing a seminar leader at a hotel in Columbia, Maryland. As soon as I started, a maintenance person came through a door that was directly behind the dais and started fiddling with the thermostat. I could see all the eyes of the audience members looking at him—not me. I knew there was no sense in trying to compete with this distraction so I decided to take advantage of it. I stopped the intro and walked over to the maintenance person and asked him to read the introduction. Without missing a beat he did so, and quite well I might add. The audience went nuts and the seminar leader came on to a very lively audience. By acknowledging what the audience was thinking about, the introduction was far better than the planned version would have been.

ACKNOWLEDGMENTS TO TOUGH SITUATIONS

There will come a time when you will either be in front of a hostile audience or a hostile question will pop up during a relatively calm presentation. This is a tough situation at best and you have to handle it with kid gloves. Humor can save the day and maybe even help you become president.

When a hostile situation arises, you have to be especially careful that you don't antagonize the questioner or group further by making a flippant response. You can use humor to distract the antagonism, but you should always make a serious reply to the question at hand.

Example:

Let's say you are speaking at a stockholder's meeting and you are telling them about all the wonderful new products that are coming out. Then someone yells out, "What about the supreme turkey of a widget you came out with last year?" Now you are on the spot. If you ignore the question you will look like you are hiding. If you use a comeback that attacks the questioner or makes fun of him or her you will turn the rest of the group against you. So what do you do? Use a prepared one-liner or some mildly amusing admission of guilt and then immediately go into a serious response to the question.

> We are donating all those widgets to the Navy because they have a shortage of boat anchors this year [pause for laughter]. But, seriously folks, based on all the available research we had at our disposal the widget looked like it would be a good solid seller for us. Then when the gizmo industry took a big hit, we no longer had a market for the widgets.

Then get back to your agenda.

If you expect to be in a position like the above speaker, try to anticipate the hostile questions that could arise and prepare responses for them. You might not be able to anticipate all the questions that could come up, but by preparing in advance you are giving yourself an infinitely better chance of responding correctly. Another good resource is *What to Say When . . . You're Dyin' on The Platform* by Lilly Walters.

One of the most famous examples of good preparation came during Ronald Reagan's 1984 bid for reelection. Reagan made a very poor showing as he stumbled through his first debate with the democratic challenger, Walter Mondale. The media jumped on this and Reagan's age and possible senility became a big issue until about two-thirds of the way through his second televised debate with Mondale.

A question was posed to the president that ask him if he was concerned about how his age would affect his ability to do the job. Reagan's prepared two-line response virtually nailed the lid on Mondale's coffin and squelched the age issue even though he was four years older than he was in the last election. He said, "I'm not going to inject the issue of age into this campaign. I am not going to exploit for political gain my opponent's youth and inexperience." Some say this comment won him his second term of office. That's the power of preparation.

WATCH YOUR CLOCK SO THEY DON'T WATCH THEIRS

One of the quickest ways to bomb is to go overtime or try to stuff too much information in too little time. I have done talks where I was a big hero at 30 minutes and a bum at 42 minutes. One time I even got in trouble with the meeting planner. She was sitting in the front row laughing the whole time then afterwards said, "You went too long." OUCH!!

When that incident happened, I was feeling the pressure to fill up the time I had been booked for. That attitude is a mistake because it pays no attention to how the audience is feeling. Now, I counsel the meeting planner to let me be the judge of when to quit. Most open-minded planners will go along with me on this. They understand that I'm not trying to be lazy and quit early. I am trying to give their audience the best presentation they can handle under the circumstances.

If the audience is really great, it sometimes makes you want to go overtime because things are going so well. Don't do it. Leave them wanting more and you

> *I don't mind you looking at your watches, but I hope you won't get out your calendars.*
> Anon

> *The secret of being a bore is to tell everything.*
>
> Voltaire circa 1718
>
> *A fool utterith all his mind.*
>
> Proverbs 29:11
>
> *What orators lack in depth they make up to you in length.*
>
> Montesquieu, 1767

It appears speakers who won't shut up have been a problem for quite a while.

will always be welcome back. If you are susceptible to losing track of time, recruit someone or have the meeting planner assign someone to stand in the back of the room and signal you when five minutes (or whatever length of time suits you) is left.

One of the worst things you can do is to try to fit all your material in a shortened time period by speaking faster. The audience won't be able to absorb it anyway and you'll look foolish besides. I regularly cut material without missing a beat when my time gets shortened or the audience is exhausted because of a long day or evening. To do this without becoming flustered takes a little preparation and a few tricks up your sleeve.

The first thing I do to make things easy on myself is to prepare a talk that is five to ten minutes shorter than the allotted time period. Rarely is your time ever lengthened, but it is routinely shortened. Even when it is not shortened it is shortened. If you are supposed to go on at 1:00 p.m., you will very seldom actually start talking until 1:10 p.m. People take time to get seated, then you have a few announcements, and then your introduction, etc., etc., etc. If you have allowed for these delays, you don't have to cut any material at all.

When your time gets cut more than 10 minutes, you must take appropriate pre-planned actions. I rank my material in order of importance to that group. I know. I know. It all should be important, but there is always something that is more important than something else for a given group. If you have studied them enough in your pre-program research, you should have less trouble deciding what material could be cut in case you are asked to shorten your talk. After you have ranked your material for a particular talk, write down how much time each segment takes so that you'll know how much time you save by cutting a particular chunk of material.

The other **supertrick** I use when I have a long story to tell is to have a quotation ready that makes the same point as the story. If my time is cut, I simply use the quote instead of the story and save several minutes.

Keep a clock on stage with you that you can glance at to keep yourself on track. Or, get a speaker timer that you wear like a pager that vibrates to let you know time is almost up.

There are two schools of thought about looking at your watch while on stage. I'll give them to you and you decide which is right. The first school of thought is that you *should* never look at your watch while on stage because it will cause the audience members to start looking at their watches. The second school of thought is that you *should* look at your watch to let the audience members know that you are aware of time. This supposedly allows them to listen to you rather than worry if you are going to go too long.

I don't know which one of these schools is right, so I simply make a statement to the audience sometime during the talk (usually the beginning or end) that I will not go overtime. Then I keep track of time with my hidden timer on stage.

To recap, keep your humor relevant to the points you are trying to make. Have a few saver lines ready to go and prepare responses for "expected," unexpected occurrences. And keep track of time. If you do these things, you will never have to worry about bombs falling on your NO ZZZZZs presentation.

It is what they can show the audience when they are not talking that reveals the fine actor.

—Cedric Hardwicke

Movement and appearance

Edward T. Hall, the noted social anthropologist, claims 60 percent of all communication is nonverbal. Communication analyst Albert Mehrabian says we are perceived in three ways: 7 percent verbally, 38 percent vocally, and a full 55 percent visually, including gestures, posture, stride, facial expressions, movement, dress, and eye contact. These guys undoubtedly know more about it than I do. What I

CHAPTER 10

want you to learn is that gestures and body language can be used to help tell your story without using additional words, they can make you feel better, and they can make your audience like you more.

Gestures include all physical activity before, during, and after your talk. A gesture can be just about anything. It could be a hand on the hip, a wrinkled brow, a raise of the eyebrows, or leaning against the lectern. In fact, communications expert Mario Pei estimates that humans can display up to 700,000 different physical signs. I'll start numbering them now: 1) eyelash curl, 2) fingernail growth, 3) double chin wiggle . . . Of course, I'm kidding, but that is an awful lot of movement to keep track of, don't you think?

According to Dorothy Leeds in her book *PowerSpeak*, "Audiences are making their hard-to-shake first impressions as you are setting up, waiting to be introduced, and walking to the platform to begin your speech." When you walk into the room you should be smiling, upbeat, and at least appearing to be calm. You want them to be *in fun*, don't you?

If I had to pick one technique in this whole book for you to master, this would be it: smile. You can get more (s)mileage out of this simple facial gesture than any one of the more than 250,000 of which you are capable. This ultimate gesture that is recognized all over the world projects warmth and the message that friendship is possible.

Studies reveal that when you smile, even if you force your smile, you will feel better. The same studies also reveal that smiling faces are perceived by others to be more friendly and likeable. Virtually every presenter I coach gets told to smile more. It's one of the easiest ways to reduce your nervousness and it will definitely make the audience more receptive to you.

Remember to thoroughly check out the gestures for a given country before you present there. Gestures vary from country to country and one you commonly use in the U.S. can cause confusion or be offensive (see "International," Chapter 2).

Before you go too deep into the study of gestures it may be a good idea to have yourself videotaped doing a program. You may be doing just fine. It would be better still to look at tapes that were already recorded before you read this chapter. The process of thinking about gestures may cause you to change how you naturally gesture. This will give a false picture of you on the videotape.

Once you get the tape, turn off the sound and study it yourself to see if you are doing anything distracting or if you notice any areas where a gesture may have helped get your message across.

If you need help, I provide the service, as do many speaker coaches, whereby you can mail the videotape in for an objective evaluation of your gestures—and other parameters as well. Getting a tape reviewed is a convenient and less expensive way to begin using a presentation consultant (see "Get Coaching" Chapter 12).

Don't get too worried about gestures. Focusing wholly on them will keep you from thinking about what you are saying. Just keep in mind—overall it is better to gesture too little than too much or to use wrong or bad gestures. Some gestures can be distracting. Any gesture can be distracting and tiring if used over and over.

If you want to be funny with gestures, many times odd body angles will do the trick. Those of you that remember Jackie Gleason and his "away we go" exit or Steve Martin's "Walk like an Egyptian" routine, know how exaggerated body angles can be funny.

STAND UP AND BE COUNTED

You've heard of stand-up comics, right? There's evidence from a study done by The Wharton School of Business at the University of Pennsylvania that you should be a stand-up presenter. These results came from a controlled study of a situation where the presenters tried to persuade people to invest in a new business venture.

For the first group, the presenter sat down and talked across a table. For the second group, all the facts and figures were identical, but the presenter stood up and used visual aids. Can you guess the results? In the first group, 58 percent of the people agreed to invest in the new business. Not bad, right? It's not too bad unless you compare it with the second group where 79 percent of the people agreed to invest.

Another study at the University of Minnesota found that a stand-up presentation using visual aids will cause your customers to be willing to pay 26 percent more money for your exact same product or service.

When you stand up, you instantly command authority, attention, and interest. People know it's time to listen. When you are standing, you can move about, which also keeps attention. Rigid, feet-glued-to-the-floor presenters will elicit loud snoring in short order. People also love visual aids, and you are the best and most reliable one in your presentation.

Trick to save you: Don't sit with your legs crossed before it's your turn to speak. If your legs go to sleep, you will have to limp (or crawl) to the stage (on the other hand that would get their attention, wouldn't it?).

STAGE POSITIONING

Where you position your body on the stage can have a subtle yet significant effect on the audience. Center stage is a powerful area. Moving downstage (toward the audience) right and downstage left can tell the audience without words that you are going to be funny or that you are going to say something that evokes emotion. You should be consistent with your stage movement so that you deliver the same types of messages when you are in certain areas of the stage. For instance, if you always go downstage left to tell funny stories and then switch to an emotional story while you are downstage left you may confuse the audience.

When moving on the stage, make sure that your movement has a purpose. If you take a step, go at least three steps in that direction to cue the audience that you are moving for a reason. Don't wander around or take a step here and a step there. Again, you will distract and confuse the audience.

When making an important point, move toward the audience. Three steps forward from center stage would be a very powerful position that would command attention (especially if you walked right off the stage and fell on your face).

Upstage (away from the audience) left and right are weak positions. They can be used when you feel you are overpowering the audience or when you want to remove attention from yourself. I use these positions when I direct the audience to do some task, such as talk among themselves. Upstage center is a strong position, but one that makes you appear disconnected from the audience. I usually avoid this position.

When I want to be playful and/or really get the audience involved, I'll go right into the crowd. I might have to come down off the stage, but to me it's worth it. I'm really connected and I feel like one of them when I'm out there. I am also sending a message that I really know what I am doing. I don't need any notes. I don't need any visuals. I don't need anything but interaction with them. They love it!

The main thing you have to watch out for when you are out in the audience is that in large rooms with lots of attendees many people can't see you, so they start to lose interest if you stay out there too long. This is counteracted if you are being projected on a large screen and you have an on-the-ball and well-rehearsed video crew. (If you don't alert the video crew ahead of time of your intentions, they will be scrambling to follow you and it won't look good on the screen.) When you are being projected, think about toning down your overall movement because it's not easy to follow you wildly around the stage with a video camera.

BAD HABITS

You can have a pretty good presentation going and damage it severely with distracting habits. I've been around for a while, yet I still watch myself on videotape whenever I can to identify anything I may be doing unconsciously that may hurt my presentation.

- Some problem areas you want to watch for are

- Pacing back and forth

- Jingling coins in your pocket

- Jingling bracelets or jewelry

- Playing with your hair (normally done by women)

- Playing with objects (pointers, markers, etc.)

- Holding on to the lectern or table for dear life

- Rocking front-to-back or side-to-side

- Staring

- Standing rigidly in one place (this would surely create ZZZZZs)

- Speaking with your head down or bowed

- Frowning

- Locking hands together or twiddling thumbs

- Tapping your fingers

- Pushing up your glasses

Almost all of these problems can be improved significantly and immediately. The simple realization that you are doing them will start the improvement process. To eliminate them completely may take a little extra effort or the help of a competent presentation coach.

Trick: Get in front of a mirror. Hold light dumbbells or heavy books in your hands. Start delivering your talk. When the books or dumbbells move, you have located real gestures. When you first try this in an effort to eliminate bad habits, you will notice that your mouth won't go. Don't worry. Eventually the bad habit will give up and your mouth will do just fine. Note: Use a heavy enough dumbbell so you don't smash yourself in the head when you try to adjust your glasses.

CLOTHING

Fun presenters can wear fun clothing—but within the limits of your industry. I'm not going to pretend to be Mr. Clothes Horse (I've been accused of looking too corporate), but I will offer a few tips that should help you out.

- When presenting, don't wear clothes that are uncomfortable even if they look great.

- Wear clothes somewhere in the upper fringe of the limits for your industry, i.e., stand out, but not way out.

- If you really want to be remembered, consider trademark clothing, i.e., you are known for wearing funny ties, glasses, hats, etc.

- Don't wear loose jewelry or anything that is a distraction. Be especially careful of this if you are being videotaped (see Appendix C).

- Double check and double sew all critical buttons and catches.

- Consider where your microphone and transmitter could be attached when purchasing presentation clothing. You may want to buy the clothing slightly large to decrease transmitter pack bulge (or if you gain weight).

- Take just about everything out of your pockets to reduce bulges.

- If you are much older than your audience, dress in your most stylish outfit (don't go overboard).

- If you are much younger than your audience dress in your most conservative outfit (don't go overboard).

Trick: Remove your glasses to change the mood. You might deliver straight information, then remove your glasses to tell a personal story. Don't make a big theatrical deal out of it and don't repeat it too often in the same presentation. <u>Note</u>: Glasses are articles of clothing, but they could also be considered props.

Trick (Men): Unbutton your coat to show an extra degree of openness. Take your coat off and roll up your sleeves for a let's get-down-to-business look.

Is Anybody out There?

The body language and facial expressions of the audience are just as important to you as your own gestures and movement. They can be a good indicator of how the audience is feeling. If they are squirming in their chairs, looking around, yawning, or slouched, it is time for you to stop or do something to gain their interest. Bob Lucas, manager of professional development at the National Office of the American Automobile Association and president of Bob Lucas and Associates, says, "If your participants are painfully looking at their watches then they are not learning."

Watch carefully for signs of boredom and/or general disagreement. If members of the audience have their arms folded across their chests, refuse to make eye contact with you, or if they have cross looks on their faces, chances are you are not connecting.

When you see these signs, you must do something different. Take a break if you have to, but do something. If you simply drone on, matters will only get worse. Always have several of the attention gaining techniques listed in Chapter 5 ready to go just in case.

If you are successful in regaining the interest of the audience, you will see a definite change in their body language and facial expression. They will turn toward you and lean forward while giving you good eye contact. You will also see heads nodding when you make your points, and laughter and other responses will be heartier.

You will learn a great deal about how good you are as a presenter just by watching your audience. If you want to get better at this, here are two good resources: *How to Read a Person Like a Book* by Gerard I. Nierenberg and Henry H. Calero and *Body Language* by Julius Fast.

BONUS TIPS

- The larger the crowd, the larger and slower the gestures.

- If you have a small crowd, or if you are videoconferencing or on television, use smaller gestures.

- Work to eliminate distracting or nervous gestures, but don't kill yourself to add new ones. They will take care of themselves.

- Let your words trigger your actions. If you are counting, hold out your fingers. If you say no, shake your head no.

- Hold your hands open and wide apart to show sincerity and honesty.

- Hold your hands behind your back during question-and-answer sessions (don't overdo it).

- Avoid excessive hands in pockets, clenched fists, pointing, hands on hips, and the infamous fig leaf position where your hands are crossed in front of your groin.

Only when you have crossed the river can you say the crocodile has a lump on his snout.

—Ashanti Proverb

Involvement and interplay

OK. So I had to really stretch to find a quotation to start this chapter. Quote books don't have many headings labeled *involvement* or *interplay*. What this quote means to me is that if you stay aloof from the audience and talk *at* them, you are not close enough to see the tiny gems of value and individual differences they bring to your presentation. I want you to cross the carpeted river and be with them.

CHAPTER 11

You have got to make your audience feel as if they are part of the program. In an effort to discover what works best, adult learning theory has come to the forefront of the meetings industry. It has shown me that for my message to be received most readily and for it to be remembered for at least five minutes after I'm gone, I must interact with the audience and get them involved. Not only does involvement make your words more efficient, (i.e., you need fewer words to make the same point) it is also a fun way to spend your time with the audience.

There are three ways to involve your audience—physically, mentally, and emotionally. There is usually some degree of overlap, and if you can use all three ways at once, that is even better. We will concentrate here on simple techniques that will allow you to easily add involvement to your presentations.

The first thing I want to tell you is that I love this stuff. I have a blast joking around with the audience. I either go out into the audience or have audience members come on stage with me whenever I can. I believe in making them the stars of the presentation and in turn they make me the star. They make me the star by giving me higher evaluations, buying more of my products and services and acting on my ideas.

AXE THE LECTERN

To get started in your efforts to involve the audience I recommend that you take a big axe with you to each one of your presentations and chop the lectern into tiny little pieces. That way you won't be tempted to stand behind it. The behind-the-lectern speaker is quickly going the way of the dinosaur. Make every attempt possible to avoid delivering your information from behind a lectern (unless protocol and/or logistics absolutely demand that you do). To be most effective, you want to eliminate any barriers between you and the audience. If they can see you, and if you are physically close to them, they will have a greater rapport with you. They will be able to notice your facial expressions and body language much better than if you have a physical barrier in between. A friend of mine who is a top-notch humorist was asked to do his presentation in a room that had a dance floor between him and the audience. Needless to say the presentation suffered immensely.

Standing Ovation

Now let's look at some simple ways to involve the audience physically. One of the all-time favorites is called the *Standing Ovation*. I'm not talking about the standing ovation that the crowd gives you at the end of a presentation. I'm talking about a standing ovation that the crowd gives to its own members. This is so popular that you have to be careful that another presenter at the same event is not using it (at least BEFORE you do). Although it has been somewhat overused, it is still quite effective, especially in front of a fun-loving crowd, so don't be afraid to try it. I'm not exactly sure where this technique originated, but the best known person who uses it is Matt Weinstein of Playfair, Inc. (Notice how I credited Matt. Art Buchwald says to credit a person the first three times you use their material and then to heck with it. Wait! I've credited Matt more than three times for the standing ovation, so forget about him. I ACTUALLY INVENTED THE STANDING OVATION. Of course, I'm kidding. This book is about humor, isn't it?)

Instructions for Standing Ovation:

1. Ask questions of the audience (feel free to change wording around to suit, but follow the "Tough/We're going to make it better" theme).

Question: Is there anyone out there who has had a tough day? C'mon up front with me. We're going to make that rough day better right now.

Question: Is there anyone out there who has had a tough week? C'mon up and we'll make it better.

Question: Is there anyone out there who has had a tough month? You come up too.

Repeat on through the millennium if you want. Just get people up on stage with you.

2. Encourage the audience to recall the last time they heard a performer get a really great standing ovation. Then have them give a great big standing ovation to their fellow audience members who are on-stage with you.

To be sure that this works, I always schmooze with audience members before the program and line up volunteers. You would look kind of stupid if no one came up front with you.

I WON! I WON!

Another fun way to get the audience involved physically is to give out prizes. My favorite way to do this is to tape my business card underneath several randomly selected seats before anyone is in the room. Sometime during the program I will tell the audience that I have some gifts for them and they are hidden in the room somewhere. I also tell them they should not bother looking for them because they are sitting on them right now. Then I direct the audience to feel under their seats for the business card.

When the winners find the business cards they get to come up on stage to redeem their prizes, but there is usually a catch. I make up some funny questions to ask them. They get the prize no matter how they answer.

If you are pressed for time, you can hand the prizes to people in the first row and have them hand them one by one back to the winners. This gets many people involved physically because they have to handle the prize. (It's not a bad sales technique either. You might use your product for the prize if you want the other audience members to touch it and want one too.)

May I Help You?

Many audience members would love to get a piece of the limelight by helping the presenter. Take advantage of this fact by giving out jobs. You could have an audience member writing on the flip chart for you. You could have another one handling cue cards or timing the presentation. This is also a good method to handle audience members whom you fear might be disruptive. If you give them something to do, you will have better control over them and you will be able to give them the attention that they want.

Try to make sure potentially troublesome audience members are seated close to you so you have some measure of control. If they are seated in the back, any noise they make will cause the rest of the audience to look away from you.

Old Yeller

I don't know about you, but I like audience members yelling at me. I really do. I have them call out to me on command. I might say to them, *When I snap my fingers, you all yell out, "Hey Tom, Why do we do that?"* or *"Hey Tom, you're a bum."* For this to sound good you must give them a solid cue. That is why I put in the cue about snapping my fingers. This lets each audience member know when to start yelling.

Some other ways to get the audience involved physically are to pull audience gags (discussed in depth in Chapter 13), give them snacks, or let them throw things around the audience. Many trainers throw a soft, easily catchable ball to an audience member who asks a question. After the answer, the audience member throws the ball back to the presenter, who in turn throws it to the next audience member to ask a question.

Mental Involvement

One of the best ways to get your message to sink in is to get the audience thinking. This may sound elementary, but when you are up there spewing words *at* the audience, they may not have time to think. That is one reason pauses are so effective. They give the audience a chance to catch up and apply their own thoughts and value systems to what you are saying.

Asking questions of the audience is a great way to force them into the *think* mode. *Has anyone ever been to Cleveland?* A simple question like this zooms an individual audience member's mind to Cleveland if that person has been to Cleveland. If that person has not been to Cleveland, he or she will be tuned in mentally to see what you have to say about Cleveland. *Have you ever had your keys in your hand one minute and the next minute they were gone?* This question is the *Has-this-ever-happened-to-you?* variety. To corral the most audience members with a question like this, all you have to do is use a question that you know (from your pre-program research) will relate to most of the audience.

Johnny Carson (before he retired), Jay Leno, and David Letterman all use questions about current news to grab their audiences mentally. They ask *Did you read today or did you hear today about . . .?* Johnny, Jay, and Dave know that if the audience has heard about the current event they will feel a common bond and if they haven't heard about it, they will listen more carefully. To make sure these talented and funny talk show hosts reach the largest portion of their respective audiences, they almost always explain or recap the news item before they make the joke. This gives those audience members that haven't heard about the current event a chance to *get* the humor.

Most audiences hate *Hey Stupid* questions. These are questions like, *Hey stupid audience! How many of you would like to make more money?* or *Hey morons! How many of you would like to work less?* These kinds of questions are trite and will quickly label you as a snooze-inducing presenter. I like to make fun of these questions. Here's how I do it:

[Say with deadpan expression] *I am known as one of the foremost experts in the world—on dumb questions.* Acknowledging the fact that you know they are dumb questions allows you to use them. I might go ahead and use two truly dumb questions to make my point and then add a third one that is humorous (Rule of Three) like, *How many people think they are going to be better looking when they leave my session today?* This third question is a perfect one to customize for the group. All you have to do is brainstorm on something ludicrous that relates to them: *How many of you think that your widget sales will triple because of what I say today?*

Another fun, but playfully insulting, way to ask a dumb question would go like this. [Pick a fun person in the audience and walk up to him or her.] *I want to ask you a question.* [Walk away.] *You probably wouldn't know the answer anyway.* [Walk back.] *Of course, you would know it.* (This negates the insult.) Then go ahead and ask that person the question.

Question and Answer sessions are another way to use questions to get the audience thinking. You'll learn how to do that and have fun with it in Chapter 13.

Breaking large groups up into smaller discussion groups or asking audience members to get a partner for discussion is another way to force them to think. They must come up with ideas themselves while you are totally out of the picture. When you ask them to break into groups, you have also overlapped your mental involvement with physical involvement (kind of like getting a two-for-one happy hour discount). This is one of the few times it is acceptable to turn your back on the audience. Many presentation skills coaches say you should never turn your back, but I disagree. When you break groups up it is their turn to be the stars. Turning your back and moving away from them takes all the focus off of you. I usually give the audience clear instructions about what to discuss, then I give them a clear command to break up into groups, then I turn my back and walk away.

Many of your less boisterous audience members like breaking up into small groups. They are too shy to stand up and express their opinion in front of the whole audience, but they feel comfortable talking to a few others or one-on-one. A good technique to connect with this type of audience member right away is to make an announcement that puts them at ease. *We'll be doing some group discussions today. No one will be put on the spot unless they want to be.* This statement near the beginning of your presentation will immediately gain the attention of the less outgoing members.

You can add some fun to the process of splitting up the audience. Break the audience up into groups of five and tell them the group leader will be the person in the group with the most grandchildren, the most pennies in his or her pocket, or the most buttons, etc. You can be very flexible with this so that no one is forced to be the group leader. Use a different group leader selection method each time the same audience is split up. After the discussion, the group leader is charged with reporting the findings to the entire audience.

Dr. Wolf J. Rinke, author of *Make It a Winning Life* does specific exercises with the audience to force them to engage both the left and right sides of their brain. He makes extensive use of brain teasers and mental stretching exercises, many of which are integrated into his book.

| Thought |
| Thought |

One mental stretch break involves a page with three to sixteen boxes. Each box has some sort of word, phrase, or picture, which participants have to translate into something

| Show | | KNEE LIGHT |

that is meaningful and recognizable. For instance, what does the word *Thought* written above the word *Thought* represent? *Second Thoughts.* The word *Knee* stacked on top of the word *Light* means *Neon Light. Show* written down the side of the page is, of course, *Side Show,* and so forth.

Another great resource is the *Games Trainers Play* series by Edward Scannell and John Newstrom. These volumes, which can be purchased separately, contain many other ideas for involving your audience mentally, plus hundreds of educational activities, exercises, and icebreakers.

I GET SO EMOTIONAL

If you want to get real action out of your audience, then tugging on their heart strings can help make it happen. This is where your storytelling ability (Chapter 14) can really make you shine. My friends Maggie Bedrosian and Thelma Wells can take a simple set of events and paint beautiful pictures in the minds of their audience members with carefully crafted stories.

However, you don't have to tell stories to get emotional response. You can get another two-for-one happy hour special when you ask the right questions. If you want to stimulate fond feelings in most Christian audiences ask them, *Do you remember when you were a child and you could barely get to sleep Christmas Eve because you just knew Santa was going to bring you that special something?* It wouldn't, however, connect so well with people who do not celebrate Christmas (remember—know your audience). If you want the audience to remember bad feelings ask, *Do you remember doing something really bad as a child? What kind of punishment did your parents give you?* If you want to elicit sad feelings try, *Did you ever have a pet that died or did you have a friend who had a pet that died?* If you want the audience to smile, ask them this, *Can you remember the most embarrassing moment of your life?* Most people will laugh when thinking back to an embarrassment that they felt was a tragedy at the time because one of the definitions of humor is tragedy separated by space and time.

There are many emotions you can trigger in the audience just by your choice of words. Happiness, anger, sadness, nostalgia are just a few. Knowing your purpose for being in front of the group helps you to pick which emotions you want to tap. When your purpose is known, choosing words to get the desired emotional response is much easier.

Here's an example of a simple set of facts that a presenter might convey:

> *There have been 11 accidents in the past year at the sharp curve which is two miles north of Cherokee Lake on Route 857. Installation of guard rails, warning signs, and a flashing light will cost approximately $34,000. Even though we have not balanced the budget this year, I feel that we should appropriate money for this project. Thank you.*

Here is a little different version that uses emotional appeal to get the message across.

> *On July 18th of this year John Cochran was found dead. The radio of his car was still playing when the paramedics got to his overturned vehicle. John's neck was broken. It was snapped when his car flipped over an embankment. No one here knows John Cochran because he did not live here, but he died in our neighborhood. Most of you do know of the hairpin turn on Route 857 that has been the scene of 11 accidents this year alone and has injured many friends as well as strangers. We need money to put up guardrails, signs, and a flashing light. I know money is tight, but I hope you see fit to find the funds to remedy this situation before the unknown John Cochran becomes one of your loved ones.*

Can you see the difference in these two appeals? The first was simply a set of facts. Facts are important, but they rarely stimulate people to action. The action comes when emotions get attached to believable facts. You can bet the second version of the above story would have the best chance of securing that $34,000.

To create the emotional appeal in the second version of the story, words and phrases were chosen that had emotional power. *John Cochran was found dead. The radio of his car was still playing . . . John's neck was broken. It was snapped . . . his car flipped . . . he died in our neighborhood.* All these phrases were woven into the original set of facts to create the emotional response of horror about this terribly dangerous turn.

Now let's take a look at a more lighthearted and fun example.

In my keynote presentations I sometimes tell a story (when you are really telling a story don't tell the audience you are telling a story like I just did. You'll learn why in Chapter 14) about a devastating business loss that I had. The basic facts of the story are

☺   I started a business before I graduated from college.

☹   A few years later I got wiped out because of a change in the law.

☺   I came back to be successful in business again.

Here's the beginning of a short version of the story along with the emotional language I include to make the story interesting:

> *Let me take you back to 1973* (gets audience thinking what they were doing in 1973). *"Piano Man" by Billy Joel was the hit song, "The Exorcist" was the hit movie* (more references to the time period to really take them back), *and Tricky Dicky Nixon was president—but not for long* (lighthearted reference to Watergate which virtually everyone my age or older knows about). *I was attending West Virginia University on a football scholarship* (almost every audience has at least some sports interest). *Being an athlete, I had to live in the dorm, and I kept noticing that my friends who were renting apartments were paying a fortune. At that time there was a waiting list for apartments in Morgantown, West Virginia. I thought renting apartments might be a good business so I saved up all the money I made working summer jobs and bought a little three-unit converted house from an old lawyer who was retiring. I remodeled the attic into a fourth apartment to get the income up. Then I bought another, then another, then another,*

and before I was done I owned five apartment buildings and a thirty-six-unit hotel—all before I graduated from college. Then I bought a little dirt bar and converted it to one of the largest nightclubs in the state. I was sure I was going to be a millionaire by the time I was 30. Then, (said ominously so they know a big disaster is coming) *does anyone know what happened in 1986?* (I ask a question to really make them think: What could have happened in 1986 that was bad? Also it's somewhat humorous that the hot-shot whiz kid was about to take a fall.) *The drinking age went from 18 to 21 years of age. I lost $400,000 in one shot. I was totally wiped out* (audience feels bad for me, but they don't mind hearing that you fell flat as you will learn in the section on self-effacing humor). *I tore my Achilles tendon clear in two* (this causes the audience to cringe thinking about what it would feel like to have their own Achilles tendon severed) *and was laid up for six months* (they imagine how bad that would be). *My girl-friend left me* (many people have been dumped by a lover so they relate).—*Actually that was a good thing* (this is comic relief to lighten up all the doom and gloom I am laying on them) *and my dog got hit by a car* (they really feel sorry for me now—especially the dog lovers). *Don't worry, he was OK and went on to write a country song* (more comic relief). *It was the lowest point in my life* (audience members may recall the lowest point in their lives).

I then go on to explain to the audience how I climbed out of the hole using joke books and comical television shows to keep my spirits up. And, of course, how they could do the same thing if they needed to. All along the way, I find places to add emotional language to keep them deeply involved in the story and its points.

I COULD DO WITHOUT SOME EMOTIONAL AUDIENCES

You may present to audiences that have very negative emotions already piqued. They may be downright hostile. When this is the case, you need to say things that will REDUCE the emotional intensity (also see "Acknowledgments to Tough Situations" Chapter 9).

I don't often face hostile audiences, but a friend of mine is an expert on them. Larry Tracy trains business executives to communicate successfully with skeptical and even hostile audiences. Larry's expertise comes from hard-won experience. In a previous life in government, he had the job of speaking to hundreds of emotional, demanding audiences in the 1980s to defend and debate the Reagan Administration's Central America policy.

Larry tells me that hostile audiences have a great deal of what psychologists call *cognitive dissonance*, a tendency to protect existing beliefs and prejudices and reject contradictory information. He says this emotional baggage has to be bypassed before a speaker's facts can be comprehended, and that only a speaker perceived to have empathy has a chance of reaching such an audience. Larry trains his clients to follow what he calls the **KAP** method—**K**now your audience's concerns, and **A**nticipate their objections and questions with realistic **P**ractice. The practice consists of a simulated presentation with colleagues role-playing as the more contentious audience members.

Larry says that speakers confronted with an angry audience should think of themselves as a thermometer, always attempting to keep the heat down. A calm voice and use of phrases such as *I understand your point* and *I certainly see where you are coming from,* as well as open body language can help cool down emotionally-charged audience members. He adds that speakers should never appear dogmatic. They should never tell an audience that they are going to persuade them or show them where they are wrong. Above all, speakers should never become embroiled in a shouting match with audience members.

He says the key to getting hostile audience members to change their view is a thorough pre-presentation analysis of why the audience has invested so much emotional capital opposing the issue. This analysis may show that audience members have been previously misinformed and speakers—after showing they are reasonable, credible, and open-minded—can then provide new data, allowing audience members a face-saving means to change their mind.

INTERPLAY

I love to interact with the audience and it is much easier now that wireless microphones are so readily available. I can go right into the audience, I can sit in one of their chairs, I can sit on an audience member's lap if I want to (by now I hope you have realized that I am inclined to be totally irreverent if I know the audience can handle it).

You don't have to be as wild as I sometimes am to get the job done. You can calmly go into the audience with a wireless handheld microphone. Let the audience members ask their questions directly to you while you hold the mic to their mouths so that everyone else can hear. (Don't forget to bring the microphone back to your mouth for the answer.)

Another technique I use frequently is to speak directly to one audience member. It goes like this, *Sharon, this is just between you and me.* Whenever I do this, I can see out of the corner of my eye everyone else killing themselves to eavesdrop on Sharon and me. They feel like they are getting to hear something secret.

One-on-one interplay is also good when you are teasing or doing a little roast humor on someone in the group. *Joe, lots of people believe that you are one of the top sales managers in the company. . . . Lots of people believe in the Easter Bunny too!*

I'll go right up to someone in the audience and touch them on the shoulder while I'm talking (don't do this in Asia). I might say (reading their nametag to get the name) *John here may have the highest sales volume, but if his net income is no good, John is not a happy guy.*

Some speakers make up skits and give the audience members easy, but funny, parts to play. This is just an advanced form of role-playing.

Don't be afraid to get right in there and get your audience involved—physically, mentally, and emotionally—and you will be on your way to becoming a NO ZZZZZs presenter.

Bonus quotation lesson: Here are three different quotations that make the same point. Different audiences would relate to each differently. Always think about the make-up of your audience before you select your quotes.

> *Everyone has the will to win; what is important is the will to prepare.*
>
> —Bobby Knight

> *I will study and prepare and perhaps my chance will come.*
>
> —Abe Lincoln

> *You can't set a hen in the morning and have chicken salad for lunch.*
>
> —George Humphrey

How to practice

A construction foreman asked his young son what he wanted for Christmas. The boy said he wanted a baby brother.

Sorry, son, there isn't time to get the job done by Christmas.

Can't you put more men on the job, dad?

CHAPTER 12

No you can't. You have to practice by yourself. One of the greatest humorists of all time and I'm proud to say one of my mentors, Dr. Charles Jarvis of San Marcos, Texas, is often asked for material and delivery tips by other speakers.

One of his stock answers is "I can't be with you when you go to Dubuque." What he means is that no matter what tips he would give (and he is always graciously helpful) the speaker would have to be able to perform when there is no one around to help. The speaker has to practice.

PRACTICE ALONE

I have a personal rule that I tell a story anywhere from 30 to 50 times before I tell it in a presentation. Really that applies to each part of my presentation whether it is humorous or not. I do the same depth of practice for each bit I use. When you practice parts of your talk that many times, a magical thing happens. All the *ums* and *ahs* that may be scattered about seem to disappear. Your volume and confidence increase. Your talk takes on a more conversational nature, which is exactly what you want. The more extemporaneous a talk appears to be, the better it will go over. When you practice this much, you can also get rid of most of those stifling notes that tie you to the lectern. Another really neat thing may happen when you rehearse a whole lot. You might start to see your notes in your mind.

You must become so familiar with the material that you can present it in what appears to be a spontaneous, unrehearsed fashion. The only way to get to that point is to rehearse like crazy. I recently did a customized talk for an association. I finished writing it one month in advance so the rest of that month could be spent rehearsing (this doesn't mean I didn't leave room for addition of up-to-the-minute material).

Not all of those 30 to 50 practice sessions per bit are recited out loud, but most of them are. I do run over stories and bits in my mind when I'm in a setting that would be prohibitive to doing them aloud (like during someone else's boring speech). For the most part though, I belt it out as if I'm actually on stage. The reason to practice like this is that you will discover difficult-to-say word combinations that look just fine on paper or seem fine when you are going over the bit in your mind. If you don't practice out loud, you are likely to stumble when you run across one of those pesky combinations. I used to have trouble with the word *particularly*. Through practice I can now say it well. In the beginning, however, by recognizing the fact that it was a troublesome word, I replaced it in my talks so that I didn't have to worry about it.

Practicing bits and stories is really great because you can do it in little pieces of throwaway time in the shower or in the car. Just remember to do most of your practicing out loud so you have a pre-arranged agreement with your mouth to spit out clearly what your mind is thinking.

Some people like to practice in front of a mirror. This is good for practicing facial expressions and seeing how your clothes look, but I don't like to practice my talk to a mirror because my eyes are locked on the mirror instead of being free to roam as they would be in a real presentation.

I practice frequently in my basement too. I even hold a microphone to simulate the exact setting I will be in during the presentation. I practice switching the microphone between hands, which could be necessary if I'm gesturing, pointing, or writing. I'll switch hands sometimes just so I'm not boringly the same to look at. I purchased a used overhead projector for my local public seminars, and also to have handy to practice transparency handling, which most people are rather messy with. I practice how to get my laser pointer out of my pocket and back into my pocket smoothly. I basically practice everything I know I'm going to be doing in a presentation.

If I have the chance, I will carry out a quick run-through in the actual room I'll be using. Being in the actual room helps reduce any major logistical surprises right before the presentation. If I'm in a hotel, I usually get the security guard to let me in the room the night before so I can see what I'm up against. This really helps my visualization of the event when I go to bed that night.

USE YOUR FRIENDS . . . CAREFULLY

After you've done the best job you can preparing new material and practicing, try it out on friends and small groups. Don't tell your friends you are testing. Just plunge into the joke or story and see if they laugh or give you the kind of response you expect. You must learn to distinguish polite and real laughter on your humorous material. On your straight material you must be able to read a genuinely enthusiastic response compared to the "I'm-being-nice" enthusiastic response. Your study of audience body language will help you with this. If you are the boss, don't try things out on your subordinates. Try them out on your peers. Your subordinates may feel obligated to laugh or give you favorable opinions.

The best test for humorous material is to deliver it to the company sourpuss. If he or she laughs, you know you've got a winner. Also, be careful to recognize that some people laugh at anything. Don't let them convince you you've got a good joke or story until it's been tested on many different people.

While you are in the testing phase, try out different deliveries. Only change one element of the joke or story at a time and watch closely the reactions you get. If you make too many changes at one time, you will never know which change was the one that got the better response.

RECORD YOUR PRESENTATIONS

You will find that this testing process is continual even after you start using your material in front of live audiences. If you pay close attention, you will notice that when you say something in a slightly different manner it may get a better response. If you can remember how you said it, you can say it that way next time too. This continual testing enables a story or a piece of material to evolve over time. However, it is very difficult to remember exactly how you said something during your presentation. That is why most pros tape record whenever they can.

I try to at least audio tape every presentation I give. It is amazing how much you can learn by doing this. You don't have to get fancy either. I started with a $15.00 recorder. I just sat it on a table near the stage area. If you can afford a higher quality recorder and microphone that is even better, but it is not necessary. Video tape is even better and, with the decreasing costs involved, a camcorder and microphone are within reach of most serious presenters.

If you are starting with audio tape only, you won't have to worry about your body language, posture, or stage movement. All you have to do is listen to what you actually said, if it was humorous, and how the audience responded. I used the term *actually* in the last sentence, because many presenters think they said one thing, but the tape proves they said something completely different.

If you really want to learn the most from audio taping your presentations, have the tape transcribed. I know this is a pain in the neck, but you won't believe how much you will learn until you do it. You will see on paper all the *ums* and *ahs,* extra noises, and words and syllables you uttered. Most people are in shock when they look at a transcription of what they *actually* said during a presentation.

This transcribed version is a good tool to help you eliminate unnecessary details and superfluous words. Remember—you don't want to use any more words than you need to achieve your intended goal with any audience.

After you have the transcribed version in hand, go back and listen to the same audio tape. Mark the transcription when you hear something that got a good response. Stop the tape and practice saying that line over until you can duplicate how you said it on the tape. Then go on to the next piece of material. If something didn't work as well as you expected, mark the transcription there too. You can then go back and rework the words or drop them.

Audio taping can help you in your pre-program practice too. If I find a joke or story that I like sometime during my 30 to 50 trial runs, I tape record the story. I then transcribe the tape and play with the word placement until I make it better and then I practice it some more. The material is always better after this process. Yes, I know it's time consuming, but it does work. The good part is that once you do this process with some stories and pieces of material, you can use them for years with just small changes along the way. The time spent up front though is what gave you a good piece of material to start with.

Audio tape will also show up voice, diction, and grammar problems that could be hurting your overall performance. I'm still finding them myself. One time at a major convention, I said the phrase *all right* 80 times in a one hour presentation. It was still a great presentation, but it will be better next time without the superfluous words.

Monotone delivery is probably the biggest killer of audience interest. If you suffer from this affliction, you can overcome it with diligent practice. Get your trusty tape recorder out and make a conscious effort to practice with a wide variety of pitch, loudness, and tone. When I coach speakers, I have them read from children's books as if they are talking to kindergarten kids. I force them to exaggerate their voice tones for maximum range and interest. This kind of practice over a period of time will get rid of the monotone presentation killer. It will land your voice in an interesting range that adults as well as kids will enjoy.

Pay particular attention to your question and answer segments to see what kind of questions you are getting. You can either make sure you cover that material the next time so that the question doesn't come up, or you can work up witty responses for the next time it does come up.

If you have video tape available, you have even more information to work with. In addition to your words you can now evaluate your stage movement, body language, gestures, and facial expressions. So that you don't get overwhelmed, it is best to watch the tape once just for fun to get that out of your system and then look for specific elements on future viewings. I even recommend listening to the video without watching the picture at least one time. The picture will overpower the words in many cases and you won't notice the verbal problems as easily. Then watch the video without the sound. Distracting gestures, odd mannerisms, poor body language, and poor facial expressions will then be highlighted without the distraction of the audio track.

Just as with the audio tape, you can use the video camera to practice before your presentation. When you do this, don't look at the camera. Just pretend it's not there. Imagine the audience is before you and practice making eye contact with imaginary audience members as you deliver your program (if you start signing autographs for your imaginary audience members you may have been practicing too long).

Good eye contact means you look directly at a single audience member for several seconds. Don't hold contact too long or it will turn into an uncomfortable stare, and don't glance quickly from face to face. A typical problem is to go overboard on my advice to look at the friendly faces in your audience. You shouldn't fixate on one or two people for the whole presentation. You can create more friendly faces by giving everyone a couple of shots at maintaining good eye contact with you. In small to medium audiences you should be able to look at everyone at least once during the presentation. Don't forget the people on the sides and in the back rows.

Audio or video tapes are also good to remind you of the timing of jokes and stories especially if you haven't told them in a while. Audio tapes are really more convenient for this purpose because you can listen to them while doing something else like driving or riding the train to work.

Part of your practice will consist of reading and part will consist of listening to other speakers. You can improve tremendously by taking little bits and pieces of delivery technique you pick up from others and using that to help craft your style. I'm not telling you to steal their material. I'm telling you to pay attention to other great speakers and watch *how* they do

> ***Barney Miller:*** *Don't you understand you can't go around stealing other people's things?*
>
> ***Purse Snatcher:*** *If they were mine, why would I want to steal them?*

things, not *what* they do. When you hear another speaker do something you like, try to extract the technique, but plug in your own material. Then practice, practice, practice!

Decide how much time you are willing to spend reading or listening to humorous and heavy content material. I love humor so I try to read some when I get up in the morning and more when I go to bed at night. I listen to tapes when I'm in the car. It makes me feel really good and it helps me to develop new material too. What a deal!

GET COACHING

When you really get serious about improving your presentation skills, you will probably want to get some professional coaching. A good speaking coach will be able to objectively evaluate where you are now and help you formulate a plan to get where you want to be. There are no quick fixes, but you can make significant improvement quickly, maybe in as little as a few weeks, if you work at it and have the proper direction. (The old joke is that the only way you can get fixed in one session is if you're a dog.)

A speaker coach will evaluate you either in person or with the help of video and audio tapes. He or she will need to interview you to see what you think your strong and weak points are and to see exactly what you want to accomplish. The coaching necessary to prepare for a one-shot presentation on television would be completely different from the coaching you would get to be a better trainer.

I like to use video when I train speakers, although it is not absolutely necessary for improvement. A speaker coach may use any number of different techniques to try to help you toward your goals. You might be asked to stretch or do deep breathing exercises. You might even be asked to read from a child's book. Your coach will do whatever is possible to help you improve.

Your investment for private coaching can run from twenty dollars per hour to several thousand dollars per day. If you are a beginner, you probably don't need the high priced Madison Avenue intensive training program. However, if you are a CEO with a major keynote presentation coming up that could help secure millions of dollars worth of business, then an intensive program might be right for you.

Another good way to get practice is to join or start a Toastmasters club (see Appendix B). They are excellent training forums for basic speaking skills. You can also get great practice by volunteering to do free talks for civic groups like Rotary and Kiwanis.

If you are serious about making a career of speaking, join the National Speakers Association (also see Appendix B).

Do everyone a favor before you stand up in front of any audience: **PRACTICE!**

Part II
Types of Humor

The only way to amuse some people is to slip and fall on an icy pavement.

—Ed Howe

Thirty-four ways to be funny

There are many forms of humor you can incorporate in a presentation. Most forms are easy to find and you do not have to be a professional comedy writer to use them to your advantage. You can be an editor of existing humor where you simply pick funny items to use in your presentation, either as comic relief from Z-producing material or to make a point.

CHAPTER 13

ACRONYMS AND ABBREVIATIONS

An acronym is basically a form of abbreviation where the letters of the abbreviation form a new word, e.g., *HUD* means the Department of Housing and Urban Development. Many acronyms and abbreviations are universally known, such as the *IRS* and the *CIA*. There are many more that are unique to your audience. All you have to do to make them humorous is to change one or more of the words that go with your well-known abbreviation or acronym.

Here are some examples:

IQ   Idiot Quotient

CPI   Consumers Poorhouse Indicator

IRA   Individual Rest-in-Peace Account

TQM   *Totaled* Quality Management

With a little thought, it is very easy to customize acronyms and abbreviations to your audience.

Now, here are some examples and explanations from a custom talk I did for a hotel franchise:

OCC in the hotel industry means *Occupancy Rate*. I changed it to *Oh! C'mon Clinton* because certain taxes were being proposed by President Clinton that would affect their industry. I always try to connect with the audience by mentioning the topics that are foremost on their minds. This gives you the greatest chance of succeeding with an item of humor.

ADR to hoteliers, means *Average Daily Rate*. This was changed to *All Dated Rooms* which is something no hotelier wants to hear. This would mean a fortune would have to be spent to upgrade and modernize the rooms.

IOC was the name of the group I was addressing (International Operator's Council). This was changed to *I'm Ordering Chinese* and *I'm Out of Coffee*. These phrases aren't particularly funny in themselves. They were coupled, however, with the fact that these people had just completed rigorous and exhausting inspections by the franchisor. That is what made it funny.

ANA is one of my generic favorites. *ANA* represents *Al Nippon Airlines*. I mention to my audiences that it's a good thing that this company had an American advisor before they created an acronym because the original version was . . . *ANAL* (this is revealed on an overhead projector just after a pause following the word *was* and I get good laughter). I extend the humor with the line, *How'd you like to see that on a 747 coming at you?* This gets even bigger laughs.

For the hotel job, the acronyms were on an overhead transparency and were displayed using a reveal technique where individual overhead lines were covered until it was time to *reveal* the funny version (see Chapter 16). You don't have to project acronyms to use them in a presentation. You could also print them in handouts or just say them out loud.

ADVERTISEMENTS

You can concoct fake ads, or use real ads that are funny in your presentation. They can be read aloud, projected, or distributed as handouts. I got an idea for a funny ad from an attorney friend of mine who was hired by a legal temporary service. I used the following flier as a fun way to keep my practical joke company's name in front of clients who were involved in the legal profession.

PRANKMASTERS PINCH-HIT LEGAL SERVICE

We Fill in When You've Had too Much Gin!
Call us anytime you can't make it. From traffic court to Roe vs. Wade we are an effective substitute for REAL representation.

And you don't have to worry if we don't know what the case is about. We'll let the client fill us in on the way to the courthouse—or at the very worst at the first recess.

● Tee off late? No Problem!
● Long lunch with your best friend's spouse? No Problem!
● Hate your poor uneducated client? No Problem!

Don't feel obligated to go to court just because you've had 10 continuances. We'll go for you.—Our Pinch Hitters are pager and necktie-equipped and come from all walks of life so they can easily relate to your client whether low-life or CEO. Even low-life CEOs are No Problem!

Did you ever draw a judge you just can't stand? Don't worry, the case will be over before he figures out who we are.

How many times have you gotten up in the morning and said to yourself, "I just don't feel like going to court today"? Now, unlike Kevin Costner, you have a way out. Just pick up that phone and Dial: 1-(800) I'm Tired

In most cases with no preparation at all we can do just as well as you would have anyway. In many cases someone from our company is also the opposing attorney, which really gives us the competitive edge. Occasionally we'll also sit in for the judge and members of the jury. We call this our GRAND SLAM of legal services.

For more complex cases we also are affiliated with the Norm Crosby School of Court Reporting for when your reporter's fingers are just not up to it.

We can also provide (at a very low cost) grandstanders who will cheer or cry on command all for the good of your client.*

Don't be fooled by expensive imitations. We are cheap. Only $100/hearing plus bus fare. Order Today!

You can't find any better legal substitutes anywhere. I'm Tom Antion and you have my word on it!

* Stage manager and box lunches required.
Copyright © 1989 Prankmasters

Fake advertisement for a legal service

Watch for funny ads that relate to your business or presentation topic in magazines and other periodicals. Cut the ads out and photocopy for distribution as a handout or make them into slides and overheads.

Jay Leno has a series of books called *Headlines I, II,* and *III.* Besides having really funny headlines from newspapers and magazines, the books have lots of blooper advertisements along with commentary from Jay. My favorites are the funeral monument company that advertised a lifetime replacement guarantee and the sporting goods store that advertised a Back-to-School special of high-powered rifles.

ALLITERATION

Alliteration is the repetition of the same sound at the beginning of words or in accented syllables. The sounds are usually consonants. Alliteration used in advertisements and titles all the time because it tends to catch your eye and ear. One of my humorous topics which has four "p" sounds, is titled *Pranks for Profit: Confessions of a Paid Practical Joker..* Here's an example of a positive message delivered with alliteration:

> *We Bagged the Baldridge award Because our Brainy, Beautiful Businesspeople are the Best.*

In a negative message you can soften the blow of the message without appearing frivolous or uncaring.

> *The strike by one of our suppliers has put a Crunch on our division. Even though we're Crunched, we're still Creative, we're still Credible, and we will Conquer this problem.*

ANACHRONISMS

A person, place, or event that is placed in a time period in which it does not belong is an *anachronism.* For instance, Paul Revere riding a motorcycle or George Washington sitting in front of a computer would be anachronisms. You see advertising strategies using anachronisms all the time, especially around Lincoln's and Washington's birthdays and Columbus Day.

I saw an ad for fluorescent light bulbs that had Thomas Edison working on a phonograph. The caption read: "If Thomas Edison wouldn't have wasted his time on this [incandescent bulb], his phonograph might have been a CD player."

The relationship between new and old is always interesting. Anytime you can highlight that relationship you will evoke mild humor and create more attention on your product, service, or point.

Here's a good fill-in-the-blank format. Would [big name from the past] have _____ if he had _____? All you have to do is make a simple relationship and your message will be funny and memorable. *Would George Washington have thrown his money away in the Potomac if he had ABC investment company on his side?* Once you get the relationship down, you can adjust the form to suit your presentation. The George Washington/ABC investment anachronism could turn into a good, usable one-liner. *George Washington wouldn't have thrown his money in the Potomac if he had come to us for advice.*

ASIDES

In the theater, an aside is something said to the audience that is not to be heard by the other actors. If the aside was delivered on a television sitcom, the actor would look right at the camera and talk to the viewers at home instead of talking to the other actors. To a presenter, an aside means a temporary departure from the main theme or topic.

If you get good at this technique, the audience will think you are a genius. The

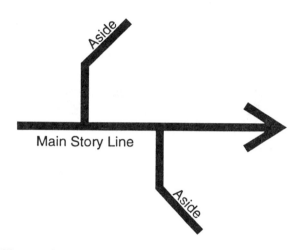

Illustration 13-1 Master storytellers use this technique to WOW the audience.

way it works is that you begin telling a story or delivering information on a certain topic. Then you go off on a tangent (aside) indirectly related to the main theme. When you have finished the aside, you pick up the main theme where you left off and keep right on going. The audience may think you are lost or confused when you first leave the original topic, but when you return to the main line after the aside, they realize you are in total control. This is very impressive. Great storytellers are able to take you down several auxiliary paths, but still move you along the main path from beginning to conclusion.

I tell a story about some medical work I had done where the doctor said to me, *This will just pinch a little bit.* This phrase sends me down a whole different path talking about how my dentist had said the same thing and then pushed the Novocaine needle up into my brain, twisted it around, and pulled it out.

I then come back to the main line of the medical story until I get to the word *gauze.* This word sets off another tangential story about my mother ripping gauze off me. Then it is back to the main line again.

You can alert the audience of an upcoming aside by saying the word *incidentally* before you veer off the main path. Get good at asides and you will add a new dimension to the way you tell stories or deliver information.

AUDIENCE GAGS

Audience gags are offbeat jokes that occur unexpectedly during a presentation. Dr. Joel Goodman, of the Humor Project does one where a telephone rings during his presentation. He answers the phone that was hidden in the lectern and pretends to talk to his mother. The same joke would be called a *running gag* if the phone rang at several other times during the program.

Ten Wanted Men

I staged a gag at a seminar one time that was loads of fun and took less than one minute to complete. Before the program, I picked out about 10 fun-loving audience members to help me. I gave them secret instructions that were to be carried out on a certain cue during the program. To start the gag, I had my assistant interrupt the seminar to give me an IMPORTANT note. The note read (I used a serious expression):

> *It appears that someone is in attendance today with another man's wife. There is a large and irate man on his way here right now. If you want out, there is a backstage door you can use to escape quickly.*

At this point, 10 men jumped up out of their seats and ran keystone cop style out the door. Once they realized what was happening, several women jumped up and ran out too. It was great fun and the gag sure woke up everyone who had a heavy lunch.

Stone the Speaker

Here's another gag I do when I really want to focus attention on an important point. Either before the program or at a break, I recruit audience members who are sitting near the front. I give each one a piece of crumpled paper and instruct them to throw it at me when they hear a certain word. Some presenters tell me that is the dumbest thing they ever heard of and that they would never do it in a professional presentation. They say that until they understand the rationale. Do you remember I said I pull this gag when I want to focus attention on an important point? Guess who is riveted on what I say until they hear the key word? Of course, all the recruits with the crumpled paper. Then, after they throw the paper and I make a big reaction, the rest of the crowd is totally focused in an effort to see what is going on. That is when I make my key point. I have virtually guaranteed the attention of each audience member.

Dr. Heckle and Mr. Sly

What is one of the biggest nightmares a presenter can have? That's right—a heckler. Since I consider myself playfully sly, I bring my own heckler and place him or her in the audience. If you enjoy seeing an audience squirm, like you would if you were doing an impostor routine (see next section), this is the way to do it. Get an obnoxious friend or actor and give him or her some believable, but outrageous, things to say. The faces of the audience will be indelibly etched on your retina. It is hysterical. You can't laugh though or you will be discovered too soon. Make sure the meeting planner and security know what is going on with this one so they don't call the police, although that can be fun too (no I'm just kidding). You could, however, have security in on the gag and have them drag the crying, screaming person out. The dragging or carrying should be done in a comical manner or after the gag is obvious so that the audience doesn't get upset.

What is He Talking About?

One of my favorite gags is the false guest speaker. This routine is used when you want to reduce some pressure in the audience or when you just want to have some fun before you get on with the serious stuff. Many times an impostor can get away with saying outrageous things you wouldn't want an employee or executive to say. When the joke is revealed the current problems of your organization just don't look as bad when compared to the nutty things the impostor was saying. The length of the bogus speech is easy to vary to suit your program. Some speakers have a canned act and speak on a generic topic like stress reduction. They then go off on bizarre tangents to the point of lunacy until the joke is revealed.

A better version includes a presentation that is customized for the group. An insider or accomplice provides industry buzzwords and authentic issues to the impostor so the speech starts off in a believable and relevant fashion. The speaker then rambles off on unrelated topics that are woven into the real information to lead the audience down the path to bewilderment.

Really good speakers open up the microphone for a Question and Answer session in which they ad-lib or give pre-written comical answers to expected or planted questions.

The speaker doing an impostor routine has to be ready for anything. One thing to avoid, unless you are really good at ad-libbing, is being pinned down before the program on questions you couldn't possibly answer. To avoid this situation, I usually rush into the in-progress meeting carrying my luggage as if my plane was late. Then I let them have it. The downside to this type of entrance is that you do not have a chance to check the room setup and microphone before you go on. Make it clear to the meeting planner how important these items are if you decide to try this gag.

He Tripped Me!

And now for the ultimate audience gag. Drum roll, please. I do an old, old banquet gag that I recycled for the 90s. I call it *Cuss Your Lunch* which stands for Cuss(tomer) Service Your Lunch.

This gag started out in my practical joke company, where I have done literally hundreds of performances as the Clumsy Waiter at banquets, luncheons, and wedding receptions. These performances were done mainly for fun and they were not messy unless, of course, I wanted them to be. When I started speaking more and more to business audiences I wanted to find a way to incorporate this outrageous routine. Now *Cuss Your Lunch* is a live training session on customer service, but the participants don't know it. I get the company to arrange an appreciation luncheon for the managers or employees of the customer service division. I am planted as the waiter at the function. The participants really feel what it is like to get rotten service. There are two ways this can end. One way is to prat fall to the floor and make a really big commotion. I claim that some innocent attendee tripped me. The banquet manager or head waiter then comes in and fires me. Then I reveal the joke and immediately go into a customer service presentation based on what they have just experienced. The other way to end this presentation takes more time and effort, but is more fun. In this case, I storm out of the room after being fired. I immediately go somewhere and change into a spiffy suit. I change my hairstyle, take off my glasses and return to the meeting as the guest speaker whose plane was late. The looks on the participant's faces are something you have to see to believe. If you want to see for yourself, you can hire me to do this for your company. Ha-ha.

Don't be afraid to have fun with an audience. Gags are a good way to do it and they can really help you drive home your point too.

BLOOPERS

Bloopers are clumsy mistakes that are usually made in public. The television show *TV's Bloopers and Practical Jokes* and many blooper books are indicators of the interest we have in other people's goofs. Here are two from *All Time Great Bloopers* by Blooper Snooper Kermit Schafer and one from *More Press Boners* by Earle Tempel, and how you might use them in a presentation.

● *A while back I heard about a DJ on WIOD in Miami, Florida who said, "This is Alan Courtney speaking. Don't forget, tonight at nine, our special guest . . . (pause) . . .will be . . . I forgot." Well, I haven't forgotten why we are here today . . .* or (for an introducer) *I couldn't possibly forget who is here with us today.*

- *Mayor Daley of Chicago was being interviewed on TV following the riots during the Democratic convention. The mayor stated, "The police in Chicago are not here to create disorder, they are here to preserve it." I hope I don't create or preserve any disorder in my presentation today.*

- From The San Leandro, CA *News: I saw a notice in the newspaper the other day. It said, "Industrial Boulevard is empty because it is a road to nowhere. Work is underway to extend it." If we keep developing the obsolete widget, we will be on the road to nowhere too.*

CARICATURE

When certain prominent features of something or someone are highlighted and other features are diminished, that is called caricature. Studies have found that it is easier to identify a political leader from a caricature than from a real photograph. This is actually a special form of exaggeration (see "Exaggeration," this chapter).

You can use caricatures of yourself in your own promotional material or in your programs to make fun of yourself. You can do the same thing to make fun of your competitors or your competitor's products by amplifying whatever feature you want to emphasize.

Caricature artists are not too hard to locate. Many times you can find them by looking in the yellow pages under the categories of "Entertainment" or "Party Planning" because they frequently perform at parties.

Caricature of Tom during a presentation

CARTOONS AND COMIC STRIPS

As we talked about in the section on international audiences, the most universally accepted formats for humor are cartoons and comic strips.

There are three ways to use cartoons: first, you can tell the audience about a cartoon you saw; second, you can cut the cartoon out of its publication and show it; and third, you can make up a cartoon yourself.

I saw a cartoon once where a lady was holding a gun to her purse. The caption said "Give up the keys!" I use this example in my *Business Lite Seminar* when I want to illustrate the use of humor to help ease the tension in embarrassing situations. (I have also used this line many times when I am with a woman who is fumbling through her purse.) When I tell the audience *I saw a cartoon,* it helps them paint a mental picture of what I am describing with words. Describing a cartoon is an easy method for using cartoons without having them physically available or needing audio/visual equipment to show them.

Showing a cartoon is a more powerful way to convey its humorous message. This is especially true in international audiences where the visual aspect takes on a greater significance. In a very small crowd I might hold up the cartoon or I might pass it around. In larger audiences, the cartoon should be projected (don't forget to get permission from the copyright holder) so everyone can see it clearly. I like this method better anyway because I can control when it pops up on the screen. I want everyone to see the cartoon simultaneously so their laughter will be cumulative. Try to fill the frame of the visual with your cartoon or comic strip. You will create a greater impact.

Cartoons are found in many places besides the funny papers. *Newsweek* magazine always has several current ones near the front. *The New Yorker* magazine is famous for its cartoons. Trade magazines usually contain industry-related cartoons and don't forget your local bookstore's humor section. There are many other sources you will come across in your everyday reading. Just start paying attention to each cartoon you find and think about how to use it to your advantage.

The third way to use cartoons is to make them yourself. When I first started teaching this subject I could not take advantage of this method unless I hired an artist. Things are different now. There are a number of inexpensive computer software programs available, one of which is Corel Draw. This program has 18,000 pieces of electronic clip art, many of which are cartoons. I can make custom overhead cartoons for my speaking engagements for about thirty-five cents each. All I do is pick an applicable cartoon, add a custom caption for my client's audience, and print it. I used to use my laser printer to do the printing on overhead transparency material. Now, color inkjet printers are so cheap I can print in vivid color for about the same price.

COMIC VERSE

Often a short poem will illustrate your point better than hours and hours of talk. Poems can be inspiring and motivating as well as funny, and they also add variety to your presentation. You must flawlessly memorize any poetry you use. Any stumbles will ruin the effect of the verse. If the verse is long, you may want to consider reading it, but total memorization will have more impact. Poetry, whether funny or not, should be used sparingly in any business presentation.

Always look for the points that a piece of comic verse could illustrate. You normally don't want to use any kind of humor that does not support the points you are trying to make.

Point: Get going to achieve your goals. You have the tools, but you must pick them up and use them.

Sitting still and wishing
Makes no person great.
The good Lord sends the fishes
But you must dig the bait.
Anonymous

Point: Look forward, not backward.

The lightning bug is a brilliant thing
But the insect is so blind.
It goes on stumbling through the world
With its headlights on behind.
Anonymous

Point: Everyone starts at the bottom. That won't keep you from being great.

Do not worry if your job is small
And your rewards are few.
Just remember that the mighty oak
Was once a nut, like you.
Anonymous

Tom's rewrite of the last verse (to make the audience feel superior to me)

Do not worry if your job is small
With rewards you cannot see.
Just remember that the mighty oak
Was once a nut, like me.

Point: Ride out the tough stuff in life.

When the tides of life turn against you,
And the current upsets your boat,
Don't waste those tears on what might have been,
Just lay on your back and float.
Ed Norton
The Honeymooners

Point: If you have a problem, do something about it.

> *Life is real, life is earnest*
> *If you're cold, turn up the furnace.*
>
> Herman Munster

Limericks

Point: Be careful whom you deal with.

> *There was a young lady from Niger,*
> *Who smiled as she rode on a tiger.*
> *They came back from the ride*
> *With the lady inside,*
> *And a smile on the face of the tiger.*

Point: Are you just coming along for the ride?

> *A silly young man from Port Clyde*
> *In a funeral procession was spied.*
> *Asked, "Who is dead?"*
> *He giggled and said,*
> *"I don't know. I just came for the ride."*

Point: Quit fighting.

> *There once were two cats in Kilkenny.*
> *Each cat thought there was one too many.*
> *So they scratched and they fit*
> *And they tore and they bit,*
> *'Til instead of two—there weren't any.*

In the famous words of Marie Antoinette

> *Keep cool when all's done and said*
> *Above all remember, don't lose your head.*

COSTUMES

No, you don't have to go on-stage in a gorilla suit, although you could if you wanted to. A costume can be anything from a flashy tie, to a feathered hat, to a full blown shiny Marca Polina outfit (the feminine Marco Polo) complete with an illuminated magic wand, that my friend Sally Walton wears when she talks about the magic art of "Communicating Across Cultures." Costumes add a flare and excitement to your presentations and certainly help to make them more memorable.

If you don't like to wear costumes, get the audience members to wear them. Better yet, get the "big shots" to wear them and you will probably be the hit of the meeting. I was doing a customer service talk for a pizza franchise and I had one of the senior managers march into the meeting wearing a filthy, doctor's lab coat with ketchup all over it (fake blood). I had another senior manager come in with a crisp, new lab coat. I asked a simple question, *Which manager would you like operating on you?* Of course, all the junior managers yelled out that they wouldn't let either one of these people operate on them. Everyone was laughing and joking around, but the point was made. They must keep their employees looking clean and neat because nice customers won't want to be served by grungy food service workers.

Costume characters can be hired to hand out fliers at your event, entertain, and generally create an air of fun and excitement. The local heart association has a "blood drop" costume they use when they are soliciting funds. There are literally hundreds of costumes available through costume shops or by mail order (see Morris Costume in Appendix B). Just make sure, as always, the theme of the costume matches the theme of your presentation or event.

DEFINITIONS

You can use a quick comical definition to liven up a talk. As always, make sure the word defined is relevant to the point you are trying to make.

Here are some definitions I like:

Banker: *A fellow who lends you his umbrella when the sun is shining and wants it back the minute it begins to rain.* —Mark Twain (similar quotation by Robert Frost).

You wouldn't use this one if you were talking to bankers. But, if you are a banker talking to nonbankers, you could change it thusly: *Some people say that a banker is a person who lends you his umbrella when the sun is shining and wants it back the minute it begins to rain. That is not true. I would lend you my umbrella anytime at X percent above prime with two points.* (Possible extender line) *If you want to borrow MONEY, that's a different story.*

City Life: *Millions of people being lonely together.*—Henry David Thoreau

Conservative: *A man who just sits and thinks, mostly sits.*—Woodrow Wilson

A man who is too cowardly to fight and too fat to run.—Elbert Hubbard

A man with two perfectly good legs who has never learned to walk.
—Franklin Delano Roosevelt

Death: *To stop sinning suddenly.* —Elbert Hubbard

Jury: *Twelve persons chosen to decide who has the better lawyer.*
—Robert Frost

Radical: *A man with both feet planted firmly in the air*
—Franklin Delano Roosevelt

Song: *The licensed medium for bawling in public things too silly or sacred to be uttered in ordinary speech.*—Oliver Herford

Zoo: *A place devised for animals to study the habits of human beings.*
—Oliver Herford

There are literally thousands of these definitions available in comedy books, quotation books, and books for speakers. In many cases you will have several to choose from on any given topic. I probably had at least 20 choices on the subject of "Conservatism" alone.

EXAGGERATION

Expanding or diminishing proportions can be a fun way to create humor. It's similar to a caricature artist that outrageously exaggerates the features of an individual, while still keeping the person recognizable.

> *An exaggeration is a truth that lost its temper.*
> Kahlil Gibran

I did a talk one time for Secretaries Day at a large insurance company. I was making a point about how hectic it always was for the secretaries. It went like this, *You're answering the telephone, the fax machine is ringing, you're making copies, and you're filing every policy clear back to 1910.* The secretaries could relate to each item mentioned. They obviously did lots of filing, but certainly not as far back as 1910. Exaggerating this date was funny to them and drove home the point that they always had lots of work piled up.

The key to using exaggeration is to inflate or deflate whatever you are talking about so much that it is obviously an exaggeration. In the last example you wouldn't want to use the year 1994 if you were doing the talk in 1995 because it is very likely that an insurance company would really be working on a file for a year or more. That's not funny.

Of course, who am I to tell you what is funny. I spent two terms in the third grade—Truman's and Eisenhower's.

FAKE FACTS AND STATISTICS

Stating falsehoods as if they are absolutely true is another fun way to play with the audience. However, you must make the statements obviously false by your words and your facial expressions. You don't want to leave any doubt in the audience's mind about whether you are being funny or not.

I was doing another Secretaries Day function and I told them that studies had been conducted indicating the only reason executives became executives was because they couldn't make it as secretaries. They loved it!

To build up your joke you should use official sounding sources for the information: *A study done for the Alaskan Pipeline Workers Union indicated that 97.2 percent of Alaskan Pipeline Workers wear No Nonsense panty hose.* When using this type of humor use exact numbers for comic emphasis (see "Numbers" this Chapter).

JOKES

In his book *Comedy Writing Step by Step,* Gene Perret, one of the best known comedy writers in Hollywood, says, "A joke is anything that makes people laugh. It can be a series of words, a look, a shrug of the shoulders, even a moment of silence—but if it makes people laugh, it's a joke."

I agree with Gene, but I try to avoid using the term *joke* when training people to do presentations. Here's why. When I ask my seminar participants for a show of hands of who can tell a joke, only a few people raise their hands. In fact, most people claim they can't tell a joke. Their claim indicates to me that they are simply not practiced and are maybe a little afraid of the term itself. I assure them that using humor in professional presentations is NOT about telling jokes. It's about using many easily implemented forms of humor to help attain the goals of a presentation. This highfalutin' explanation is usually enough to distract them so I can teach them how to tell jokes. Consequently, you won't see me using the word *joke* very much in this book. I'm too busy teaching you how to make people laugh.

If you like to *tell jokes* there are presently 97.5 zillion joke books available on every topic in the world. Acquire the ones you like and pick appropriate jokes to help you make the points of your presentation.

JUXTAPOSITION

Juxtaposition is the placing, side by side, of two ideas or items usually for the purpose of comparison or contrast. I staged an event at Washington National Airport where I had a huge man (450-pounds) and a very small man (3' 11") dressed as chauffeurs. They were waiting at the gate for a man from Japan arriving for his first visit to the United States. To take the comical juxtaposition one step further, the small man was holding a gigantic sign with the Japanese man's name on it and the extra large man was holding a similar sign, except it was about the size of a business card. Believe me, we had the attention of everyone in the gate area. What a visual!

Now let's look at two specialized types of juxtaposition:

Oxymorons

Warren S. Blumenfeld, Ph.D., in his book *Pretty Ugly* states, "I {passively tried} to warn you oxymorons had {almost absolutely} no socially redeeming quality except that they make people {smile out loud} and are addictive." His first book on the subject was called *Jumbo Shrimp*.

According to Dr. Blumenfeld, "An oxymoron is two concepts {usually two words} that do *not* go together, but are used together. It is a bringing together of contradictory expressions."

Terms like *old news*, *extensive briefing*, *direct circumvention* and *random order* are oxymorons. Also concepts like *an advanced state of decline* and *expecting a surprise* are oxymorons.

Pleonasms

A pleonasm is the bringing together of two concepts or words that are redundant. A pleonasm is the bringing together of two concepts or words that are redundant. How many times do I have to tell you? I stole that from Dr. Blumenfeld, but I've already credited him a couple times and Art Buchwald says that's enough.

Combinations like *frozen ice, sharp point, killed dead, sandy beach, young child, positive praise*, and *angry rage* are pleonasms.

Here are some ways you can use comical juxtaposition in business world presentations:

● Use a large copy of your company logo or company name on a slide or overhead, or in a drawing on your flip chart. Next to it, place extremely small logos or company names of your competitors. Use this as a greeting slide to a meeting or let it pop up as a slide or overhead at a strategic point in your presentation. You could draw an outline of a large duck around your company logo and little duckling outlines around the competition. You could say: *Our company was born to lead and the others were meant to follow.*

● Use an oxymoron in conjunction with a simile to drive home the point that something is a little out of kilter.

You could say, *Acme Co. claims that its market share is increasing, yet their sales are down while everyone elses' are up. It's just like a Jumbo Shrimp. It just doesn't make sense.*

● Invite a tall person and a short person on stage when you call for audience participation. If you are considerably shorter than the tall person say, *I don't want you to talk down to me.* If you are considerably taller than the short person say, *I don't want you to feel like I'm talking down to you.*

LETTERS

You can really have fun with the audience by reading phony or funny business letters, bogus telegrams, notes from the meeting planner, and other contrived pieces of correspondence. You can also get them involved using this technique by recruiting audience members in advance to help you with these gags.

To: Bob Parsons
From: Harry McDonald Administrator
       Pycoming Valley Health Care System

Dear Bob:

We would like to thank you for the quick thinking your manager displayed during our recent surprise inspection. Had our employee Donna Kaufman been caught out of uniform, we surely would have been cited by the health department.

Hiding her behind the pastry cart in the walk-in freezer was a stroke of genius. She would have come through with just a few sniffles had the inspection not taken so long. We did have a little explaining to do over in the Emergency Room but at least we didn't get cited!

Again many thanks and keep up the good work.

Sincerely

Harry McDonald

Fake Testimonial Letter

There is a high-powered rifle aimed directly at your mouth. It will go off if you aren't done by 11:15 A.M. Thanks for being with us today.

Sharon (meeting planner)

Note from meeting planner (Have audience member hand you piece of paper. Read it aloud.)

Testimonial Letter found in a book published in 1857

Dear Sirs:

Four weeks ago I was run down so much that I couldn't even spank the baby. After taking three bottles of your Elegant Elixir, I am now able to thrash my husband in addition to my other housework.

God bless you!

TELEGRAM

Sorry I couldn't make the meeting-STOP I know company can't survive without me-STOP

Using every second of my vacation in Maui to prospect-STOP

I know I am an inspiration to you all-END

                         Joe

Bogus telegram (from person well-known to the group)

Fake Surveys (Have the meeting planner or registration attendant interrupt to give you "the results of the door survey.")

We did a random sampling of those in attendance today and these are the results of the survey. (You can make up questions and answers that apply to your group or adapt the generic ones below.)

1. *In response to the question, "What do you want to accomplish at today's meeting?," 2 percent said they wanted to hear about the upcoming sales strategy, 3 percent said they wanted to learn closing techniques and a full 95 percent came to find out who the band would be for the Christmas party.*

Note: This is an example of the comic principle called *The Rule of Three.* The first two responses above were straight lines and the third was the zinger.

2. *In response to the question "What did you think of the food at today's luncheon?," 4 percent said they thought the main entree was too spicy, 7 percent said the shrimp were overcooked, and the rest of you, 89 percent to be exact, belched. I guess that tells it all.*

Funny Question

3. *In response to the question, "How many of you think you will be better looking when you leave my session?,"* [pick on fun members of the audience, but clear it with them first] *Joe Watkins said, "I don't need to be better looking. I've got brains." Janice Stephens said, "I couldn't be any better looking. Eat your hearts out." Bob Harley said, "Beauty is only skin deep, but ugly goes all the way to the bone."*

Make no *bones* about it (I hate dumb puns) we're moving onto the next section.

MAGIC

Magic tricks are a fun way to add some lightheartedness and WOW factor to your presentations. A stop at a magic store will put hundreds of simple tricks at your disposal that will astound your audience while helping to reinforce your points. The comedy aspect of the magic usually comes from the "patter" (what the magician says while doing the trick). You can even buy books of comic patter. Many magic tricks are now on video, which makes them really easy to learn. An excellent tape for rope tricks is *Daryl's Rope Tricks # 7.* Your local magic shop probably has it and if they don't they can probably order it. Morris Costume (see Appendix B) is also an excellent source for magic tricks, videos and books.

MALAPROPS AND USAGE BLUNDERS

Just as Mark Twain thought that a person should be able to spell a word more than one way, Mac, a friend of mine, believes he should be able to fracture the English language to suit himself. Who am I to argue with him? He is so brilliant that he invents new words and combinations of words without even trying. They always make me chuckle. When a problem arises, he calls it a *snagfu,* which is a cross between snag and snafu. If we are talking about business promotion, the business should make good use of *slogos*—slogans and logos. The main thing he always remembers is to stay calm, cool, and *collective.*

Most people play badminton. Mac plays *batmitten.* Mac had a pretty rough childhood so he tells me he didn't grow up with all the *accoustaments* I had. To get ahead in the world he believes you need *insertiveness* training, and when you start to get that middle-aged spread you better get some *lifo suction.* If he was *corroborating* on this book he would certainly *collaborate* my story.

Mac has been known to drink a few beers now and then and he was complaining recently about the cost. He claims that a six-pack has increased from $2 to nearly $4. He told me he now has to drink 12 beers to help him forget about the cost of 6. But he wouldn't want to bore you with *sadistics,* so let's get on with the discussion.

A malaprop is an absurd misuse of words. It can be from words that sound alike (*sadistic* and *statistic*) or from explanations that don't make any sense. Consider some of the classic examples below:

Casey Stengel

○ *I want you all to line up in alphabetical order according to your size.*
● *I guess I'll have to start from scraps.*
○ *If people don't want to come to the ballpark, nobody can stop them.*
● *It's déjà vu all over again.*

Goldwynisms

In the 1940s the movie mogul, Sam Goldwyn, misused language so much that malaprops became known as Goldwynisms.

○ *A verbal contract isn't worth the paper it's written on.*
○ *I read part of it all the way through.*
● *I never liked him and I probably always will.*
○ *Every Tom, Dick and Harry is named William.*
○ *For your information, I would like to ask a question.*
○ *Now, gentlemen, listen slowly.*
○ *In two words: im-possible!*
○ *Include me out.*

The great comedian Norm Crosby, who is best known for appreciating *standing ovulations* when he performs, has made a living out of the ingenious misuse of words. In real life though, malaprops are usually uttered by people who don't even realize their *fox paws*. A friend of mine, who is a fund-raiser for an unnamed, stuffy Washington, D.C., art society, told me of a hilarious incident that took place during a meeting. The humorless director stood at the conference table in an effort to put an out-of-control meeting back on track and said, "I fear our discussions are *tangenital* to the issues at hand."

TANGENITAL!—My friend looked around at the other attendees who were all fighting back laughter. She had to excuse herself from the meeting to keep from laughing right in the face of the old windbag.

A flexible presenter who was truly in touch would have 1) realized her mistake, 2) laughed at herself, and 3) used that unplanned comic relief to get everyone's attention so that she could regain control of the meeting. Someone really experienced would make the mistake on purpose.

I have learned, in my years of writing comedy skits, that many times the mistakes are much funnier than the planned program. Now I plan mistakes when appropriate. To make this more foggy, I'll explain in one sentence. I learned that when I plan something and then I mess up the plan, the plan becomes funnier than the plan I planned to use, so now I plan to mess up the plan so the plan is planned to be funnier than a plan that is not planned to be messed up. Get it? Good, because you need to hear loud and clear what I'm writing here so you *bunglestand* it.

Malaprops can be used for fun or to grab attention while making a serious point. Take for example Sam Goldwyn's classic, "A verbal contract isn't worth the paper it's written on." I don't know if Sam said this one on purpose or not. I wasn't around in the 1940s to ask him. I do know that the message is clear and has stood the test of time. If he had simply said, "Contracts should be in writing" who would remember?

Use malaprops in your presentation, but make sure the malapropism is obvious, or your audience may think you are not too bright. If you do get caught in an accidental misusage, you **MUST** acknowledge your blunder. If you don't, you will absolutely lose your audience who will be thinking about the blunder for several minutes after the fact. They will also note that you are trying to be an absolutely perfect robot that couldn't possibly make a mistake. This will turn them off and make communication extremely difficult.

All you have to do to acknowledge the blunder is to refer to a quotation from Mark Twain and turn it on yourself. Say a self-effacing humorous prepared ad-lib: *If Mark Twain can spell a word in more than one way, I should be able to say a wrong word at the right time.* If you don't like that one, make an ad-lib up on your own.

To make effective presentations, you must appear human to those you speak to. Humans make mistakes. That's part of life. As Archie Bunker says, "Case closed, *ipso fatso.*"

ONE-LINERS

One-liner is a general term for very short pieces of humor. Using one-liners is probably the best and easiest way to begin adding humor to your presentations. These brief bits of humor are quick and easy to deliver and they don't have to be all that funny to be effective. If you are a little apprehensive about using humor, this is the place to start. The audience likes one-liners, because they can get a quick mental break from content heavy material. Also, if the audience is there to get high levels of content, they don't feel you wasted their time with long stories and jokes.

One of the handiest sources for one-liners is a small and inexpensive paperback called *Today's Chuckle: 2500 Great One-Liners for Every Occasion* by Paul Harlan Collins. Most resource books are broken down into categories. This book has categories such as, *Affairs of State and Other Political Indiscretions* where you might find the one-liner: "Politicians are like polkas. They have different names, but they all sound alike," or *Money and the Meaning of Life* where you would see truisms like: "Prosperity is that period between the last installment and the next purchase." There are 25 categories in all and I can't imagine a talk that wouldn't benefit from one of these selections.

You'll run across one-liners everywhere once you start looking. Some will even have two lines. Don't worry. Write them down, too, and start adding them to your presentations using the formula mentioned in Chapter 5 ("Make a Point with Humor"). If you want to be more bold and if the point of the one-liner is clear, use them by themselves. Just for fun, I'm including some of my favorites:

● *Thanks to automatic teller machines you are always conveniently close to being broke.*

● *Behind every successful person stands a bunch of amazed co-workers.*

● *Computers can do complicated mathematical calculations in 1/100,000 second, but the invoices still go out 10 days late.*

● *My accountant is shy and retiring. He's $250,000 shy. That's why he's retiring.*

● *How are you supposed to teach a kid what clockwise means when he's wearing a digital GI Joe watch?*

PARODY

Parody is a humorous imitation of a person, event, song or serious piece of writing. I have a great time when I use this technique in a presentation and so do the audience members. The way I use it is to change the words of a recognizable song. I get the audience members to sing along with me by putting the words in their handouts or giving out a song sheet. The latter method keeps the whole segment hidden so I can surprise them. I get the words to customize the song from my pre-program research. Here's a singing introduction Art Gliner (one of my mentors) and I worked up when we co-presented for a group of aspiring professional speakers (sung to the Tune of *Roll out the Barrel*):

> *Roll out the humor,*
> *Antion and Gliner are here!*
> *Roll out the humor,*
> *Learn how to boost your career!*
> *Use lots of humor,*
> *Speakers should never be staid.*
> *Do you have to use some humor?*
> *Just if you want to get paid!*

Simply take any recognizable tune, change the words, and sing it yourself or get the audience to sing along.

PROPS

The term *prop* is a shortened version of the theatrical term *property*, a word used to describe any object handled or used by an actor in a performance. As a presenter you are a performer whether you believe it or not. You have an obligation to use whatever means necessary to get your message across to the audience.

I think of props as any physical item that is on stage with you. Your flip chart is a prop. Your lectern is a prop. Overhead projectors, pointers, notes, chairs, markers, pens, and other audio/visual aids are all forms of props. Conversely, props are a form of visual aid.

Why Use Props?

Props help warm up the audience. They can be used as a substitute for notes. They help focus attention on the points you are trying to make along with illustrating them for you. They make better connections than your words with the visually oriented members of your audience. They create interest, add variety, and make your points more memorable.

Props can be used pre-program to pass around in the audience in anticipation of the program. You see this at large arenas when beach balls and Frisbees are being tossed around in the crowd. I pass out snacks and/or custom-designed crossword puzzles about the group that I make on my computer. The puzzles make especially great icebreakers because the members of the group get together to help each other with the solutions.

Do you hate relying on notes? Props can be a substitute for written cheat sheets. To illustrate this in live seminars I use three hats as an outline for a program. The first hat is a gag ball cap that has really long hair attached to it so that I look like a hippie when I wear it. The second hat is a black top hat. The third is a safari hat. Each hat prompts me to talk about a thoroughly rehearsed bit or chunk. Putting on the longhaired ball cap immediately reminds me to talk about when the company was young and aggressive. After that section I remove the ball cap (if you have a fun and playful audience, you could put it on an audience member's head), then I put on the black top hat. The top hat prompts a section on the mature growth years of the company. I then put on the safari hat which kicks off a section on searching for new business. The whole talk is done without any notes at all. You only have to memorize your opening and closing and practice each of the sections independently as you learned in Chapter 5.

Didn't someone say a prop is worth a thousand words? Maybe that was a picture, but it's just about the same thing. Many times a well-selected prop will illustrate your point much better than you could ever do in words. It also focuses attention directly on the point you are trying to make because it is something novel that is occurring during the presentation. People can space-out easily on your words, but a unique prop is hard to ignore. Also, the visually oriented people in your audience will perk up and get more value when you use props.

Memorability is another good reason to use props. People remember pictures far longer than words. That is why the great storytellers try to use words to create images in your mind. They know the images will be remembered when the words are long forgotten. If you're not a great storyteller yet, you can use props to help create these pictures.

Types of Props

There are many different kinds of props that can be used to your advantage in a presentation. Extra large or extra small props are funny. Noisemakers are funny. Even though you are attacking the sense of hearing, you are attacking it in a unique way that makes it memorable. Costumes and magic tricks make good props.

I have a friend who speaks on telephone skills. He uses a giant telephone receiver to make a point about the importance of phone skills. I used a clown prop to make the serious point that if we went through with this merger it would be like being in a thunderstorm with a clown umbrella (for those of you that don't know, a clown umbrella is only about 8 inches in diameter).

Noisemakers are fun. I recommended that a sales manager get one of those expressway revenge devices that makes machine gun, ray gun, and bomb noises when you press a button. *If XYA company* (remember no Zs) *gets in our way, this is what will do to them* (he pressed the machine gun button while holding the device near the microphone). He got his point across.

I've worn gorilla costumes. I've brought full-size mannequins on stage and kicked them around. I've done simple magic tricks. I'll do whatever is necessary to get my point across in a more memorable and interesting fashion.

You don't necessarily have to do wild things to use props. A very creative friend of mine was going to talk about the keys to creativity. She opened by holding up keys, then discarded them in favor of a combination lock. Her point was made.

Tips for using props

● Normally you should keep your special props hidden until you are ready to use them.

● Make sure the prop can be seen from all parts of the room.

● **ALWAYS** talk to the audience, not the prop.

● Make sure the audience is focused on surprise props before you unleash the surprise. (If using a fake peanut can with pop out snakes, hold the can in full view for an extra second before you open it so the audience doesn't miss it).

PROVERBS AND FORTUNE COOKIE HUMOR

(Note: Determine if this is politically correct for your audience.)

You can throw in a cute diversion to a boring speech by attributing a saying to an ancient Chinese philosopher. Since these sayings are not attributed to anyone in particular, feel free to change or update them to fit your situation and to enhance their humor.

(The term *"original"* below means as original as something can be after being recited and translated for several hundred years.)

Original: *You cannot prevent the birds of sadness from flying over your head, but you can prevent them from nesting in your hair.*
Update: *You cannot prevent the birds of sadness from flying over your head, but you can prevent them from pooping on your Gucci blazer.*

Original: *He who walk on eggs should tread lightly.*
Update: *He who walk on eggs should find out the price per dozen.*

Original: *People who live in glass houses should not throw stones.*
Update: *People who live in glass houses should pull down the blinds.*

QUESTION AND ANSWER SESSIONS

Question and Answer sessions are great opportunities to show off your sense of humor, get audience participation, and make two powerful closings. Did I say *two* closings? Yes, I did say *two* closings.

One of the biggest mistakes I see presenters making has to do with the handling of Question and Answer sessions. The presenter does a good program, has a powerful close, opens the program up to questions, answers them well, and then fades off the stage into oblivion. The lack of a second powerful close after the question and answer period could negate much of the impact that was created throughout the program. Make sure you have two good closes whenever there is a possibility of a Q & A session.

OK. Now let's see how we can have some fun. A good way to open up a Q & A session is to say, *The last time I opened up for a Q & A session, the first question I got was "What time is it?"* or *"Can I be excused?"* or *"Aren't you getting tired up there?"* Say anything except the old boring *Now let's open it up for questions.* To be a fun presenter you must take every opportunity to do something different from the norm.

To prepare for Q & A sessions you should spend some time anticipating questions and creating humorous answers to use before you give the real answer. Be careful not to sound like a smart aleck when delivering the humorous part of the answer. When a witty response is offered to an audience question it appears to be spontaneous but, as we learned in Chapter 9, you can easily be ready with well-rehearsed responses.

If you want to take more control of the humor used in a Q & A session, you can easily do that too. Here are two solid methods that I use all the time. The first is to plant stooges in the audience. The second is a variation on an old standby Q & A method.

Plant Stooges

When I say that you should plant stooges in the audience, I usually mean that you should select one or more of the audience members to help you with the gag. You contact these people either by phone when you are doing your pre-program research or during the time you are schmoozing with audience members before the program. You simply ask them for some help during the talk. If they agree, tell them to raise their hand during the Q & A portion of the talk. They will be asking the fake question you have given them. The question itself may be funny or your preplanned answer could be the zinger. Either way should get a laugh.

Here's the hard part. You must supply the question. The more customized it is to the group, the better it will be. It might be funny if you got the president of the company to ask a really dumb question like, *How much did we pay you to be here?* It might be funny if you got one of the top salespeople to ask when they get to take the company jet to their next sales call. Who knows what might be funny to your group? I sure don't. I will give you a little hint though. The answer to what might be funny to the group you are addressing will most likely come to you while you are doing your research on the group. That is another reason pre-program work is so important. Sometimes all the humor is handed to you. All you have to do is plug it in.

Solicit Questions

If you want even more exacting control over the humor used in the Q & A session, you can use a very common Q & A technique. Solicit questions from the group to be submitted on 3" x 5" cards. All you have to do then is slip in a few fake ones. That way you get to be in control of reading both the question *and* the answer. This would be the way to go if you had worries about your stooges performing well or if you didn't recruit any stooges. This would also be a time when you could do the fake survey mentioned earlier in this chapter under the "Letters" section.

Trick: Purposely omit material that you know will evoke certain questions. When the questions come, give a preplanned answer that appears spontaneous. They'll think you are a genius.

Do you see how easy it is to take a run-of-the-mill (I hate clichés) part of a presentation and make it memorable. I hope so. Let's look at another way.

QUOTATIONS

Quotations are safe to use because if the quotation is not funny, it doesn't matter since you are just reciting it. You did not write it. It can still be used to make your point. You can use the power of the name of the person who did write it. People will be more likely to laugh or at least chuckle if a famous person made up the quotation.

If you are not sure to whom the quotation belongs, it does not matter at all. Unless I am absolutely certain who said something, I always give myself an out. I usually say *I BELIEVE it was _____ who said*. This keeps me out of trouble for attributing the quotation to the wrong person. Sometimes I say, *My great, great grandpappy used to say,* or *My old aunt Maude used to say.* However, if you know for sure who said something and their name carries weight, go ahead and use it.

There are literally thousands and thousands of notable quotations available to you. Check the bibliography for the names of some quotation books I use and look in the Internet section in Chapter 16 for searchable quotation web sites. Here are just a few examples of some of my favorite quotations:

● *Men occasionally stumble over the truth, but most of them pick themselves up and hurry off as if nothing had happened.* —Winston Churchill

- *I am a friend of the workingman, and I would rather be his friend than be one.*—Clarence Darrow

- *I never made a mistake in my life; at least, never one that I couldn't explain away afterward.*—Rudyard Kipling

- *Get your facts first and then you can distort them as much as you please.* —Mark Twain

- *Many of us spend half our time wishing for things we could have if we didn't spend half our time wishing.*—Alexander Woollcott

- *He is more apt to contribute heat than light to a discussion.* —Woodrow Wilson

- *Everything comes to him who hustles while he waits.* —Thomas Edison

- *When you have got an elephant by the hind legs and he is trying to run away, it's best to let him run.*—Abe Lincoln

- *It takes less time to do a thing right than to explain why you did it wrong.* —Henry Wadsworth Longfellow

- *When you get to the end of your rope, tie a knot and hang on.* —Franklin Delano Roosevelt

- *In the first place God made idiots; this was for practice. Then he made school boards* (take out school boards and substitute anything that fits your purpose).—Mark Twain

Don't feel bad about twisting the quotations to meet your situation. Mark Twain will never say a word about it. Neither will anyone else if you introduce your quotation by saying, *Someone once said,* or *My great, great, grandpappy used to say.* Then change the quotation around any way that suits you.

ROAST HUMOR AND INSULTS

Being roasted is an honor, but you must be careful to honor people while you are roasting them. Joke about things that are obviously untrue, then exaggerate them to make them more obvious. Or, you can outrageously exaggerate things that are true.

When choosing the butt of a roast joke or story, pick big targets. Never make fun of a small target (janitor, secretary, etc.). Make fun of the boss. He or she is still the boss after all the teasing and will look like a great sport for going along with it.

Members of *in groups* can joke about their peers and insult each other all they want. Bob Hope makes fun of Ronald Reagan. Everyone knows they are buddies.

If you widely spread an insult or collection of insults, the group can laugh together. No one is individually embarrassed. The same remarks aimed at an individual removed from the cohesive influence of the group might cause someone to get upset. Always clear your comments IN ADVANCE!

Unless you are participating in a full-blown roast program, always make fun of yourself first. If you kid yourself first, the audience will be more receptive when you kid them. Here are some roast examples:

To an AT & T executive:

● *If a Martian called Ed's office to contact earth, he'd try to sell them on the benefits of our new 800 service.*

Keep remarks focused on unimportant things that can't be damaging!

● *Folks we are here tonight to Roast Joe. I'm particularly happy to be here because I can now say in public all the things I've been saying behind his back.*

● *He/she is a man/woman of the world . . . and you know what bad shape the world is in.*

Insult about areas of recognized strength and superiority!

To a great family man and/or community leader:

● *Joe's neighbors/business associates/preacher, etc., all say what a wonderful couple he and his wife make . . . if it wasn't for Joe.*

To a well-known philanthropist:

● *He is a man of rare gifts . . . he hasn't given any in years.*

At a program with a long head table with lots of speakers, an emcee might say:

● *The emcee's job is not to be wise or witty. In fact, it is his job to appear dull so that the speakers on the program will shine in comparison. Tonight it looks like I'm going to have to rise to new heights of boredom.*

To the audience the emcee or speaker might say:

● *I'm glad to be here tonight to look into your faces. . . . And God knows there are some faces here that need looking into.*

SELF-EFFACING HUMOR

Self-effacing humor or making fun of yourself is quite a contrast. It is a very powerful form of humor that gets its strength from highlighting your weaknesses. It seems that people who have the ability to laugh at themselves in just the right amount are perceived as secure, confident, strong, and likeable.

With this type of humor, a little goes a long way. If you overdo it, you will look like a doomsayer who is always putting yourself down. If you can't bring yourself to use any self-effacing humor, you should learn. I must be candid here. Most people hate to deal with a *stuffed shirt*. Unfortunately, if you can't poke a little fun at yourself, that is the way you are perceived.

I think the reason self-effacing humor works so well is that weak people feel the need to inflate themselves and powerful people don't. If you have the confidence to tease yourself, you are indirectly sending the message to the audience that you are secure and powerful. Most audiences can see right through speakers who are trying to puff themselves up. It turns them off quickly. The person who is not afraid to tease him or herself is the one who makes the greatest connection with the audience because everyone in the audience has embarrassed themselves or failed at something at one time or the other. If you use self-effacing humor, the audience knows that you, the presenter, know how it feels to fail. That is a very powerful magnet.

Katharine Rolfe, president of The Lighten Up Club, takes self-effacing humor one step further. She says, "I call it *self-appreciating humor* because it conveys a positive appreciation of ourselves as humans who are simply out there doing our best and bumbling along as we go." Katharine's organization believes the key to a happy life is the ability to laugh at yourself, for then you are never without a source of amusement.

Unless you are a Don Rickles type presenter (known for his *hockey puck* teasing style of humor), you should never set yourself up as superior to the audience either socially, financially, or intellectually. You want the audience to accept you as one of them. Let them feel superior to you in some way. Your audience would rather hear about the time you fell on your face, rather than the time you won the race. That is why self-effacing humor is great. The audience likes the fact that you openly admit your weaknesses. They laugh, but they still respect you because you are self-confident enough to joke about yourself.

There are any number of things you can tease yourself about. Your physical appearance is good if you are especially tall or short or fat or bald. Just make sure that the physical characteristic is obvious to the audience. If you are disorganized, you could tease yourself about that. If you can't parallel park, you could tease yourself about that. Just about anything will work as long as you are the target. What you want to avoid teasing about is any subject that has a direct tie to your credibility. For instance, if you were a nuclear control room technician, you would not want to joke about the time you pushed the wrong button. But, if you got fired from your job as a nuclear control room technician for *almost* pushing the wrong button, then this fact might be a good topic for humor. It could turn into a great topic if you now own a landscaping company or are in some other nonthreatening position.

To use self-effacing humor, you don't necessarily have to joke about yourself. You can make fun of your family background, your profession, or anything else that directly relates to you.

I tell a story in my presentations about the time my mom came from our very small hometown of Claysville, Pennsylvania, to visit me in the big city of Washington, D.C. The audience hears about how small Claysville is and that my mom's house is way out in the sticks. We didn't have city water, or city sewerage, or cable TV. I then go on to tell how we took a dinner cruise on the *Spirit of Washington* and went sightseeing all over the capital. Here's how the end of the story goes:

> *When we got home that evening I was exhausted, so I told mom I was going to bed and that I would see her in the morning. She said, "OK. I'm just going to watch the news and then I'll go to bed." I got up at about 2:00 a.m. and there was mom sitting in front of the TV. Her head was nodding and drooping. I said, "Mom. What are you doing?" She said, "I'm just waiting for the news to be over." Well she would have waited a long time because she was watching . . . CNN 24-hour headline news.*

In this story I was not directly teasing myself. I was teasing about my small town background and about the innocent and funny boner my mom pulled when she came to visit.

Former president Ronald Reagan was a master at using self-effacing humor. In his bid for the Presidency in 1980 his age appeared to be his biggest obstacle. He attacked the problem with self-effacing humor. He would joke about his age all the time which, turned age into a nonissue. He told a group of reporters once, "Thomas Jefferson once said, 'One should not worry about chronological age compared to the ability to perform the task.' . . . Ever since Thomas Jefferson told me that I stopped worrying about my age."

Look for opportunities to tease yourself. This will be one of your most powerful tools to connect with the audience and a subtle way to show your strength.

SIGNS

I run across funny signs all the time. I try to take a mental note or take a picture of the sign for later use. John Jay Daly, a speaker friend of mine, does a hysterical slide presentation called *The Wacky, Wonderful World of Washington*. Many of the slides are of signs that he has seen around Washington, D.C. My favorite is a sign that says, "In case of nuclear attack, the ban on school prayer will be lifted." Another slide has a brass plaque on the front of a large building that says, "All Deliveries Go to Rear of Building." The next slide is the brass plaque on the back of the same building that says, "No Deliveries."

You can have lots of fun with signs. I just showed you two ways you can use them. In the last paragraph, I *told* you about the signs my friend uses in his slide presentation. That's one way. The second way is to actually show them, as my friend does, by means of projection. A third way is to have the sign or signs with you and hold them up. I just attended a Meeting Planners International function where the presenter had his own applause sign. Everyone applauded on cue and had a good laugh because of it.

Photographic Tip: When taking pictures or slides of funny signs, always fill the photographic frame up completely with the sign. The impact of the sign is much greater when you do this (see Illustration 16-1).

Some of my favorite signs:

● At a hospital in Prince Georges County, Maryland: *Hospital Policy is to refuse service to hospital patients.* (This was posted at the snack bar.)

● Funny tombstone inscription:

> *As I am now, you soon shall be.*
> *Prepare for death and follow me.*
> Scribbled below:
> *To follow you I'm not content.*
> *Until I know which way you went.*

- **Another tombstone:** *It's so soon, I'm done for, I wonder what I was begun for!*

- **On church marquee:** *Honey I Shrunk the Sermon.*

- **On door of small restaurant:** *Out to lunch.*

- **Sign in front of bankrupt store:** *We Undersold Everybody.*

These English language signs were seen outside the United States:

- **Advertisement for a Hong Kong dentist:** *Teeth extracted by latest methodists.*

- **Somewhere in an elevator:** *Do not enter the lift backwards, and only when lit up.*

- **1936 French sign:** *Don't kill your wife with work, let electricity do it.*

- **In a Bangkok drycleaner's window:** *Drop your trousers here for best results.*

- **France:** *Please leave your values at the front desk.*

- **Japan:** You are invited to take advantage of the chambermaid.

- **Switzerland:** *Because of the impropriety of entertaining guests of the opposite sex in the bedroom, it is suggested that the lobby be used for this purpose.*

I saw this sign on a display in a shoe store

All our spring colors are now in. (All shoes on the rack were white.)

Keep your eye out for funny signs so that you can tell your audiences about them or show them.

Here's my favorite sign of all time from a hotel in Acapulco, Mexico:

The manager has personally passed all water served here.

SIMILE

Simile is a comparison of two things which, however different in other respects, have some strong point or points in common. The words *like* and *as* will normally be used when making the comparison.

You might say, *Getting this contract signed is as impossible as trying to smuggle daybreak past a rooster.* Contracts and roosters don't have much in common (which is funny), but in this case the presenter is telling you what they do have in common. Getting the contract signed and smuggling daybreak past a rooster are both impossible. You could shorten the last simile by changing *as impossible as* to *like*. *Getting this contract signed is like trying to smuggle daybreak past a rooster.* In this case, the audience must make the interpretation that both are impossible. It's good to make the audience think sometimes because it forces them to be involved.

Similes help paint pictures in the minds of the audience members.
"If we sign the contract with XYA company it will be like sliding down a thousand foot razor blade."

A recurring theme with me is that humor surrounds you wherever you go. I got a great simile out of a child's joke book I acquired (if something is valuable you *acquire* it) for 10 cents at a flea market. I now use this line in presentations all over the country. I do a seminar called *Business Lite: Low Cost/No Cost Ways to Improve Productivity.* In that seminar I talk about how employees feel at work. I say, *Sometimes you go to work and you feel like a turtle with claustrophobia—you've got to be there, but you feel closed in.* I like to mix and match many types of humor in one concise chunk. Here's a simile that I just love.

> *If you put his brain on a matchstick, it would be like rolling a BB down a four-lane highway.*

Let's break this one-liner down to see how several different forms of humor were used.

Putting a person's brain on a matchstick and rolling a BB down a four-lane highway are both ludicrous juxtapositions. No one is going to put someone's brain on a matchstick or roll a BB down a four-lane highway.

This piece of humor is a simile because the two ludicrous juxtapositions are compared with the word *like*. The effect of the simile is to exaggerate how small this man's brain is.

So, three different types of humor—juxtaposition, simile, and exaggeration—were combined to make a great one-liner. These are the types of relationships you would explore if you were feeling adventurous and decided to write some of your own humor*. However, that is not what this book is about. Many of the one-liners you run across will be combinations like this. You don't have to be able to dissect them as I just did. All you have to be able to do is pick the ones (in this case similes) that make your point and use them where and when appropriate.

*Note: For more information on a great comedy writing course contact Jeff Justice's Comedy Workshop (see Appendix B).

TOASTS

Toasting is not nearly as common as it once was. However, the polished presenter should have a few short toasts ready to go if and when the occasion arises. Here are a few fun toasts and a few touching ones too:

Birthdays:

- *To your birthday, glass held high. Glad it's you that's older—not I.*

- *Here's to you. No matter how old you are, you don't look it.*

Christmas:

- *Twas the month after Christmas, and Santa had flit; Came there tidings in the mail, which read: Please remit.*

- *Here's to the Holly with its bright red berry. Here's to Christmas, let's make it merry.*

Meals:

- *Eat, drink, and be merry, for tomorrow you diet.*

- *A full belly, a heavy purse, and a light heart.*

Friendship:

- *Here's to a friend who knows me well and likes me anyway.*

- *May the friends of our youth be the companions of our old age.*

Banquet speech ending:

- *Good day, good health, good cheer, good night!*

Health:

- *Here's to your health. You make age curious, time furious, and all of us envious.*

Luck:

- *As you slide down the bannister of life, may the splinters never face the wrong way.*

- *May your luck be like the capital of Ireland. Always Dublin.*

New Year:

- *May all our troubles in the coming year be as short as our New Year's resolutions.*

- *In the year ahead may we treat our friends with kindness and our enemies with generosity.*

Marriage:

- *Marriage is an institution, but who wants to live in an institution?*
  —Groucho Marx

- *May for "better or worse" be far better than worse.*

To close this section I would like to tell you that I feel like a loaf of bread. Wherever I go, they toast me.

WORDS AND SOUNDS, PLACES, FOOD, AND NUMBERS
Words are funny

Some words are simply funnier than others. Your word choice can be the key to creating a successful witty line or a dud.

All professional comedy writers agree on the following fact. The sound of certain words can virtually guarantee a laugh. In particular, the "k" sound in words is the granddaddy of all funny sounds. In Neil Simon's play, *The Sunshine Boys*, Willy, a main character, gives his nephew a lecture about comedy:

> Fifty-seven years in this business, you learn a few things. You know what words are funny and which words are not funny. Alka Seltzer is funny. You say "Alka Seltzer" you get a laugh . . . Words with "k" in them are funny. Casey Stengel, that's a funny name. Robert Taylor is not funny. Cupcake is funny. Tomato is not funny. Cookie is funny. Cucumber is funny. Car keys. Cleveland . . . Cleveland is funny. Maryland is not funny. Then, there's chicken. Chicken is funny. Pickle is funny.

Someone actually researched why the "k" sound is funny. It has something to do with the sounds we, as babies, associated with comfort. Like *cootchie-coo, cuddle, cozy,* etc. Note that these words don't have a "k" in them, but they have the "k" sound.

Examples:

● *Those turkeys over at XYA* (remember no Zs allowed) *company can't hold a candle to our team of installers.*

● *I'll bet you a cupcake to a cucumber the blue team will outsell the gold team.*

Places

As we saw above, *Cleveland* is funny. *Saskatoon, Saskatchewan,* is funny. I live just off *Goodluck Road.* That's funny. My computer consultant used to live on *Easy Street* in Temple Hills, Maryland. That's funny. It was hard to find him because people were always stealing the sign, and it's not easy to steal an Easy Street sign.

I guarantee that if you pick up any map that has city or street names on it, within a few seconds, you will find a funny name. If you look at it for a few minutes, you'll find many. I just picked up my road atlas and opened it to the USA and Canada maps in the front. *Saskatoon, Saskatchewan,* almost jumped off the page and into my word processor. *Tuscaloosa, Alabama,* wasn't far behind along with

Kalamazoo, Michigan; Toledo, Ohio; Schenectady, New York; and one of my favorites, *Albuquerque, New Mexico.*

Now, I'm going to open the street map for Lanham, Maryland, where this brilliant work is being created. I told you I live off *Goodluck Road* and I see that a few blocks away from my house is *Elvis Lane* in *Presley Manor.* About a mile away is *Lois Lane* and I recently did some work in *Boniwood.* That isn't funny to you, but it was a scream around our office because my assistant's name is Bonnie. Humor is literally waiting for you just around the corner!

Besides cities and roads, you have at your disposal an unlimited number of funny names related to restaurants, hotels and stores like *Pigly Wigly, Kangaroo Katies, Motel 6, The Colonels Kentucky Fried Chicken,* and the ultimate "k" sound store—*K Mart.*

Food

Food is funny. I heard a comic many years ago say "Life is a Twinkie." When there is no other way to explain some office calamity I say, "I guess life is just a Twinkie." I laugh off the tension, then I seriously take care of the problem.

There are lots of other funny foods like *chicken soup, meatballs* and Bill Cosby's favorite, *Jello.* If you majored in philosophy, you might find deep meaning in the Twinkie line. However, most of the rest of us would agree that the line was pure nonsense. This kind of wordplay can do wonders to jazz up a presentation, and *that ain't chopped liver.*

Numbers

Most businesses have numerous uses for numbers, both written and oral (also see "Financial," Chapter 17). Again, some numbers are funnier and more interesting than others. A number like *zero* has other names that are funny that aren't even numbers.

Goose egg, nada, nil, zip and *zilch* are all funny ways to express the number zero. Even *zero* is funnier than the word none. Although *none* is funny when you talk about the two chances of a hostile takeover as *slim and none.* A hundred dollar bill is a *C-Note,* a five-dollar bill is a *fin.* If someone is outrageously rich, they could be a *zillionaire.*

If you want to exaggerate a little bit, or if you have some tough news to deliver that involves numbers, add a touch of levity to help soothe the sting.

One common rule of humor that does not apply to numbers is brevity. In all other types of humor you should conserve the number of words you use. Normally you want to use the fewest words possible to get to the punch line. When using numbers in a presentation, pronounce them using the *longest* version possible. This gives them more punch. The number 1,500 should be recited as *one thousand five hundred,* not *fifteen hundred;* the time of 8:15 should be *a quarter past eight,* not *eight fifteen;* 6'2" should be *six feet two inches* not *six-two.*

If I couldn't tell these stories, I should die.

—Abe Lincoln

Storytelling

If I keep writing this book the same old way, I should die. I'm getting bored with the same old chapter layout. If I'm getting bored, I can only imagine how you feel. That's the whole point of this book. Don't get in one groove in front of your audience and stay in it forever. Change things up to keep their attention and interest.

Since I'm tired writing straight text, what I thought I would do for this chapter is write an introduction to storytelling then use a *Do's* and *Don'ts* format. If you incorporate the *Do's* and eliminate the *Don'ts* I guarantee your storytelling will improve dramatically. Here we go!

CHAPTER 14

Storytelling is such an important type of humor I gave it its own chapter instead of including it in the previous chapter. Being a good storyteller can be profitable for you. It will make you immensely popular with people in business and social circles.

People are more likely to remember your points and move in your direction if the points are supported with stories. These don't have to be long stories either. Any personal anecdote is really a story.

Only use stories if you enjoy telling them. There is too much invested to do a boring or bad job of it. If you don't have a good time telling the story, your audience will probably be bored. Even if you acquire all the right techniques, your stories will still flop if you don't tell them with great enthusiasm.

ENTHUSIASM

I was doing some work for a government agency where I was hired to critique and improve the sales presentations of the program staff. It was an early morning program full of typical mistakes by typical untrained presenters. The audience was nearly asleep from the boring presentations and sugar crash they were suffering after eating pastries when they got there.

I had been watching one particular presenter prior to his segment and I was thinking to myself, "I'm going to have to really tear this guy up on his evaluations." He was poorly groomed, including big dandruff flakes on his poorly fitting sports jacket. His tie was hanging out over the top of his jacket button. His pants were way too short—I mean WAY too short. He appeared to be just a goober of a guy.

When it was his turn to present his boring legislative issues topic, I got the shock of my life. He virtually flew up on the stage. He was running around like Groucho Marx. He was spouting off facts and figures. He made a perfect ad-lib when the electrically operated overhead screen started to go up by itself. The audience woke up and they were laugh-

> *Nothing great was ever achieved without enthusiasm.*
>
> Ralph Waldo Emerson

ing and learning from this man. He actually got applause in a meeting that wasn't even a setting where applause would be appropriate.

From that experience I learned the value of enthusiasm. This man made almost every technical error a presenter could make, but I gave him the highest evaluation of all the other presenters. If you are ultimately enthusiastic about your topic and let it show, many of your errors will go unnoticed. It's the same way with storytelling and presenting in general. Your enthusiasm can make or break your overall performance.

WHAT TO DO AFTER IDENTIFYING A STORY

When you come across a story in a book, or when you have a personal incident you think will make a good story, ask yourself the following questions:

● Is it clean?

● Can I use it in a professional presentation to make a point?

● What point does it illustrate?

● What other points does it illustrate?

● How many categories should I file it in so I can find it when I need it (see "Sources and Organization," Chapter 15)?

- What should I say to lead into the story?

- What should I say following the story?

- Where should I put it in my presentation?

- Is it better than something I am already using?

Just thinking about the answers to the above questions will make your storytelling better. Many presenters just slap any old story into their presentation, any old place, because they like the story. That is not the way to do it.

The following list of *Do's, Don'ts, Rules,* and *Tricks* is meant to break the important points about storytelling into digestible chunks. Each point is very important. I'm glad I got bored with the format of this book now because it gives me a chance to really emphasize each point about storytelling. Don't try to implement all these tips at once. You'll never remember the details of your story. Pick one or two to practice until they become ingrained. Then add another tip to make the story even better. <u>Note</u>: These points are not in order of importance.

Do's

- Use stories to illustrate points and state the point in addition to telling the story. Always make your story relevant to the subject at hand.

- Select stories to match the intelligence, experience, occupation, and age of the audience as well as the nature of the occasion. You don't want to talk over the heads of the audience members and you don't want to bore them with stories that are too simple.

- Space stories at intervals to provide a change of pace and to reemphasize your message. Remember from Chapter 5 the listening pattern you want to create in the audience.

- Tell about your troubles, stupidity, or ignorance. People like you when you use self-effacing humor because they see themselves mirrored in your weaknesses.

- Eliminate inconsequential detail. Use the fewest number of words that convey the message in an interesting fashion. Writing the story out will help you see words that can be eliminated without hurting the story.

- Keep your humorous stories short. The size of the laugh is inversely proportional to the number of words used to get to the punch line.

Rule: The longer the story, the funnier it must be.

You must make jokes and humorous stories believable up to a point. Use factual, specific details that the audience can relate to, i.e., say the brand name like *Lots-o-Suds* rather than *a laundry detergent*. The more truthful and specific the story sounds, the more your audience will get caught up in what you say.

> *I told them the truth and they fell for it.*
>
> Judge Harry Stone
> *Night Court*

Specify the location of a joke or story. If your story takes place in a restaurant say, *"I was at Jerry's Sub Shop in Rockville, Maryland, the other day."* This gives the audience something concrete to think about, which makes them more involved mentally.

When crafting a story, use people, places, and things the audience knows. When the audience is familiar with the elements in your story, they will become even more involved. As soon as you mention the company cafeteria, their minds race to the cafeteria to meet you and find out what happens. However, don't use humor that is too *inside*. Only a few people will understand it.

Emphasize the adjectives and verbs in your stories to make them sound more interesting. Try it. Look around where you are right now and describe anything you want. Really put punch behind the adjectives and verbs and see how your description comes to life.

Use specific and interesting verbs and adjectives. Say I was *exhausted,* not I was *tired.* Say, her head was *nodding* and *drooping,* not her head was *down.*

Learn your stories. In a normal speech if you forget the exact thing you wanted to say, you can improvise and go on. But if you leave out an important detail in a story or if you accidentally give away the climax too soon, you have a mess on your hands. I tell a story at least 30 times in private before I'll test it in front of an audience.

Use true facts from your own life. This makes it easier for you to tell the story because you lived it and you can learn it faster too. Also, someone else can't steal your story as easily if all the facts have to do with your life.

Use appropriate emotional language to *hook* the listener as described in Chapter 11.

- Construct a humorous story so that it concludes abruptly with a climactic word. Don't utter another syllable or sound after this climactic word. You might squelch the laughter you worked so hard to get.

Exception: Some stories get laughter all along the way. More of these stories are used by humorists who are expected to be funny all the time.

- Work out different lengths of the same story to fit different time segments. (Yes, I've snuck a *Don't* in the *Do's* section.) *Don't memorize your stories word for word.* This way you won't feel forced to say every word, every time you tell the story. You can change the length of the story easily by adding or subtracting detail.

Super Trick: Have a quotation ready that makes the same point as your story. If your time is shortened, you can cut out a story and replace it with a quote.

- Slant your story to the intended audience. When telling a story to a group of executives you would probably want to use different language and emphasis than if you were telling the same story to a group of secretaries. Change nonessential elements of the story to make a better connection.

- Use terms like *Imagine this, Have you ever had an experience where . . ., Let me take you with me to . . .,* to draw the audience into your stories.

DON'TS

1. When Setting up a Story

- Don't say the words *funny*, *reminds me of*, or *story*. These words are so overused they alert the audience that a story is coming. This causes audience members to resist your story rather than get caught up in your story. They say in essence, "Let's see you make me laugh," or "OK, here comes another story."

- Don't say, *I heard a good one the other day* for the same reason you don't say *it reminds me of*. The audience will resist and challenge you to make them laugh.

- Never say, *I don't know if I should tell this one.* If there is any doubt whatsoever that a story is not appropriate for a particular group, leave it out.

Better ways to set up a story

The best way to start a story is to get right into it. You should be into the story before anyone realizes it is a story. That way they are already deeply involved and don't have time to resist. You could say:

● *There was this man . . .*

● *On the flight here . . .* Don't say, *A funny thing happened on the way to the meeting today.*

● *Driving in this morning . . .*

● *In the cab today . . .*

● *I was talking with . . .*

● *Let me take you back . . ., Come with me . . ., Imagine . . ., Visualize this . . .* These are a little different because they do alert the audience that a story is coming, but they get them so involved emotionally that any resistance is counteracted.

2. When Getting Out of a Story

● Never say, *But seriously folks.* If it was a funny story you don't have to say, *Hey Stupid! That was a joke.* It also implies you were lying.

To exit a story, don't say anything about it being over. Just make a slight change in delivery, tone, rate, expression, etc., and go on.

3. When telling any story don't

● Use too many stories on the same topic. Each successive one will lose impact.

● Tell a story where you are the hero. If you are the hero, make it appear that it was dumb luck that made you so (self-effacing humor). If you are a bonafide hero, forget what I just said, but make sure you add a healthy dose of humility for best connection with the audience.

● Use terms foreign to the experience of the audience.

● Try to come off as an expert if you took a whirlwind tour of someplace.

● Die of printed page poison. Written stories must be changed to be recited aloud. When you find a story that you like in a reference book, you cannot say it exactly as it is written or you will sound stupid. You must knock out the "he saids" and "she saids."

● Don't give a history lesson when telling a humorous story. Put yourself into the story to make it believable. Fake truth is essential to humor even if story is totally false.

> *Sometimes the truth can be so unnecessary.*
> Remington Steele

The exception to the need for fake truth is when you are telling an exaggeration. Then anything goes.

Example:

> *I had a terrible day at the beach. I came home with 14 harpoon wounds.*

To use that line, it doesn't matter if you've ever been to the beach in your life. It's just a funny line teasing yourself about being large (like a whale).

TRICK: Look in different directions to indicate different characters. The audience will associate a stage right or stage left look with the different character.

TRICK: Use above trick along with changing your voice tone to indicate different characters.

TRICK: Do what the written story says. If it says Joe cleared his throat, you clear your throat at that point in the story.

SPECIAL RESOURCE: If you really want to get into the nitty gritty of storytelling, check out the *National Storytelling Association* (NSA). (**Note:** This is not to be confused with The *National Speakers Association* which is also NSA.) This group, formerly known as the National Association for the Preservation and Perpetuation of Storytelling (NAPPS) has a bimonthly magazine and tons of resources for storytellers. They can be reached at (800) 525-4514, (423) 753-2171, Fax (423) 753-9331, or by mail at P.O. Box 309, Jonesborough, TN 37659.

EXTRA SPECIAL BONUS GENIUS TECHNIQUE

Split your story. Start a story near or at the beginning of your talk, but don't finish it. Build suspense by cutting off the story at a key point or just before the climactic finish. This builds anticipation. Finish the story at the end of your talk.

If you incorporate even a small percentage of the above tips, your storytelling and value as a presenter will increase dramatically.

Part III
Sources,
Organization,
A/V and Computers

*Have a place for everything and keep the thing some-
where else. This is not advice, it is merely custom.*

—Mark Twain

Sources and organization of material

Humor and usable material literally surround you. It is your job as the "Pilot in Command" of your presentation to pick and choose the anecdotes, one-liners, stories, visuals, etc., needed to support the points you are trying to make. Part of this process is collecting and organizing your material so you can find it when you need it.

CHAPTER 15

SOURCES OF MATERIAL

Daily Information

Every day, you are bombarded with tons of information both serious and humorous. You are also involved in life incidents that, with a little thought, can be turned into stories or one-liners to be used in your presentations. The information on-slaught comes from many directions. Television, radio, newspapers, magazines, books, audio and video tapes, trade journals, the Information Superhighway, billboards, and the U.S. Mail all contain more good material than you could ever use.

Sometimes really great and on-target pieces of information will hit you right in the face. I was reading *Newsweek* last week and ran across an article about a church that encouraged hysterical laughing during their sermons. One of my topics has to do with the value of laughter in your life. I'm not sure yet how I'm going to use that article, but I tore it out of the magazine and filed it along with other information on that topic.

Some information you run across will be more subtle, but when you actually start watching for usable material, you will get better at recognizing it. I read in another *Newsweek* article that the cost to business of stress-related health care was skyrocketing. The writer made the observation that now there are so many stress reduction programs that people are getting stressed out trying to pick one. I didn't know what I would do with that observation, but I did know that I liked it so I cut it out and filed it under *stress*. I started collecting more information on stress which led eventually to the creation of a new program, *Technostress: Don't Let Computer Chips Drive Away Your Blue Chip Staff.*

The key to getting a shot at using material you stumble upon is to write it down or secure it immediately. I mean IMMEDIATELY! If you don't like making notes, get a microcassette recorder and dictate the idea. I can't emphasize this point enough. Great ideas can come and go in an instant. If you don't do something with them when they hit you in the face, you are likely to lose them forever. I usually carry a mini razor blade knife or pocket knife so I can cut things out of newspapers, magazines, newsletters, etc.

Jot down little life incidents, too, such as your electricity going out in the middle of the night, which caused your alarm clock to malfunction, which caused you to be late for work, which caused you to run in late to your presentation that morning (time for a canned ad-lib—*I would like to tell you that the reason I was late is that the Commander in Chief called me for some advice. I would like to tell you that, but I have been sworn to secrecy. So the story I have been given by the Secret Service is that my electricity went off last night and the alarm clock didn't go off*).

Let's see how you might use this same incident in a presentation. First let's recall some of our story telling questions from Chapter 14.

●   Is it clean? Yes it is clean.

●   What point does it illustrate? It could mean that there was a malfunction in the house which caused a short and the main breaker prevented the house from catching on fire.—**Point:** Have fail-safe mechanisms in place to protect your business not only from physical damage, but from business breakdowns too.

● What other points does it illustrate?—**Point:** Electricity is something we take for granted. When it's not there, we suffer.

Undoubtedly more points could be made, but let's look at how taking electricity for granted could be used to help make a point in a presentation.

A few weeks back my electricity went off in the middle of the night. I awoke the next morning thinking I had just had one of my best night's sleep in a long time until . . . I saw my digital alarm clock blinking at me. I jumped up and ran to find my wristwatch: 9:30 a.m. I still hadn't buttoned my pants as I jumped in the car and raced to work for my 9:30 a.m. presentation. Luckily, they waited for me and I got through the day. But after everything settled down, I got to thinking about how we really take electricity for granted. It's just supposed to be there. When it's there all the time, we sometimes forget what a disaster it would be if it weren't.

If it were a business audience, you could use this story to talk about long-term customers and how we might take them for granted. Or, if it were a keynote speech you could use this story to talk about balancing home and work and how we might take our spouses for granted.

You can see that the tiniest life incident can be used to help reinforce points in your presentation.

Reference Material

The reason I talked about current information and personal life events first is that they will earn you the highest amount of impact. Using your own life incidents and observations makes you unique. Why should you be asked to speak if anyone could get up in front of the group and recite the same old tired information and stories? I encourage you to spice up your presentations with your interpretations of news events and information and your personal experiences.

However, I go back again to the idea that you must change up. An entire presentation based on you could be considered self-aggrandizing and boring. It is perfectly acceptable and necessary to include observations and humor of others to support your points. This information is easily found in reference material for speakers, many of which include both serious and humorous material. Most of these resources are categorized by subject and they put thousands of pieces of material at your fingertips.

I also have more than 400 books in my humor library now and it's growing all the time. I really go crazy in the used bookstores and at flea markets. For instance, at a yard sale, I found a book of baseball anecdotes that only cost me a quarter. When the time comes that I need a baseball story this book is waiting on my bookshelf to help me hit a home run. (I can't believe I used another dumb joke like that!)

Here are just a few references I rely on when preparing a presentation. <u>Note</u>: Some may be out of print, but you can look in used bookstores and ask book search services to find them (see Appendix B).

☆   *The Book of Business Anecdotes* by Peter Hay

☆   *Speakers Library of Business Stories, Anecdotes and Humor* by Joe Griffith

☆   *How to be the Life of the Podium* by Sylvia Simmons

☆   *Witty Words* by Eileen Mason

☆   *Dictionary of Humorous Quotations*, Edited by Evan Esar

☆   *Humorous Stories About the Human Condition* by Eric W. Johnson

☆   *The Public Speakers Handbook of Humor* by Helen & Larry Eisenberg

☆   *2715 One Line Quotations for Speakers, Writers and Raconteurs* by Edward Murphy

☆   *5600 Jokes for All Occasions* by Mildred Meirers & Jack Knapp

Your local library is an excellent source of humor. I found over 100 listings on humor in my small town library. They had tapes, records, books, and videos available at no charge. You can look for humor in the library under the following topics: *Humor, Wit and Humor, Humorous Stories, Humorists, Humorous Poetry, Humorous Recitations, Humorous Photography, Proverbs, Caricatures and Cartoons,* and *Quotations.*

Keep in mind that you can't always use the humor in these sources *as is.* You must update, personalize, and localize much of the humor to increase its effectiveness. Here's an example of a joke that came from *5600 Jokes for All Occasions.* You will first see it in its original form from the book and then see the slight changes for the usable version.

Original - exactly as written:

Do you find that advertising brings quick results?

I should say it does. Why, only the other day we advertised for a night watchman, and that night the safe was robbed.

Update:

Advertising can bring quick results. The other day my company advertised for a security guard and we got robbed that night.

To make the update for this old-fashioned joke, change the first line from a question to a statement to eliminate the dialogue between two people. Then change the old fashioned term *night watchman* to the more modern term *security guard*. Also eliminate some of the extra detail and say it was your company that did this so it's personalized. Now you have a quick usable two-liner that makes a point.

You can do the same thing with funny stories, funny articles, quips, and quotes you find. Just don't take someone else's personal experience and claim it as your own. The best way to do this is to give credit and piggyback off their humor (see more on this topic in the next section of this chapter).

Many newspapers have humorous quotations and sayings for the day along with cartoons and funny news stories. You could even paste up fake headlines on newspapers to tease someone in the group. When I'm doing a talk, besides reviewing national news, I try to get the local paper in advance. I also buy a paper as soon as I get to the city of the presentation so I can pick up on any local news items to refer to in my talk. This helps me connect with the audience because it surprises them to find out I know so much about events in their area.

You can find great humor on television situation comedies, comedy channels, HBO specials, talk shows, etc. Just be ready to jot down notes when you hear something you like. Video and audio tapes can be found at places like Blockbuster Video, your local bookstore, music stores, or Nightingale Conant Corporation (see Appendix B).

Other Speakers

Other speakers can be a great source of humor. I got a line from Zig Ziglar that I use. I say *I was talking to Zig Ziglar the other day* (which I did at a National Speakers Association Convention) *and he told me the definition of a hypocrite. That's someone who complains about all the sex, drugs, and violence—on his VCR.*

If Zig is the best known speaker using that line and someone else hears me use it without giving credit, it would taint the rest of my program. I would look like a Zig Ziglar copycat. If I give credit, I am showing integrity by doing so and using the line will not have an adverse effect on the rest of my presentation.

If the joke, story, or one-liner is one that you see all the time in joke and reference books, feel free to use it without worrying about crediting anyone. When it is showing up everywhere, it is considered to be in the public domain. Remember though, if you are seeing it everywhere, so are lots of other speakers. Don't let yourself be embarrassed by using the same humor as another speaker before you. That can ruin your whole day.

Joke services are a relatively inexpensive way to have a constant stream of current humor. Many radio and television personalities subscribe to these services whose sole job is to provide humor for professional use. These services have a limited number of subscribers so I wouldn't worry too much about your audience having heard the jokes and one-liners sold by these companies (see Appendix B for names and addresses).

Don't forget the Information Superhighway that everyone is talking about. Lots of humor is batted around all the time in online services like CompuServe and America Online. The Internet has more humor than you could use in a lifetime. Although some of the jokes are not suitable for use in professional presentations, many are. Lots of jokes are located in a newsgroup called "rec.humor.funny" and there are numerous web sites about humor (see "Internet," Chapter 16). Get a computer guru to help if you want to take advantage of this source of humor; figuring out the Internet is far beyond the scope of this book.

Old Humor Is Good Humor

Humor is only old if your audience has heard it before and if they remember it. Most people don't remember the exact details of jokes, one-liners, and stories. This is not contradictory to the fact that one of the uses of humor is to make your points more memorable.

One of the reasons people don't remember jokes and other pieces of humor is that the humor is usually heard without a context. It was used for entertainment only, enjoyed, and quickly forgotten. It was not used in conjunction with a point, which is the way you should use it in a professional presentation.

When you bring back some of this old humor, you will be tying it to your point, which makes it acceptable to use in the first place. In the second place, even if some audience members recognize the humor, they probably don't remember the punch line. If you tell it well, even those people who do remember the punch line will enjoy hearing it again.

The technique to use in telling a very old joke or story is to tell the audience it is old. This is the one time when you *should* tell the audience you have a joke or story coming. If you don't tell them that you know it is old, they will likely think you are out of touch. If you tell them you are going to tell an old story or joke, you are telling them you know it's old, but it makes the point so well that you think it is worth telling again.

As we saw in the last section, you will come across jokes and stories that can be updated. Some can be updated as easily as adding a current name. Here's an old politician joke:

> *Joe the politician said he was so surprised about his nomination that his acceptance speech fell out of his pocket.*

All you have to do to update this one is change the name from Joe to the current politician or association member you want to tease. You could also make this a joke on yourself if you know you are going to be nominated for something. *I was so surprised about this nomination that MY acceptance speech fell out of my pocket.* Here's another one that can be used for presidents or to tease any boss:

> *A man was alone in a rowboat on the Potomac shouting No! No! No! Someone on the riverbank said, "Is that guy crazy or what?" Another man fishing said, "No. That's just one of President Clinton's 'Yes Men' on vacation."*

All you have to do on this one is change the name of the river and substitute your BIG TARGET where you see President Clinton.

Industry-Specific Humor

If you are looking for stories and humor in a specific industry, you must work a little harder. Certain professions like medicine and law have many individual books, newsletters, and articles written about them. But if you are a plumbing executive, it is unlikely you could go down to your local bookstore and find a plumbing joke book.

Start a file right away for industry-specific information you find. A good place to start looking for information to fill this file would be in a trade journal for your industry. Almost every industry you can imagine has one or more associated trade journals. If you're looking for humor, sift through back issues to find humor you can use now. Virtually no one remembers cartoons and jokes more than a month or so. Watch for industry newsletters so you can extract usable material. Check your company bulletin boards regularly for funny signs and postings.

Ask others in your industry to look for stories or incidents that would be of interest to your audience (remember to give credit). Collect everything you can that is interesting and industry specific and soon you will have the best collection around.

Recap

In conclusion, I say again: Humor surrounds you if you just open your eyes to it. Your own personal life situations are always the best. Next in line would be updated and personalized humor taken from other sources. You can find instantly usable humor (instant as soon as you practice and twist it around a little bit) on television, in the newspaper, in books, on the Internet, in *Reader's Digest,* in joke services, and from other speakers (always, always give credit). You could even have your own speech or joke writers as long as you can find one that understands you and your industry.

When using any of these sources, be ready with a pencil and paper or tape recorder to grab the stuff you like. You will look through much more material than you could ever use. The old saying is that you have to sift through a lot of dirt to get to the gold.

ORGANIZING YOUR MATERIAL

Being able to find humor, stories, quotes and other speech material when you need it is very important. It is very frustrating to know you have a piece of material, but you can't find it. Some system of organizing all this material is essential to efficient preparation.

A file and cross-reference system will help you keep track of your material. I use both a computer and hard copy filing system. Both have advantages, so don't worry if you don't have a computer.

The Computer

On the computer I keep separate files for all the different topics I cover in my presentations and also

Sometimes a hard copy file is better than a computer.

for the different parts and categories of speeches like *Response to Introduction* and *Openings*. (You can also do this with three-by-five cards or in a regular file box or cabinet if you do not have a computer.)

Some information in my topic files may be duplicated in other topic files. For instance, one of my signature stories about my dog, Freeway, makes several different points. It can be used as a customer service story, to illustrate going the extra mile, reacting under pressure, or thinking quickly. Since it is a story involving an animal, it could be told to a group of animal lovers. Consequently, this story shows up in several of my topic files.

Using a computer has some big advantages. When I'm preparing a talk, all I have to do is open the file on that topic and pick the information I want to use. I copy this material to another file named for the group to which I'm speaking.

If I am in a hurry, I can locate material quickly and copy it directly where I need it. Also, when traveling I can take all my speech reference information on a few floppies or a lap top computer in case I get another talk while I'm on the road.

Hard Copy

I use folders in a filing cabinet to keep cartoons, clippings, gag items, etc., that do not lend themselves to input to the computer. Overhead transparencies and other audio/visual material can be organized in binders by inserting them into three-ring document protectors. You can also use three-ring pouches to hold much of the miscellaneous stuff you need like pencils, pens, tape, etc.

Even though the hard copy filing method is slower than the computer, it has several big advantages. The first advantage is that my filing cabinet has never once malfunctioned in 20 years. It has never had a hard drive crash. It has never given me a general protection fault (computer lingo for BIG PROBLEM). I have never had to sit for hours with a technician while it was being serviced. Never once has it been difficult to find a file. It even works in a thunderstorm and when the electricity is out.

The second big advantage is that having hard files and a big box of miscellaneous material forces you to look through the material to find what you want. When you do this, you will see many things that you forgot you had. Maybe it's time to revive some of the old stuff.

Bonus Tips

- Immediately after you talk to a group, log your material so you don't repeat any jokes or stories if you are invited back.

- Professional speaker Larry Winget gave me this great tip: Keep a master log of all your best material, humorous lines, stories, and jokes and use it as a sales tool. After a presentation, check off all the material you used. Show the master log to the meeting planner. Tell the planner if he or she has you back, you won't use any of the material you used this time. They will be impressed at seeing how much more you have to offer.

- Another good trick is to write down the names of the folks you dealt with or met at the event. Do this phonetically and include a physical description so you can greet them properly next time. They will think you are a genius.

Eyes are more accurate witnesses than ears.

—Heraclitus, circa 480 B.C.

The mind is more slowly stirred by the ear than by the eye.

—Homer (Note to reader: This is NOT Homer Simpson)
circa 750 B.C.

Audio/visual equipment and computers

WHY VISUALS ARE EFFECTIVE

The standard types of audio/visual equipment and the more modern computer generated images and multimedia can be used as alternative ways to add humor, excitement, and clarity to your presentations. Slides, overhead transparencies, and flip charts are the old, but very effective, standards. Video, CD-ROM, and other forms of electronic multimedia are becoming cheaper and easier to use. All these methods allow the media to display the humor, which takes at least some of the pressure off you, the presenter.

CHAPTER 16

Don't get me wrong. Using audio/visual devices still requires timing, practice, and a good selection of humor. It also adds equipment failure to the mix of problems you may have to face during your presentation. (Have prepared one-liners, such as those found in Chapter 9, ready because projectors and other forms of A/V can be a source of problems). Audio/visual equipment does, however, allow you the option of simply displaying humor that is in itself funny. You may choose to add spoken lines before, during, or after the display to make the humor even better.

> *Things seen are mightier than things heard.*
> Alfred Lord Tennyson

I'm a firm believer in the concept of understanding the rules before you break them. You should know how to use your equipment properly, and the advantages and disadvantages of each piece, before you try to use it to help you be funny

Coming up:
Overhead Projection, Slide Projection, Flip Charts, Video Projection, Computers and Multimedia

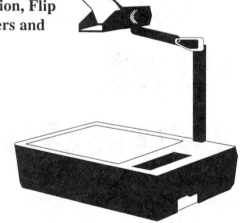

OVERHEAD PROJECTION
Why should I use overhead projection?
Controlled studies at the Wharton School of Business and the University of Minnesota have shown

● Overhead visuals (slides and overhead transparencies) produced quicker decisions, and the presenters who used them were more apt to win favorable decisions.

● Using overhead transparencies resulted in meetings that were 28 percent shorter—meaning meetings were more efficient.

● Overhead projection is considered more interesting than slides (both have 43 percent more persuasiveness).

Other good things about overhead projection:

● Transparencies are easy and inexpensive to produce.

- You can interact with the visual by writing on it.

- The equipment is easily transportable.

- The room lights can be left on, making note taking easier.

- The wall can be used as a screen if necessary.

- You can always face the audience.

Projection Setup

When using projected visuals, or any visuals, it is important to incorporate them into your presentation from the beginning. You will want to plan your visuals to enhance your presentation. You don't want them to compete with you for attention.

Decide early what percentage of your presentation will be based on visuals. This will help you decide how to seat the audience for maximum comfort. It will also help you make screen placement decisions. A very high percentage of visual use may warrant a more central screen placement. In this case, you would stand off to the side. You don't want the audience to try to look through you to see the screen.

Make sure there are one or two spare projection bulbs with the projector and that they work. You should figure out ahead of time how to change the bulb if it does burn out. It's even better to use a projector that allows you to switch bulbs instantly if one burns out. Don't forget to check both bulbs before the presentation.

Please, oh please, locate the on/off switch before you get started. If you have faithfully checked out the bulbs, this chore would have been done automatically. Nothing will make you look worse than fumbling around with simple equipment. OK, maybe continually tripping over the microphone cord might make you look worse. You may as well write on the flip chart, (since you can't get the overhead turned on) *I haven't prepared for this presentation.*

Also, have a backup plan. All your bulbs may blow, the electricity may go out, or the last presenter may pick up and run off with your overheads. You should never miss a beat if you have an equipment failure. Have an exercise ready to go while you work with the equipment or take a short break and get a new piece of equipment (you already know who to call and what spare equipment is available, don't you?). If you aren't using surprise visuals, you could reproduce them in the handout material just in case all your equipment malfunctions. In any case, never lose your sense of humor and to borrow from a famous fashion designer whose name I can't remember, "Never let them see you sweat."

Once you've switched on the overhead and have it aligned on the screen, have someone stand where you will be standing when using the overhead. Then, sit in many different audience seats to make sure everyone will be able to see your visuals. If you find seats that have an obstructed view, pull out those chairs or move them. You will have very frustrated (and disconnected) audience members if they cannot see your visuals.

When I'm going through this setup period, I am projecting a homemade focusing and alignment transparency. This transparency has vertical and horizontal lines and circles. This helps me line up the projector and transparency centering device. The transparency centering device is a glass plate housed in a plastic frame which sits on top of the lens of the overhead projector. The plastic frame is the exact size of an overhead transparency. Without looking at the screen I am able to put the transparency into this frame and I know it is exactly centered on the screen. This gives me a polished look and it will do the same for you. Don't you hate it when the overheads are slapped on any which way?

Also, when preparing overheads for a presentation, keep them all in the same orientation, i.e., all horizontal (landscape orientation) or all vertical (portrait orientation).

Projection Screen

When using projection of any kind, try to avoid rooms with low ceilings and/or chandeliers. It won't make much difference for small audiences, but for large ones it is quite important. If the screen is too low, it makes it virtually impossible for those in the back to see and, of course, a low hanging chandelier will obstruct the audience's view.

If you have a choice, ask for a matte finish screen. It gives the greatest horizontal viewing angle so people looking at the screen at an angle will be able to see the image more clearly. All screens must be tilted forward at the top or backward at the bottom to eliminate the keystone effect (top of image is wider than bottom). Many portable screens have a *keystone eliminator* at the top, or you can simply use masking tape on the lens of the projector to square off the image.

Most of the time you will try to place the screen at an angle in the front corner of the room (see Illustration 3-2). This way the screen is not directly behind you competing for the audience's attention. The lights right above the screen should be turned off so the image doesn't get washed out.

Correct Overhead Projection

The biggest mistake I see when critiquing presentations is the presenter talking to the screen instead of to the audience. There is ABSOLUTELY no reason for this. If you want to refer to the overhead to jog your memory, simply glance down at it on the lens of the projector. Then look back at the audience. Much of your impact as a presenter in North America comes from eye contact with the audience members. Don't ever lose *sight* of that. (I can't believe I used a dumb pun like that. I would never do that in real life.)

Another common problem I see is the incorrect or nonexistent use of pointers. If they are used properly, pointers are great in helping to draw attention to specific areas of your visual.

I prefer using a short pointer which I point at the projector. This allows me full eye contact with the audience. I don't have to turn away from the audience to locate the portion of the screen I'm pointing to. If I'm using mounted transparencies, I can write notes on the transparency mounts. The tip here is to touch the pointer to the transparency to steady it or lay the pointer on the projector. If you don't, and if you are the least bit nervous or shaky, the shakiness will be amplified many times on the screen. And here's another no-no. Don't point to the projector and turn around and look at the screen to see if the pointer is showing up. Believe me, it is. I guarantee it. There is no need to look.

If you feel you must point at the screen, be sure to use a long pointer. Hold it with the hand closest to the screen. Do not cross your body with the pointer. If you are going to talk while pointing, turn your head back toward the audience while doing so.

One other neat pointer is the laser. However, laser pointers are still not widely used and thus are somewhat of a novelty item, so use them sparingly. When you do use a laser pointer, you should make tiny circles over the area to which you are pointing. This is for the same reason you should lay the short pointer on the projector lens. That is, any tiny shake in your hand will be magnified many times and will make you look nervous, even if you are not. Intentional circling eliminates this problem. Lastly, with regard to any kind of pointer, don't play with it. It is distracting.

One of the most thoughtless practices I have seen while working with a company on presentation skills was that the presenter had turned the lights off to use its overhead projector. One of the main features of overhead projection is that you don't need to turn the lights off. Turning the lights off is a sure-fire way of putting the audience to sleep, and it also makes it hard to take notes. I really try to avoid dimming the lights, except for a special effect under very controlled circumstances.

Whether the lights are off or not, it is hard on the audience to look at a blaring white screen. When you are changing transparencies, do it quickly so the blank white screen doesn't reflect into the eyes of the audience. You could also use a piece of paper or cardboard to black out the screen, turn the projector off between overheads, or use light blue transparencies to take the edge off the harsh white light.

When you are doing a significant amount of talking between overheads, you may consider turning the projector off. You must decide if the particular visual will help keep the audience on track, or if it is competing with you for the audience's attention.

Overhead projectors also allow you to use two types of visual techniques that you cannot use with a single slide projector: Reveals and overlays let you give related visual information to the audience in small doses.

A reveal is a process whereby a blackout paper or piece of cardboard is slid down the transparency so that only part of the information on the transparency is *revealed*. This is useful if you want to create an element of surprise, or if showing the entire visual would create confusion. Without this technique, the audience members might be tempted to read ahead. They won't hear what you are talking about. The only problem with reveals is that, if you are not careful, the blackout sheet tends to fall off the projector as it is slid toward the bottom of the transparency.

Overlays are several transparencies sandwiched on top of each other. Each transparency adds an element to the overall picture. To make an overlay, you create the layers on separate transparencies then stack one upon the other. Use transparent tape to create a "hinge" that will allow the top layer of the over-

> *The best way to fight temptation is to get rid of it.*
> Uncle Martin
> *My Favorite Martian*

lay to open up. You can create several layers and hinge them on the other edges of the main transparency.

I recently saw a remote control device designed to change overhead transparencies. You load your transparencies in a feeder tray, hit the advance button, and your first transparency slides right into place on the projector lens. When you hit the remote control again, your second transparency slides into place while your first goes back into another tray. Pretty neat, huh? This means that now you can be anywhere in the room and still be able to change transparencies.

About the only uncorrectable problem concerning overhead projection is that it doesn't work very well for large audiences. Another minor problem is keeping the transparencies protected from dust, dirt, and fingerprints. To help with this, I enclose my transparencies in sheet protectors until I'm ready to use them and then carry the sheet protectors in a three-ring binder.

I've got one last tip on using overheads. Don't start packing up your transparencies before you make your powerful conclusion. It will weaken your ending significantly.

Here are what studies have shown: The presenter that used overhead transparencies in his or her presentation was perceived as significantly better prepared, more professional, more persuasive, more credible and more interesting than the presenter who did not use overhead transparencies.

Summary of overhead projector advantages:

● Easy to operate.

● Transparencies easy to create.

● Readily available and easily portable.

● Room lighting can stay bright.

● Transparencies allow note space on each frame.

● The presenter can easily add or skip material.

● Shorter meetings.

● Helps eliminate wasted discussion.

● Projection leads to faster group decisions.

● More meetings successfully arrive at decisions.

● Presenter perceived as more professional, more interesting, and better prepared.

● Participants understand subject much better.

SLIDE PROJECTION

Slides are considered to be more formal than overhead transparencies and the presenters that use them are considered to be slightly more professional. The downside is that along with this perceived formality goes a distancing from the audience. In general, presenters that use slides are considered more impersonal.

This does not mean you can't be funny with slides. In the section on signs, I mentioned my friend John Jay Daly, who does a hilarious slide presentation. He developed it by taking slides of interesting and goofy signs that can actually be seen around Washington, D.C.

Slides are both easily portable and getting much cheaper and faster to produce. Slides are still the only really sharp medium (besides film) that can be seen by large audiences (roughly 300 or larger). Also, slides are the one medium that make photographs look really great. By using a wireless microphone and a wireless remote control for your slide projector, you can literally be anywhere in the room and still control the show.

On the downside, slides require that the room lights be dimmed. Also, it is hard to make changes once you begin a slide program. There is no way to skip material without each slide coming into view, albeit briefly. It's also quite an ordeal to change the order of your slides.

The only way to achieve humor with a slide projector is to make funny slides. Two slides of the same funny item will have different impacts depending on the framing. The technique is to virtually fill the frame with the funny item whenever possible (Illustration 16-1).

Illustration 16-1 Fill the frame for greater impact

FLIP CHARTS

The common flip chart is probably the most used, and *underused*, piece of presentation equipment. I didn't realize how I was underusing flip charts until I read the book *Flip Charts: How to Draw Them and How to Use Them* by Richard C. Brandt. This book goes into unbelievable detail on all the cool things you can do with flip charts.

Since I do mostly keynote presentations without flip charts, I won't pretend to be the expert, but I will give you some basic information on their use and, of course, some ways to make them funny. I'm not going to talk about desktop flip charts, because I'm not a fan of little bitty presentations. I don't care if it's a one-on-one presentation. Create impact. Do a stand-up presentation using full size equipment.

Flip charts have many advantages. They are simple, inexpensive, dependable (no electricity to go off or bulbs to burn out), versatile, and the room is normally at full brightness when flip charts are in use. The biggest disadvantage of flip charts is that they can only be used in small crowds. I've never tried it, but I always thought that a dark room with slides and a spotlit flip chart would be unique. If you try this, you might want to use special blue flip chart paper so the audience's eyes don't bug out from the stark contrast.

If your handwriting is as terrible as mine, you might want to have an audience member who has good handwriting help you. This would be a great way to get involvement and it's a way to turn a weakness (poor handwriting) into something positive.

If you are using the flip chart to record audience comments, condense their words, but don't paraphrase. Also, don't say things like *That's a good one* to every audience response. Not only do these types of comments become repetitious, but if you don't say it to everyone, those left out may feel you think their contributions were dumb.

Try not to talk to the flip chart. This is more difficult than not talking to your projection screen because you are writing on the flip chart. Make a real effort to look at the audience over your shoulder if you are forced to talk while you are writing.

If you would like to include artwork on pre-drawn flip chart pages you can do that too, even if you don't have an artistic bone in your body (again, like me). Here's how: Artwork on an overhead transparency can be projected onto your flip chart page. You simply trace the image right on the page. With all the cheap and easy to use electronic clipart available, you have tens of thousands of images available. Simply print them as transparencies, project and trace, and you've got an inexpensive custom flip chart image.

If you've got a little bigger budget, you can get a poster machine. All you do is put in your 8.5" x 11" original, push the start button and out the other end comes a full color flip chart sized posters. If you can't afford a machine like this, you may be able to lease one on a per page basis. On-line plotters are also available if you have lots of money.

Here's another wild idea if you have a larger crowd. Get some helpers and on cue have them march into the crowd carrying flip charts to different areas of the audience. Appoint impromptu recorders/presenters all over the crowd and have them discuss and record their section's view on the particular subject. Have each section report their ideas. (OK, I admit this is kind of wild, but so what?) It's a lot better to push your limits toward excitement, than let them fall asleep. Here are a couple more fun ways to use flip charts.

One thing I like to do is violently rip the pages off when I'm done with them. I crumple them up and throw them all over the place. Another thing you could do is, accidentally on purpose, flip over a page to show something embarrassing like a grocery list or reminder from your spouse. You could reveal scribbling or a stick figure as if your kids got hold of the pad.

Many presenters hang flip charts on the wall to use as notes or constant reminders to the audience of the points that have been made. Why not have some fun with this? You could have a flip chart page covering a funny blowup of the CEO or some other funny picture. You would again, accidentally on purpose, make the page fall from the wall which would reveal the joke.

Extra Flip Chart Tips

● Black, blue, and green inks have the greatest visibility.

● Blue is the most pleasing color to look at with red coming in second (pleasing to look at and visibility are not the same).

● Don't do the whole chart in red ink.

● Avoid purple, brown, pink, and yellow inks.

● Use underlines to emphasize.

● Make letters large and bold.

● Permanent markers give the most vivid color, but dry out faster if you leave the cap off and bleed through to the next page. The ink is extremely difficult to get out of clothing.

● Water colors don't bleed as much and you can clean the ink out of clothing, but they give less vivid colors, and they squeak when writing.

● You might want to reproduce your major flip charts in the handout material for take-home value.

● Don't pre-number flip charts when you are looking for audience ideas. If you put six numbers on the chart and the audience can only come up with five ideas, they feel like they have failed.

● Title your charts and use some type of graphic element or artwork to make them more memorable and better looking.

VIDEO

Video has been ingrained in our society for some time now and it looks as if it will be around for quite a while. VCRs and monitors are readily and inexpensively available just about anywhere, so considering the use of video in your presentation is not really a wild idea.

Video can be used in several ways. You can purchase or rent training videos on just about any business subject. John Cleese, of *Monty Python* fame, is doing corporate videos that are interesting and informative and, of course, have a humor twist. John's videos are available from many sources. For fast and reliable service, I recommend The Humor Project (see Appendix B).

If you're the CEO of a company, you could produce a funny *day-in-the-life* tape which could be very self-effacing. Maybe you would wake up at 11:30 a.m. Then you would shower and go to lunch. After that it is time to stop in to say "hi" to your secretary. Then you might go to the golf course, on to dinner, and then to the theater. The ending scene would show how exhausted you are at the end of the day.

I use FREEZE FRAME video when I do my presentation skills training seminars and individual coaching. This technique consistently gets super high ratings because people can learn techniques better when they see them in action.

I heard of one presenter who played a video of himself telling the crowd that he wouldn't be able to be there in person. He then ran on stage and argued with himself on the video.

You could use video to show your product in action. Video can capture and convey situations that you could never reproduce on-stage.

I sometimes use a video introduction that is very funny. The scene shows a lady at a desk who is supposed to be one of the top meeting planners in the country. She is saying that she uses me for every meeting and social function her company ever has. She says, "In fact, I wouldn't use another speaker if you held a gun to my head." As she is saying this, the camera pulls back and you see me holding a gun to her head. It always gets a big laugh.

I saw Frank McGuire, one of the founders of FedEx, use a video introduction that had Ted Koppel saying how great Frank was. If you know any celebrities, video is a good way to use their testimonials over and over again.

You could briefly show home video of you doing something funny. Or you could show how proud you are of your kids (just don't overdo it).

For maximum effectiveness when using video, interact with it. Interrupt the video and discuss what you have just seen. Keep video shots fast-paced with short segments. According to *Business Week,* the average U.S. executive has an attention span of six minutes while at work. We are starting to talk to the MTV generation. TV is shaping the minds of our audiences.

An interesting phenomenon occurs when you are speaking in a large venue and also being projected on massive video screens. Audience members will actually look past *you* to watch *you* on video.

When you are in a large room, you must use several monitors or use video projection. Projection on a large screen has more impact, but it is also more expensive. Projection also requires that the room lights be dimmed.

You can even use a video camera to take shots of the crowd and put them in a video production immediately using multimedia and a video capture board. How do you do this? I don't know, but I assure you you can do it with a computer.

COMPUTERS (PRE-PROGRAM)

With lowering prices, increasing power and ease of use, computers can tremendously assist you in your quest to be a No ZZZZZs presenter. For most presentations, computers are much more useful in preparation than in the actual delivery. I use my computer to help me with every presentation I give. I use it to keep track of what hotel I'm staying at, to remind me to call the meeting planner, to make the handout masters, and to keep track of all my reference materials and humor. Sometimes I use it to make custom crossword puzzles based on the pre-program research I did for the group. Most of the graphics in this book were created on my computer. Even some of the cartoons were in electronic clipart collections. All I did was change the captions.

I could have just as easily used my computer to output these graphs and cartoons to my laser printer for instant overhead transparencies. If you want vivid color on your transparencies, you could output to a color laser printer or less expensively to an ink or bubble jet printer. If you want extremely high resolution, you can output your files to a disc and give the disc to a service bureau or transmit the files by modem. This method is considerably more expensive per overhead and, at the time of this writing, is the only affordable option for computer-generated slides.

I also use my computer extensively for research. It used to take me hours of library time to find the smallest bits of information. Now I do it all and I do it better right from my desktop.

I have an up-to-date encyclopedia on CD-ROM. In a matter of seconds it gives me information that would take at least five minutes to find by going to my set of encyclopedias. You might say, "Tom, a couple of minutes savings is no big deal."

It is a big deal when you are under tremendous time constraints, not to mention the distraction and loss of your train of thought that will occur if you get up and leave your workstation. Also, I would like to see you trying to carry a set of encyclopedias on an airplane.

I also use the online service CompuServe to do my research for me while I sleep. I subscribe to the Executive Option of CompuServe which is an electronic clipping service. It searches the current news media 24 hours a day, based on key words I enter. For instance, if I'm speaking to Hallmark Cards, I put in key words or phrases like *Greeting Card, Hallmark, American Greetings* (their major competitor), etc. The computer searches for those key terms and saves any article that comes up that includes them. All I have to do is download them to my computer and use what I need. For past articles that may have my key words included, CompuServe also has magazine databases, health databases, and many others. There are small charges for these services, but the time savings is tremendous. Ask your computer advisor about other specialized databases that may be available in your field.

For humor, you can get joke programs that are searchable. I use a program called *Just Joking* by Wordstar Co. (see Appendix B). It has 2,800 jokes and humorous quotes in 250 topic areas. In moments, I can find many usable items. By the time you read this there will undoubtably be many others on the market for both Mac and IBM computers.

If you really want to take a stab at humor writing, *Comedy Writer*™ (also see Appendix B) will certainly be useful. It is a Windows based program that helps you create humorous scenes, characters, situations, dialogue, expressions and punch lines.

Internet

Internet access is getting really easy and really cheap and it literally has tons of humor and other research material available (if you printed it all out). Keep in mind that the Internet is virtually unregulated so you may run across quite a bit of gross and totally unusable humor. Overall *surfing the net* is a really easy method to come up with humor (and any kind of serious info too). Here are some of my favorite easy-to-find humor sites:

Jokes and Humor Web Sites

www.swcbc.com/humor.html

The Mother of All Humor Archives

www.cs.cornell.edu/info/People/ckline/humor/maillist.html

Humor on the Web
www.cybertown.com/humor.html

Murphy's Laws
www.Misty.com/laughweb/murphy/murphys.laws.html

Here are a few more handy quotation sites:

Big list of quotation sources
www.Yahoo.com/reference/Quotations/

Bartlett's Familiar Quotations
www.cc.columbia.edu/acis/bartleby/bartlett/

Multimedia

In the good old days (translates to last year), *multimedia* meant using several different media in the same presentation. You might be using overheads and slides on different screens or you might be using several slide projectors on the same screen with a tape recorder providing music or narration. Now the term *multimedia* carries a whole new meaning. In present day terms, multimedia means you are using a computer-controlled presentation that may include full color, sound, video, graphics, animation, and text.

Computer-based presentations can be great, although they are definitely risky, just like any other presentation that relies heavily on equipment. The risk is lowered if you are really good at quick computer trouble-shooting and if you are the only one using the equipment. Keep in mind that computers can *help* you become a better presenter than you are now, but they will not make you a good presenter in the first place. In fact, they might just show up how bad you are if you rely on them too heavily. My advice is to have a well thought out and rehearsed backup plan in case of a malfunction.

I attended a trade show not too long ago where a major vendor of multimedia software was doing a demonstration. The equipment malfunctioned and there was no backup plan. The audience members were walking out laughing. How embarrassing! Don't let that happen to you.

Computer software and hardware change very rapidly. To keep up with the latest multimedia innovations, check the computer section of your local newsstand and/or visit one of the larger computer superstores.

COMPUTERS (POST-PROGRAM)

I use my computer for various functions after a program. I usually input the attendee list, create mailing labels, and do a mailing in an effort to get feedback and/or leads for future presentations. I do the expense billing, and I keep track of what humor or stories I actually used so that I don't repeat them if I am invited back.

A/V TIPS GALORE
Five tips on how to be funny while using A/V

- Project a funny opening overhead or slide to help people get *in fun* as they arrive for the presentation.

- Use a funny pointer. I have several small pointers that I use for overhead projection. One looks like a little hand pointing a finger, one is a bunny rabbit, and one is a dinosaur. They never fail to get a laugh when I use them. The trick is to put them on the overhead projector and go on with the presentation as if nothing is happening (deadpan expression). The bunny and dinosaur are simply erasers on children's pencils. The little hand was purchased from a presentation supply company. If I feel like pointing to the screen, I use a plastic "may the force be with you" sword. You could use a golf club or baseball bat or whatever you want. Try to find some excuse to tie the prop pointer into the theme of your presentation, i.e., (for a golf club) *If we use ABC method we are likely to score a hole in one.*

- Use the element of surprise. Don't tell the audience that a funny slide or overhead is coming.

- **BRIEFLY** show self-effacing or funny life shots of you, or your family, your kids, your dog, etc. Let them pop on the screen as if they accidentally got mixed in with your business slides or overheads. With flip charts, turn the page to accidentally on purpose show your children's scribbling or a grocery note from your spouse, etc.

- Fill up the frame with your funny object when using slides, overheads, or video. The impact is much greater.

Overhead/Slide Design Tips

One of the reasons we use visuals is that the audience can get the significance of a graph, picture, or bulleted item much more quickly than they can understand a bunch of numbers or extensive text. This only holds true if the visuals are created properly. Many of the visuals I see are so cluttered and confusing they create more *misunderstanding* than *understanding*. Here are some design tips that will keep your visuals attractive and understandable.

- **Title your visuals.** Titles should be 48-point type and above. Subtitles should be in the 36-to 46-point range.

- **Use all uppercase sparingly.** All uppercase is hard to read. It is usually only used in titles.

CUMMULATIVE SALES YTD		
Western Division	Central Division	Eastern Division
Jan 27,645.27	35,277.43	24,488.84
Feb 32,894.76	41,446.98	22,850.72
March 29,446.67	37,968.45	19,558.83
April 33,098.51	33,659.21	21,934.77
May 31,234.85	38,224.75	23,568.54
June 24,142.88	36,432.89	25,499.76
July 38,704.27	40,214.77	19,993.21
Aug 36,666.43	39,435.88	20,054.87
253,833.64	302,660.36	177,949.54

Illustration 16-2 Poor visual design that contains too many numbers.
If these numbers are critical, put them in a handout.

CUMULATIVE SALES YTD*

Western	Central	Eastern
253,833	302,660	177,949

*Through August 31

Illustration 16-3 Design is much better.
Letters are bold. Cents, monthly figures and extra words have been eliminated. Visual is clear and uncluttered.

- **Use only one or two plain typefaces.** Just because you have 800 fonts on a CD-ROM, doesn't mean they will all look good on a visual. Stay very simple with the font.

- **Bold and big is better.** Bold text is easier to read at a distance. Body text should be at least 24-point type, but bigger is truly better.

- **Add drop shadows.** Most computer programs easily add drop shadows to your text which adds an attractive depth to your visuals.

- **Use contrasting type and backgrounds.** In a dimly lit room use light text and graphics on a dark background. In a well-lit room use dark text and graphics on a light background.

- **If possible, use the same background for all visuals in the same presentation.** This gives a well planned, consistent and polished look. Many well-designed templates are available in presentation and graphic programs.

- **Use subtle graphic elements and/or gradations of color in backgrounds to add interest.** Do not get so wild with the background that it competes with your message.

- **Bullets or numbers?** Use bullets to list items in no particular order. Use numbers to express order of importance or items that must be done in sequence.

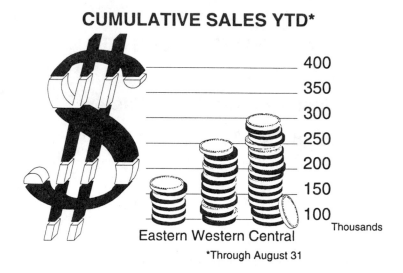

Illustration 16-4 Same information as above in graph form.

● **Use simple, short words.** Avoid technical jargon and *fancy* language. It causes the audience to turn off and tune out.

● **Use short lines.** Try to use fewer than seven words per line.

● **Use short columns.** Try to use fewer than seven lines per visual (this includes extra spaces between lines).

● **Use upper part of frame.** Try to keep your text and graphics in the upper two-thirds of your visual so people in the back can see.

● **Use one visual per visual.** Try to use only one chart, graph, cartoon, or illustration per visual to avoid crowding and confusion.

● **Triple check all spellings and math.** Misspelled words and numbers that don't add up will seriously detract from your credibility. Have some pre-planned ad-libs ready to go just in case.

● **Use color thoughtfully.** Use bright colors for small graphics to make them stand out and more subtle colors for large graphics so they don't overwhelm. Avoid red for text.

- **Use color psychologically.** According to Greg Bandy in *Multimedia Presentation Design for the Uninitiated,* certain colors evoke certain emotions.

RED = Brutal, Dangerous, Hot, Stop!
DARK BLUE = Stable, Trustworthy, Calm.
LIGHT BLUE = Cool, Refreshing.
GRAY = Integrity, Neutral, Mature.
PURPLE = Regal, Mysterious.
GREEN = Organic, Healthy, New Life, Go, Money.
ORANGE/YELLOW = Sunny, Bright, Warm.
WHITE = Pure, Hopeful, Clean.
BLACK = Serious, Heavy, Profitable, Death.

Since death is a pretty heavy way to end this chapter I think I'll give you a couple more bonus tips.

Bonus tip: When the audience is focused on your visual, you can peek at your notes without their knowing.

Bonus tip: Duplicate your visuals on your notes to reduce the urge to read from the screen or chart.

Bonus
Chapters

No one ever lost credibility by being interesting.

—Tom Antion, your humble author

Technical and financial presentations

Are you ready for a sweeping generalization? Well here it is. Technical and financial information can be boring and dry. There, I said it. Technical and financial presenters need the information in this book more than anyone. The good thing is that they don't have to use too much of the information in this book to dramatically increase their effectiveness.

CHAPTER 17

A survey of the faculty of engineering schools showed that 15% of an engineer's future success depends upon engineering skills, while 85% depends upon communication skills. The problem is that most engineering schools don't emphasize communication skills. There are so many numbers and equations flying around that no one worries too much about whether someone can explain them or not.

At conferences, many technical presenters are picked on the basis of their research. Many of them hate presenting or even being with people. That is why they chose a profession that hides them away in a lab. Some brilliant technical people think the audience just isn't smart enough to understand their concepts. They take no responsibility at all for making their information understandable and interesting. They think it's "Mickey Mouse" for them to try to be interesting.

Why are most technical presenters horrendously boring to a general audience? The technical professions train people to look for detail. If a detail is missed, the whole project falls apart. A techie once told me, "When I'm talking to you or to an audience, I'm carefully building a bridge in my mind. I'm going to tell you about every part of that bridge whether you want to hear it or not." That might be OK for a technical audience that has to go out and build the same bridge, but it is bomb city to an audience who is only interested in finding out where the bridge is going.

Was that techie at fault? Not really. He was just applying the learning template he lived by all the way through school.

To help us understand how to be successful in delivering technical information I have recruited fellow National Speakers Association member Mike Rounds who is one of the top presenters in the country on the subject of the Internet. Mike is Past President of the Greater Los Angeles Chapter of NSA and a Lead Trainer for Career Track.

CREATING A FAVORABLE LEARNING SITUATION

With the world of technology changing at such a rapid pace, it's not surprising that more and more presentations are being geared towards the technological side of learning, or the "hard skills" types of programs. The nature and content of these programs has to be different from the "soft skills" or motivational programs because the needs and the expectations of the audience are different. The attendees look upon the time spent as a learning investment. They expect high content to be delivered in an understandable and usable manner during the allocated times.

Humor, as an end in itself, will not be appreciated. It's best to use humor that is specific to the discipline and that will probably only be understood and/or appreciated by the attendees who have an intimate knowledge of the topic. (General humor will be considered as time wasting and irrelevant.)

Stories are another good type of humor. Stories to which the attendees can directly relate, and ones that demonstrate practical methodologies of what to do or what to avoid, will assist the attendees in empathizing with the information being taught. On the other hand, typical "shaggy dog" stories and tales that would normally bring the audience to tears or result in a standing ovation will fall flat when addressing a technical audience.

Most technical session attendees are used to receiving information through a highly structured and organized means. They generally appreciate a bulleted outline of what is to be covered and expect the presenter to cover all of the points promised in a timely and expeditious manner. Time will become critical because of the volume of information to be delivered without leaving out anything important.

Always evaluate your material for flow and time allocation and remember that the audience has no idea of what you leave out, as long as you address each point promised to some degree.

If you are concerned about having too much material for the time allocated, seriously consider creating a detailed handout with all of the relevant information and only address the spots of critical concern in the presentation. Technical audiences **always** appreciate having a written document with lots of details that they can refer to later.

As with every other learning situation, your presentation should be geared to the needs of the participants. The most important characteristic to consider for a one-to-three-hour session is the demographics of your participants. Demographics are not just age, sex, income, and education, although these may be very important to know. You also want to know the learners' level of knowledge about the subject, their problems and needs, and how they are going to use the information you are giving them.

There are many reasons why the one-to-three- hour session is an ideal learning setting:

● Your participants will be ready to learn.

● The environment is most likely to be comfortable and conducive to learning.

● The learners will give you their full attention for the entire session.

For all these reasons, you have a favorable learning situation. The technical teaching situation in general is one of the better and more challenging situations in which to work. The one threat to the success of your session is time, yet time also can be a wonderful ally.

You can turn time from a negative into a positive by narrowing down your subject, providing lots of information within a short period of time, looking for how-to, practical implications, and gearing your presentation to the audience. Stay away from explanations of your own situation. Instead, rephrase your comments from "The way we do it is . . ." to "You can utilize this concept by . . . ." Use the second person "you" in your talk and, more important, think in the second person. You will be more apt to influence your audience by stating your case in their terms and from their perspective. Distill your information down to the essential core. Look for the golden nugget of ideas that will convey your message.

And best of all, leave them a little hungry. If your participants are concerned about the lack of time, or how they could have listened to you for another two hours, that is a compliment.

It is far better to leave your participants wanting more than to leave them looking at their watches wondering when it is going to end. Turn the brevity of time into a plus by making your presentation concise, going after the essence of your ideas, being learner-centered rather than self-centered, and relating all your content to your audience.

INVOLVING YOUR PARTICIPANTS

Interacting with your participants generally increases their learning, holds their attention, helps you make your points, and possibly provides for new information to be shared. Technical presentations hold some different challenges because most of the participants will be writing and taking notes throughout the program. Interactive processes **must** enhance the learning process and not just provide a break or entertainment. There are lots of proven techniques, but the introduction seems to work best of all and will, as a general rule, get most if not all of the attendees to participate.

Attendees at a technical session generally have a specific need in mind when they sign up for the program. By getting them to open up and share their needs, all the participants stand to benefit from the applications and concerns of someone else. In other words, there is a sharing of goals, concerns, and needs which may become as relevant and valuable to the participants as the materials you present.

Participant introductions serve two useful purposes. First, getting people to say anything at the beginning of a session gets them involved and is a way to establish interest in what you will say afterward. And second, if the participants do not know each other they may find it useful to know who is in the room.

On the other hand, introductions can take up a lot of time. People can insert many irrelevant comments and take up valuable time talking about themselves. If your session is part of a larger program, like a conference, introductions may not fit into the workshop format. The critical consideration in whether to have participants introduce themselves is time. For instance, if there were 15 people in the room for a three-hour session, introductions might be helpful. If there are 60 people in the room for a one-hour program, the time constraint would eliminate the possibility of adequate introductions.

INCLUDING ALL THE CHARACTERISTICS OF A GOOD TECHNICAL PROGRAM

An effective technical program will meet the following criteria:

● It will provide information that is generally useful. People resent being in a session that squanders their valuable time by presenting information which is superficial, unnecessary, or can be easily obtained elsewhere. The resulting unfavorable word-of-mouth publicity will make it difficult for the program or the presenter to survive.

- It will provide specific, "how-to" information, rather than theoretical concepts. Training should be designed to effect measurable change that will improve a participant's productivity, ability, or practical skills, with a minimum expenditure of resources. It is not intended to replace or compete with a broad education generally provided by the regular curricula of colleges and universities in our society.

- It will enable participants to get all necessary information in the shortest possible time. Technical seminars and workshops appeal to those who want a thorough understanding of a subject in a short period of intensive learning.

- It will provide support materials to supplement the program. Materials should be designed to help a participant organize new information during the presentation, as well as access and review it easily afterward.

- It will provide an avenue for further learning. A good program will pave the way for future studies either through a participant's own research, the starting points you provided, or the resources provided in your materials, including any further information and bibliographic citations.

- It will entertain as well as inform. Humor, judiciously used in the context of the topic being discussed, contributes to a lively and interesting presentation, and enhances the learning process.

- It will provide a "status report" to participants on a regular basis. Periodic summaries of topics covered will help people organize their new knowledge. Giving quick previews of upcoming subjects and using question-and-answer sessions will actively engage the participants in the learning process, instead of allowing them to slip into a "passive recipient" mode.

- It will provide an opportunity for the practice of learned skills. If a program is designed to teach participants new abilities, opportunities should be built into the agenda for them to practically apply those skills.

- It will provide for participant comfort. Regularly scheduled breaks will go a long way to alleviate restlessness or boredom in your audience. Changes in training technique like moving from lecture to exercise to audio-visual presentation to discussion sessions, etc., will serve to keep participants interested and assist them in learning, due to the fact that different people are more receptive to different modes of learning.

CHOOSING THE APPROPRIATE PROGRAM LENGTH

The most important consideration in determining how long a technical seminar or workshop should be is the time required to cover the subject in sufficient detail. Some subjects require two or three days to tackle the complexities of a topic, while that amount of time would be superfluous in others. The burdens placed on the presenter(s) should also be considered. In a single-day program, chances are that one individual can handle the entire presentation. If it is longer, either more presenters will be necessary or more participant activity must be scheduled to ease the strain on the presenter.

In the world of speaking, there are speakers and there are trainers, and the two differ greatly in their content, styles, and goals. Trainers are far more concerned with the accuracy and relevance of the material content than a speaker will ever be and yet, they must be as entertaining and motivating as any other.

Technical trainers can seldom count on standing ovations, peals of laughter, or thunderous applause. What they can count on is being followed to the restroom and being asked questions. They can also count on people standing around waiting to tell of their experiences on the same topic.

Evaluations of trainers by attendees are usually sparse as well. Most trainers have discovered that the attendees have their own agenda when they arrive and their acceptance and satisfaction is totally dependent upon whether or not you live up to those preconceived expectations, whether they are a part of the program or not.

Evaluations will most often be extremely critical of facilities and temperature and will reflect learners' representations of what they think the trainer should be, irrespective of the material content.

Nevertheless, technical training can be one of the most rewarding of all presentations because you may have the opportunity to observe the participants taking "hard skills" with them that they can apply immediately to make their lives and businesses a fuller and richer medium for their personal growth and happiness.

Thanks, Mike, for a great section. Now here's what Doug Fox, another top technical trainer, does when it comes time to lighten up one of his programs.

One of the frustrating things about speaking is that sometimes the group on the other side of an air wall is having more fun than you and your attendees. There's nothing like making a serious point and hearing a huge roar of laughter coming from the adjacent room. It makes a speaker feel awkward, *How come they are having so much fun and my folks aren't even laughing?*

Well, I found the solution. I keep a set of three juggling balls concealed by the side of my computer (I do lots of computer presentations). If the group next door starts laughing loudly, I stop in the middle of my presentation and pause. I then say to my audience, "I hate when other people are having more fun than we are. I think we should get even." I then pick up my juggling balls and start to do a variety of juggling tricks. I juggle for about 20-30 seconds. I stop and everybody claps and cheers. Then, I turn to the offending folks across the air wall and say "Take that!" and I go on with the seminar.

USING TEAM PRESENTATIONS

Here I go again! One thing you can say about me is that I know where to go when I need help. Vern Hoven, from Vern Hoven Tax Seminars has found that presenting technical or financial topics with multiple speakers is an unusual, and exceptionally successful, alternative to the lecture. He told me to be sure to tell you that this is **not** the same thing as a panel discussion and it will work in many other settings beside technical and financial. Vern even told me that he gets less tired doing an eight-hour team presentation than doing four hours solo. Here is a checklist for team presentations that Vern says will help you out.

● Generally, have a left-stage speaker and a right-stage speaker. This requires the audience to physically move their eyes when listening, which keeps their interest.

● Make sure each member of the team is committed only to making the other speaker the hero. If one of the speakers tries to make his or her reputation at the expense of the other, there will be a disaster. Upstaging the partner is definitely no good. Don't do team teaching with a partner that you don't have 100 percent confidence in concerning commitment to the team. No stars are allowed!

● Inform the audience at the beginning of the day that a team presentation will be used. Otherwise the audience will think that the off-stage team member is "interrupting" the on-stage member.

● Let each team member start the day with a long enough segment to build his or her separate rapport with the audience.

● Use various team teaching concepts for variety. Eight hours of team teaching is no different than four hours of speaker number one and four hours of speaker number two.

For example:

A. Let each team member have one solo segment during the morning session and one in the afternoon session.

B. Try to change presenter every six minutes or so when team presenting.

C. Be spontaneous, not scripted, when both are experts in the same specific topic.

D. Some point/counterpoint action is fun, but watch out so that one party isn't perceived as too liberal or too conservative.

E. Use the technique of having one member ask the question (or set up the issue) and the other supply the answer. Keep in mind that this has the most risk of looking stilted and artificial. To make this work, the question asked must somehow be already in the minds of the attendees.

● To prevent the impression of rude interruptions by one team member, both team presenters must "interrupt" the other. This is done with meticulous advance planning by scripting who is in charge of each separate topic and when the transitions and interruptions are to occur . . . to the minute! Also make sure that at least every fourth comment praises the other partner. Note: There is actually very little spontaneity in team teaching.

● Allow the other presenter to leave the front while the on-stage speaker is teaching a longer segment. But, both speakers need to know the entire specific speaking schedule, in case the call back to the office takes too long and the on-stage speaker doesn't get back on time.

There should be one place for the off-stage speaker to sit, usually in front, or to the side nearest the exit, when the on-stage speaker is presenting. Of course, when interrupting, or during point/counterpoint, both should be in front. Sometimes though, you can make the whole room the theater! Choreograph the presentation by having the nondominant speaker interrupt from the side of the room, back of the room, etc.

● Evaluations are still needed for each speaker, but I have found that the evaluations are normally identical for both, and normally the lower scorer will be pulled up to the higher scorer's level. If one speaker is lower, the other speaker must help build up the lower speaker's score.

● Each speaker should have a separate cordless microphone and make it a rule that the mic will not be removed from the room! If it was accidentally left on, comments not meant for the audience's ears could be disastrous.

Do team presentations work? Vern's evaluations show that team teaching is more memorable to the audience than solo teaching.

So there you have it. There are no more excuses for ever delivering a boring technical or financial presentation again. Just follow the tips of Mike Rounds and Vern Hoven and you will be on your way.—Oh! Taking up juggling like Doug Fox wouldn't hurt either.

Dead men sell no tales.

—Carolyn Wells

Dead speakers sell no wares.

—Tom's rewrite

Sales presentations

If any time is critical to create excitement in a presentation, this is it. If you can't get someone excited about your idea, product, or service, it is unlikely you will ever be great in sales. I'm not necessarily talking about the wild excitement you see at some multilevel sales rallies. That kind of excitement might get you kicked out of a conservative organization. I'm talking about your ability to create the appropriate level of excitement to cause your client to want to sign on the dotted line.

One of the best sales tools I know of to create excitement is humor. Let me again qualify that. I mean appropriate humor. I say this because I also believe that

CHAPTER 18

if you won't take the time to gain the skills needed to determine appropriate levels and types of humor, you will do yourself more harm than good. It's just as we determined when we talked about touchy subjects. The rule is, "If in doubt, leave it out." According to Ed McMahon in his book, *Superselling,* there are three facts when it comes to sales:

Fact 1: We tend to buy from someone we trust.

Fact 2: We tend to trust someone we like.

Fact 3: We tend to like someone who makes us laugh.

His conclusion: You can become a more effective and successful salesperson by using humor in your sales presentation.

GETTING THE SALE

Humor can help you get the sales presentation in the first place. It will also help you stay upbeat in the face of rejection, overcome inevitable problems that arise during a presentation, break down sales resistance, and create loyal customers who will buy again. Let me tell you how humor has greatly helped me.

One of the ways professional speakers gain business is to do *no fee* demo talks in front of potential buyers. I was doing one of these talks for an advertising association in Washington, D.C. After the presentation, a lady came up to me and invited me to call her. She said my information would be perfect for the employees at her government agency. I called three times that week and did not get a return call. I called three times the next week and did not get a return call. I called three times the next week and the week after that. Finally, I got sick of calling so I sent her a funny fax.

She called back within the hour. I went down and got a $3000 contract and another one the following month for $2000. She said my fax really made her laugh in the midst of the constant pressure she was under and that's why she called.

Was my success in this case only because of the humor? No. It was a combination of humor and persistence.

You might be wondering how I could call someone 12 times in a month and not be considered a pest. In the first place, she specifically invited me to call. To me that means I'm

Just the Fax

Adrian: I know your workload is heavy. Please call me before you get completely crushed.

Tom

going to call her the rest of her life until she tells me to quit. In the second place, I knew she was a fun person because I saw her really enjoying the program where she met me. In the third place, I was lighthearted and fun on each phone call. I used mild exaggeration humor by saying things like, *I know you've got a six-foot stack of paperwork on your desk* or *I'll bet people are pitching tents in the line outside your office door.*

I do all sorts of things to help land the sales call. I sing on a prospect's voice mail, I send funny post cards, E-mail, gag gifts, and foods like candy, popcorn, doughnuts, and bagels. I always send humorous notes. I want my name to pop up when they need a speaker, seminar

> **Seasoned Sales Pro:** How ya doin'?
> **Green Recruit:** Not good. I've been insulted in every place I've made a call.
> **Seasoned Sales Pro:** That's funny. I've been on the road 40 years. I've had my samples flung in the street, been tossed down-stairs, manhandled by jani-tors, and rolled in the gutter, but insulted—NEVER.

leader, or consultant. Constant, interesting, and fun reminders will help you get the call when they have a need.

Humor is great in helping you stay upbeat in the face of outside pressures; multiple presentations; long, hard hours; and rejection. Let's face it. No one closes 100 percent of their sales. The sales profession is a profession of rejection. In fact, your ability to handle rejection probably has more to do with your success than any other sales skill.

I read humor books when I get up in the morning and before I go to bed at night. I listen to comedy tapes in the car. I watch funny videos and comedies on TV and at the movies. Laughing a little bit helps you forget about the last deal that was Soooooooo close before it fell apart. More importantly, laughing gets you in the proper, upbeat, and fun mood before you speak to the next prospect.

Being in the right mood is another critical factor in your success. If you could go back and analyze your sales successes you would most likely find that they came in clusters. Your excitement from one sale carried over and made you do a great job in front of the next prospect. Your ultimate success depends on your ability to create that excitement *at will* regardless of the outcome of your previous sales attempt. Adding humor to your life will help you do just that.

Joyce Saltman, a top presenter in the health care field, says, "Humor makes you look healthier. It even makes your cheeks rosy." She says this is important in sales because people are reluctant to purchase a product from someone who looks as if they will be dead before the warranty is up.

Humor is also great for helping you overcome problems that arise during a sales presentation (see "Pre-planned Ad-Libs," Chapter 9). You certainly don't want your one big chance in front of Megabucks Corporation to be blown because of minor problems.

I'm not suggesting you substitute clever one-liners for solid preparation. I'm suggesting that your ability to use appropriate humor in the face of adversity will send a subtle, but clear, message to your prospect. The message will be that you are polished and unshakable when a problem arises. Some salespeople are afraid of humor because they think they won't be taken seriously. In fact, being able to use appropriate humor makes you more powerful. Most experienced buyers have been around the business block a few times. They know that good buyer/seller relationships experience unforeseen problems all the time. Your cool, lighthearted demeanor will be giving them the impression you can calmly handle whatever might come up.

Another advantage of humor is that it can help break down the status barrier between the salesperson and the client. It helps build a rapport and a sense of *we* instead of *you and me* which makes your point of view, as the salesperson, much more persuasive. David Rich reports in his book, *How to Stay Motivated on a Daily Basis*, that even Las Vegas has learned the power of a smile. David says that black jack dealers who smile while they deal consistently bring in 5 percent more revenue than nonsmiling dealers. He says the reason is that people are more likely to play longer when they believe they are playing with the dealer against the house as opposed to playing against the dealer. David's advice: "Avoid the smiling dealers."

When people are laughing, they don't feel like they are being sold. Their resistance to the sales message is greatly reduced. That's why it is important to weave your humor in with the sales message rather than tell a joke at the beginning and then forget about humor.

If you add more humor to your daily life as we talked about a few paragraphs back, you will begin to notice humor to incorporate in your sales presentation that is both funny and supports your points. All you have to do is write it down and organize it so you can find it when you need it.

Joe Girard, who is recognized as the best car salesperson of all time, has no shame at all. He believes in showmanship to the maximum. He'll get down on his hands and knees and beg the person to sign the contract for the car. He'll lie down on his back and say, "I'm going to die if you don't buy this car." Of course, he gives a fair price and good honest service, but his humor and showmanship are what make him the greatest car salesman ever.

As wild as Joe gets, even he admits you must know your audience. Joe says, "You don't use these antics on really conservative types because they won't take you seriously."

I pay close attention to the demeanor of my sales prospects and I use test humor just as I do in my written introductions (see Chapter 4). I use any mild lighthearted comment and watch or listen closely for the prospect's response. If he or she brushes it off and gets back to business, you do the same. If he or she laughs or comes back with humor, you know you can use more humor as the sales process continues.

Prospects may not respond to humor all the time. Usually they are just too busy. When I hear a different tone in their voices, or observe some aloof body language, I normally just say Oh, you sound as if you are really busy. This is what I want to talk to you about. Do you have time? And they usually respond with "Thanks. I am busy. Let's talk another time." However, be alert if this happens several times. It could be that the change in their response indicates a change in their attitude toward you or your product or service. You need to act fast and ask a few delicate questions to see if something has shifted and, if it has, if there is anything you can do about it.

FOLLOWING UP AFTER THE SALE

Humor and lightheartedness can be used after the sale to maintain a nonthreatening presence with the customer. This also helps create loyal customers and repeat business. Customers see that you didn't disappear immediately after getting their money. My office assistant bought a new Saturn automobile a few years ago. About every three months she gets a letter from the salesperson who sold it to her. He writes her a poem. No doubt it is the same poem that goes out to all his customers, but so what? His name is always in front of her. For a few cents he is creating a loyal customer. In addition, the Saturn Corporation is always sending her customer satisfaction surveys to show they care.

Use product-related stories

You can bring your product to life in the eyes of the client with stories. I learned about this from the general manager at John Wanamaker Department store in Philadelphia, Pennsylvania, where I was doing a customer service presentation.

The manager was telling me about the time he and his wife were shopping for a handmade quilt to give as a wedding gift. They went to several different shops in eastern Pennsylvania. The people working at the shops were uninformed about and indifferent to the questions they asked about the history of the quilts. They eventually came upon a shop where the proprietor went into great detail about the person who actually made the quilt and about the origin of the material, thread, etc. Guess where the manager bought the quilt?

Of course, not all customers would want this level of detail. But the ones that do may be influenced to buy immediately if you are ready with this kind of information about your product, idea, or service.

You should also develop interesting or humorous stories or one-liners about how your product was used. For example when I was in high school, I used to sell matchbooks with advertising on them to small businesses. On a sales call I would put a used match in my wallet which I would pull out with great ceremony and say, "This is THE match that lit the bonfire we had just before winning the homecoming football game. You can have a match similar to this one." That would get the clients smiling. Then I sold them one or two cases of matchbooks.

Think up ways such as my one-liner to talk about your product, idea, or service to keep it in the customer's mind with a nonsales sales pitch. Product-related stories or jokes lend a favorable light to your product without increasing sales resistance.

TIPS GALORE
Tips for one-on-one or small boardroom presentations

Arrive slightly early to conduct up-to-the-minute research.

Make friends with the receptionists and/or secretaries. These people will pave the way to your success when it comes to access to the decision makers.

Pick up and/or read prospect related info from the lobby (you should try to get this in advance).

Notice the decor or any sign of humor or lightheartedness so you can refer to it if the prospect appears to be unhurried and friendly.

Stand up during your presentation. According to the University of Minnesota study mentioned in Chapter 10, your customers will be willing to pay 26 percent more money for your exact same product or service when you do a stand-up presentation using visuals. You can always find an excuse to stand. You might write on a white board or flip chart, etc. If you sit and the prospect happens to stand, you will be in a very weak position.

● Control the environment as best you can to avoid barriers between you and the client or attention-busters such as windows, doors, etc.

Try to make connections with what you learned from the lobby.

Pay close attention to the demeanor of the prospect and try to match it.

Tips for Larger Presentations

● Control your food service. Filling the prospects full of donuts and pastries will have them snoring within an hour (you might want them groggy if you have a lousy deal to present—Ha-ha). Also, health conscious individuals will be turned off if you don't provide some healthy choices like bagels, veggies, etc.

- Control your signage. When inviting large groups of prospects to your location for a presentation, make sure they are directed exactly where to go. Nothing will sour them more than nonexistent or confusing directions. You may want to stage live people movers to help direct your prospects.

- Control the seating. If it is a long session that will include lots of paperwork, you may want to include tables. Just don't make the tables too large. You don't want the prospects too spread out.

- Play music as the prospects arrive and at breaks. This makes the meeting special and negates the *deafening silence* effect. Even if you are not in your own venue, you can play the music on a tape player or boom box and put the microphone in front of the tape player's speaker. This will send the music through the sound system of the room.

- Plan for fun. In most sales presentations there is room for some degree of levity. It is up to you to plan for appropriate humor just as you plan other parts of your sales presentations.

More sales tips

- Don't forget to make your sales pitch. Some salespersons get so wrapped up in telling jokes they forget to go for the business.

- Use testimonials. They can be delivered live by happy clients who are willing to help you or in writing or by video or audio tape. You could make a funny video which includes bloopers.

- Keep your ego out of the sale. Remember—the sales profession is a profession of rejection. In most cases, it is not you that is being rejected.

- Develop and use impressive color visuals. According to a study by the Wharton Business School, presenters who used them were more apt to win favorable decisions.

- Develop humor to support your points, products, and services. Go for quality humor and stories instead of quantity.

- Develop ad-libs for equipment failure and other expected unexpected occurrences.

- Add some type of attention-gaining device every few minutes to keep your clients alert.

Women were made with a sense of humor so they could love men instead of laughing at them.

—Will Rogers

Tips for women presenters

I know what you are saying out there. "Tom, who are you to be writing about women's issues? What could you possibly know about women as presenters?" Tom's reply, feeling a little attacked, is: *I love women. My mother is a woman. I don't have any sisters, but all my aunts are women. I've got many female cousins who are women. Most of the women I've dated have been women. Actually, I've worked with and coached female presenters for years. So, the answers to your questions are—NOBODY and A LOT.*

CHAPTER 19

I know nothing of what it actually feels like to be a woman in front of an all-male, egotistical "What's this little girl going to tell me?" audience. I do know quite a bit, however, about how women can be more successful in front of male, female, and mixed audiences, but I've had my say about that in Chapter 2. I also know that it is very important for women to be good communicators. According to a survey in *USA Today*, the number one factor in the success of women who have made it in management is communication skills.

One thing I hope you appreciate about me is that I don't try to be the pseudo-expert when real experts are available. That is why I have assembled a group of top female presenters to help me with this chapter. I've tried to select a good mix of presenters, including corporate executives, humorists, a trainer, a speakers bureau owner, and entertaining business speakers, so there would be something for everyone.

Nance Rosen, Senior Corporate Executive

Using humor in business? It's easy if you're very beautiful and really rich. Well, actually everything is easy if you're very beautiful and really rich. So let's assume we're talking about the rest of us who have to earn our living speaking mostly to men (who remain the hulking majority in the senior suites of the executive floors).

I have two strategies. One strategy works with smart, secure men who have calm digestion when they work with women. (In other words, they can at least stomach us). These fellas come to work to get the job done. Along the way, they enjoy our sense of humor just the way we enjoy theirs. I find that people who are smart and funny are almost always fair minded. Best of all, these men treat you to the golden rule of corporate comedy: "I'll laugh at yours if you laugh at mine (jokes, that is)."

Because I like and respect these guys, I treat them to both my brains and my brawn (at least my funny bone). For example, at The Coca-Cola Company I was asked to *produce* a presentation on conflict management for a group of mostly male managers. I took the word "produce" to the extreme. That is, I made a big production out of what was a simple assignment. Within three days, I wrote a fairy tale about two working dogs who were having trouble cooperating with each other. My story also featured doggy bosses and various doggy colleagues (including the Chief Financial Dog). Overnight, my favorite audio-visual house (Heliotrope in Santa Ana, California - and no, I don't get a commission) created slides of all these dogs doing all kinds of things. Of course they were clothed and propped. Isn't everyone's dog clothed and propped, or am I alone in creating a perfect world when given the opportunity?

Anyway, David at Heliotrope and I had too many dogs trying to sit on a couch, another dog incorrectly adding up numbers on a blackboard, and more dogs driving cars in the wrong direction, that sort of thing.

When I made the presentation, I would click onto a slide and stand silently while the audience, startled by the dogs in a new position, howled with laughter. People were actually screaming, and some were even crying. After the roar died down, I would tell a segment of the story using, of course, names of people in the room as characters in my play. That caused more laughter.

The salient points about how to manage conflict were made as my story moved along. Not the least of these tips was that humor could reduce tension in almost any situation. Afterward, the real, non-canine, CFO of the division told me that it was the best presentation he had ever seen in all of his decades of working with The Coca-Cola Company. Big risk, I suppose, but huge reward. At the time, I felt it was worth the energy because I liked these people.

Now, as I said before, I have two strategies when it comes to humor in business. The one I just described works with smart, secure men. The other, which I call my Jack Webb strategy is for everyone else. Remember Jack Webb on *Dragnet?* His favorite line was "Just the facts, ma'am." Well, that's what I try to give those guys who are uncomfortable with female experts. My experience is that for some male audiences, a woman really can't win over the crowd with humor. Under these circumstances, the winning approach is to be straightforward and let your solid preparation showcase your competence. Sure, you can joke some about sports if you genuinely have the knowledge to back up your comments. (You certainly don't want to be caught talking about *Tuesday Night Football,* do you?) But, tread lightly if you really need to sell to people who would prefer not to buy from you.

In two decades of business, I have made only one presentation that stands out as a painful reminder that sometimes women are not welcome, even when we're hired. I had been hired by a (female) administrator to develop a marketing plan for a large orthodontic practice. For weeks I gathered data, interviewed patients and their families, and worked with the staff. I was President of the Medical Marketing Association as well as the owner of a successful advertising agency, so I knew the subject matter thoroughly. When I finally met with the chief orthodontist, who had spent weeks avoiding me, I started out with some light small talk.

He interrupted me mid-sentence saying "Look, I don't have to listen to you. Just give me the information." He was right. He didn't have to listen to me. In fact, he couldn't. We were on such different wavelengths that no verbal communication skills could be successful. I was grateful that my written report was comprehensive since it had to speak for itself. The funny part of this story is personal. Two years later I was shopping with my daughter Molly in a local toy store. Who should come in with his lovely wife and twin babies but the orthodontist! In that setting, he gave me a warm greeting and proudly introduced his lovely family. He engaged Molly in conversation and complimented her for being so well spoken. We must have chatted for 15 minutes before all the kids finally got us moving again.

It goes to show that people whom you know in business can be quite different in social settings. I have often thought that should I have met this gentleman first socially we would have had a better business rapport. Or, perhaps if I had been hired directly by him rather than by his administrator, he might have been one of my success stories. Or maybe not.

After 20 years, my experience proves that the best reason to use humor is to keep yourself laughing. Sometimes you keep laughing all the way to the bank. Sometimes, you keep laughing all the way home. But, like growing old, it's much better than the alternative.

Nance Rosen, a former senior marketing executive at The Coca Cola Company, is now a syndicated business radio talk show host. She is the author of Megamanagers are Made in Tuff Times & Other Business Fairy Tales.

Denise Koepke, Trainer

I have trained over 3,000 people of many different mixes of age, sex, and occupations on numerous topics. I have even crossed-trained male techies in sales skills (what a challenge!). There are many different ways of leading off a session based on the profile of the audience. It is critical to judge the audience and the best way is to be there early and greet and chat with as many as possible. This gives you the chance to take a reading on attitudes before the group dynamics begin.

I am a female that has been in sales most of my life. I tend to be lighthearted in style when teaching serious information. This can be a definite edge or the kiss of death when you are a subject matter expert. The males that have been in a strongly male-dominated market will have an immediate disbelief in my technical abilities (I train a lot of these guys as of late). They tend to be the most fun eventually, but the process of getting there takes skill and time.

The first step in this process is not to use any giddy "female" behavior. Don't be too serious either. I'd recommend being a "professional neutral" in the greeting process. After you know everyone, you can be "light" until you begin teaching. This indicates that the class will be different than the last class the attendees may have taken. In my case, this may be the first formal class they have had since high school.

The beginning involves a tough, up-front approach of what's in it for them, why they should listen, and why they should listen to me. (I have a strong background in communications that lends itself to this type of opening.) I follow with what I expect them to walk away from this session knowing. I use general terms to indicate the knowledge level I expect them to have. I explain the time limits and obtain a buy-in that those time limits are acceptable (after they agree, they usually adhere to them). Then I begin my presentation as usual. I will not start to be entertaining until one hour or so into the session. I then try a little humor to test to see how it is received. If it is received as adults, then I know I can go a little further next time. Then I test again. If it is not received as adults, I back up a notch. This strategy is very important to keep from getting so far down the road that you can't gracefully back up. With these types of groups it is difficult to back up without sounding like your elementary school teacher, which is an invitation for trouble.

As a female there are sometimes comments like "Can you come teach me yourself?" and other off-color or just slightly off-color statements. I handle these as true compliments (and why not, I'm not getting any younger!). When these comments are received more sincerely than intended, it seems to humble the commentator immediately. But if others join in, a simple "Thank you" followed by moving on is all that is needed. Without a rise, it dies a quiet death.

If there is someone in the group who speaks out or challenges the information, I am not defensive. I do not challenge them back. I ask them questions about their comments or information sources before I answer. When I feel fully informed, I answer if I can. If I can't, I say so.

Most people that are challenging my information have conflicting information or they are testing the waters to find out if my belief system matches theirs. I don't assume they are challenging me solely to get the correct information. When the class sees that I don't overreact easily, it goes a long way in keeping control.

After those hurdles are jumped, I am established as an expert in whatever topic I am speaking on (different from a know it all). I have fun and challenge the group with their experience and knowledge. It then becomes a different session with a lot of synergy in most cases. I love it!

Denise Koepke is President of Remote Control Management, a professional speaking and consulting firm specializing in Telecommuting, Selling, and Sales Management Skills. She is the author of Corporate Telecommuting: Is it Right For Your Company?

Barbara Sanfillippo, Speaker

In my 10 years as a professional speaker, I've addressed all types of audiences. Audience members have included conservative CEOs, middle management, salespeople, and clerical staff. By far, my most typical audience consists entirely of male CEOs and senior managers.

Male senior executives are concerned about their image and have seen and heard it all, and therefore are a challenge to loosen up. If I can get them to say something out loud simultaneously, they will laugh, which allows the energy to shift in my favor and I start to command their attention. For example, when bringing up a point on employee recognition, I might say, "There's something about recognition I hear CEOs say that absolutely drives me crazy. When I count to three, I want you all to shout out, 'What drives you crazy, Barbara?' OK! One, two three!" They always chuckle as they shout out the question and, of course, I play up my response. "I thought you'd never ask me. 'When CEOs say, "But Barbara, it's their job to provide excellent service and sell our products. Why should

I pay them any more?"' How many of you feel that way?" This technique also works well when you customize the question and response to a common problem or inside joke.

The other technique is to pre-interview a lively audience member by phone and have him or her "briefly" take the mic and share a light story. This works particularly well if a majority of the audience members know this individual and can often lead to playful banter and ad-libbing.

If the goal is to entertain and have high impact, I've learned it is important to use my entire body to act out characters, change my voice, and take up space on stage. Acting coaches have helped me tremendously. I literally transform myself into a witch, hunched over with a harsh whiny voice, or a young girl full of wonder. The audience enjoys getting close to a speaker. So whenever possible, I leave the stage and walk out into the crowd for a few minutes.

Props can work well with both mixed groups and all female audiences. I tend to stay away from props with my male CEOs, or use them only minimally when my goal is to establish credibility. For example, when I recently addressed a mixed group of junior level supervisors and engineers I slowly and dramatically climbed a ladder on stage. As I stepped up, I emphasized the importance of continuing to take risks, always looking ahead, and not getting stuck by our fears. You could hear a pin drop as I carefully stepped up the ladder. The ladder definitely had strong visual impact.

Generally speaking, I find mixed audiences and all female audiences more willing to play. With conservative male groups, I seek to set a playful but commanding tone to instantly win their respect. This group does not want to look foolish in front of their peers. I ease into the play rather than sock it to them quickly.

Based in San Diego, California, Barbara Sanfilippo is a nationally and internationally known speaker in the areas of sales, service, and motivation. She is the author of "Five-Star Service Solutions" and holds the prestigious Certified Speaking Professional (CSP) designation from the National Speakers Association.

Lilly Walters, Speakers Bureau Owner

I am a female who speaks and owns a speakers bureau. As much as I dislike the reality of it, audiences still tend to prefer men. For a woman to be a hit on the platform she needs to be much better than a man. I know, I know, thousands of feminists are ready to shoot me. But the reality is, when my buyers make their final decisions, more times than not they are still hiring men. They may ask for a woman when they call in, but they often end up hiring a man.

Academic researchers have found that women actually lose immediacy points for joke telling. Students tend to be more strongly influenced by the amount and type of humor used by male lecturers than by female. The researchers also note that female students are influenced less by jokes and wisecracks than are male students, and more by the use of stories and anecdotes. The lesson to be learned seems to be that female presenters should incorporate humor through the use of stories and anecdotes, especially for predominantly female audiences. For predominantly male audiences, the judicious use of jokes which are relevant to the audience or subject matter should be added.

My personal reflection on this research is that we as women are still not as secure up there as men. It is not the learners and their styles at fault, it is us. Some of us have tapes running in our minds that say "demure" and "feminine," which is fine, if you can add passion. Passion is what sells concepts to your audience. Look at Mother Theresa—plenty of passion, but she uses it with strength. The result is very womanly presenters that captivate the audience. For you technical types that say, "What is demure and feminine?", a little passion is advantageous for you too. It is one of our unique strengths as women, so capitalize on it.

Lilly Walters is a best-selling author, a business executive, and a professional speaker. She is the Executive Director of Walters International Speakers Bureau. Together, Lilly and Dottie, Lilly's world famous speaking mother, publish <u>Sharing Ideas,</u> the largest newsmagazine in the world for professional speakers.

Hope Mihalap, Humorist

Once business audiences hear us, they love us. But an obstacle we women humorists face in the business world is, in one word, comediennes. Comediennes, or female night-club comics, have created an impression that women humorists have to struggle to overcome. As humorists, not comics, we talk about life and about ourselves. The trendy material used by many women in comedy clubs or on cable television has made corporate meeting planners wary—much more so than they would be of male speakers. While men often get away with slightly off-color material, rough talk, or brash political barbs, women cannot—nor should they. No matter who uses this sort of material, it's not particularly creative. Since good women humorists try to avoid these pitfalls, you can count on more creativity and original wit from them.

Our best humor is self-related—and, in the case of women, this doesn't make it applicable only to female audiences. Bill Cosby talks about family humor and is celebrated for it, and the highly acclaimed Robert Fulghum writes about simple human values. I have found that ethnic humor, naturally about my own ethnic group, goes over wonderfully in the business world, as do stories about my family and work experiences.

My job then is to convince corporate meeting planners that 1) basic human values and personal relationships are not only rich in humor, but full of lessons that are important and applicable in the workplace; and 2) they don't need to be afraid of me because I'm a woman! Good material is good material, no matter who delivers it.

Hope Mihalap is an award-winning humorist with an ear for accents and an eye for hilarious situations. She has received the prestigious international Mark Twain Award for Humor and also the Council of Peers Award of Excellence (CPAE) from the National Speakers Association—the Oscar of the speaking world.

Sheila Feigelson, Speaker and Humor Consultant

Here are some of the things I am aware of as I speak to both mixed groups and groups of only women. I don't think I have ever spoken to an all-male group, except for my immediate family of three sons and one husband!

My most frequent speaking topic is *Not Just For Laughs, Putting Humor to Work!* The underlying mission of my work is to help people explore the whys and ways of inviting laughter into their lives both on and off the job, purposely plan for the presence of humor, and have a good time together. A particular interest of mine is the role of humor, fun, playfulness and shared laughter in promoting more effective and productive meetings. My background as a junior high school teacher and trainer of teachers at The University of Michigan helped me realize how powerful a sense of humor and fun can be for creating the kind of climate that invites participation. When we had fun in the classroom, all of us were more effective.

Now, about changes I'm aware of making for audiences comprised of either all women or of both women and men. I am very aware of my physical presence in both settings. I wear clothing that is comfortable and flattering without drawing undue attention. I am VERY aware that when a speaker is wearing something that causes the audience to be concerned or uncomfortable, the audience will not be paying attention to what the speaker is saying. I once saw a woman speaker who was wearing a nice suit, but she had on a blouse that caused me to worry for her. I felt that at any minute, it was going to come apart and reveal that which she would be very embarrassed about. And I had no way to tell her! The entire time, I was just hoping that her blouse would stay closed. Fortunately it did, but the near-miss was very distracting. I didn't hear much of what she said. I did tell her afterward that she would probably want to make sure that the pin holding her blouse together in the front was more secure. I also suggested that she probably ought not to wear that particular blouse! Even if it had come open, I'm sure the men in the audience would have been equally embarrassed. It just wasn't appropriate.

There ARE some differences I'm aware of when I am with an all-women audience. I make more references to things female, e.g., make-up, the women's room, clothing challenges, moods, gynecological exams. I have a wonderful story about an exam that I once had during which I got the doctor and nurse laughing hysterically. I tell it only to women because only women know what it feels like to be on the gynecologist's table getting a pelvic exam. They don't have to stretch their imaginations to try to figure out what it looks and feels like. We're all comfortable with the images. I don't tell this story to a mixed audience because I'm afraid that the males would be caught up in trying to figure out what I might look like in that situation. They'd be mentally undressing me, and that would make ME feel uncomfortable. That's also a reason why I don't like to see women in short skirts on the platform. It's an invitation to be distracting.

Another thing I'll do with an all-women's group has to do with my shoes. I am of an age now when comfort has become more important than the appearance of my feet. One time I was a keynote speaker for an audience of 500 women. I wore an attractive suit and appropriate mid-size heels. Following the speech I conducted a two-hour workshop. I changed into flat shoes for that session in order to be more comfortable. Part way through, I realized that those shoes were causing me to stand in a way that was bothersome to my back. So, at the break, I put on my tennis shoes which I had worn while driving to the engagement. When the audience returned from the break I just stood there, lifted up my leg so they could see my foot, and said, "How do you like these shoes for the rest of the session?" They laughed and then applauded! Let's hear it for comfort! I'm not sure if I would have done that with men in the group, but I may have. I would probably have had second thoughts. Vanity is ever present to some degree!

One of the suggestions I make in my presentations is for people to carry some humorous item with them, either in their wallet, purse or briefcase, that can be pulled out at an appropriate moment. It's called "being prepared to be spontaneous." Joel Goodman, of the Humor Project refers to it as "Planned Spontaneity." I often show my funny glasses and tell people that "I carry these with me all the time. It doesn't mean I use them every day. Sometimes just knowing I have them with me is all I need to make me feel good. It's kind of like wearing new underpants with no holes or stretched out elastic bands! No one knows except me, and it feels delicious!"

This last sentence, about the underpants, I would say very comfortably to a group of women. With men in the audience, I would always think twice, and often decide to omit it. Again, I believe it has to do with not wanting them to picture what I might look like in my underwear. Most women don't have to bother with that. We KNOW the look and feel of fresh, new, un-holey female underwear! This is "girl-talk." This is not to say that men don't enjoy fresh, new underwear as well. But I'm not quite as comfortable talking about it from the platform with them. "From the platform" is an important phrase here. I'm comfortable talking about a lot of things one-on-one and in small groups. But there is a difference between talking among a small group of friends and a larger group from a platform. I believe we need to remember that our words and actions take on more significance from the platform.

In most cases, I'm comfortable in mixed audiences, but being with an educated, all-female audience is the MOST comfortable of all. Maybe it's because all females have some experience with a period: either they're early, late, irregular, menopausal, and blah, blah, blah. . . . I really am convinced that I can connect with any woman, based on the fact that we both have what I call "Period experiences." And this crosses all classes, races, nations. . . . Isn't that amazing?

Sheila Feigelson of Ann Arbor, Michigan is a professional speaker and humor consultant who helps people find simple ways to lighten up their meetings, organizations, and daily lives. She is the author of a forthcoming book on how to put fun to work for more effective meetings.

Lola Gillebaard, Speaker

When I just recently did a presentation for my husband's Rotary Club as a Valentine's gift at a meeting where spouses and significant others were invited, I was once again reminded of what happens when couples are together for a humorous luncheon program at a predominantly male club. The couples are so busy watching to see what each other laughs at that they never really relax and just have fun. Also, men and women act differently when their significant others are present, and are not nearly so fun-filled as when alone. This doesn't happen if the program is in the evening; it's as if the couples give themselves permission to relax and laugh in the evening because the workday is over.

In contrast, at the spouse program I had done early in the morning the day before for the National Sugarbeets Association, 300 wives of farmers almost tipped over their chairs in laughter as they wiped their eyes. Just days before that, I had done a program for the California Society of Hospital Pharmacists, all men, at five o'clock in the afternoon. They laughed heartily. Both the sugarbeet wives and the hospital pharmacists were at a convention in a vacation town far away from their workplace. They were staying in a nice hotel, the food was good, and they did not have to prepare it whereas most of the Rotary people had to get back to the office for an afternoon of work.

So what's the point? As humorists, we must remove the work anxieties from the minds of the audience by what I call a pep rally. Some would call it a warm-up for your program, much like a comedienne does for the star at the comedy store. In other words, put some really funny material at the beginning and get them involved, not individually, but as a group. For example, at the Rotary Club I had them shout together loudly, "You know you're getting older when . . ." We practiced it until they were really loud and then I gave 12 zingers to complete the sentence. The audience was mine when we finished this exercise.

What's it like to be a female presenter? It's fun. Men are more reserved than women as a rule in the beginning, but it's my job to win over the audience, whatever it takes. Also, being an older woman is definitely an advantage. I can get by with more in front of both men and women and the women are not jealous. In other words, I am not a threat.

Lola Gillebaard is a professional speaker based in Laguna Beach, California. She is a past president of the Greater Los Angeles Chapter of the National Speakers Association. Her one woman show "Life's Funny That Way" has received rave reviews nationwide. She is also a recipient of the <u>Readers Digest</u> Writer's award.

Patricia Fripp, Speaker

A woman may have to work a bit harder to get the attention of and buy in from a mostly male audience. The thing that has helped me most in all of my jobs, from hair stylist to professional speaker, is my personality. I believe in the "shmooze" factor. I talk to the crowd, warm them up first, get to know them, have fun, and build on the "like factor." If they see you care about them, they are more likely to pay attention to you. This shmooze factor is especially important if you are trying to be funny.

I spoke for 80 Knife and Fork Clubs. These clubs consist mostly of elderly people who go to listen to speakers. I would always chat with the crowd and say things like, "The hairdresser must have been busy today, you all look so good." I was repeatedly told I was the only person who had ever come down from the head table and actually talked to them. Consequently, I got great ratings. The individual who books speakers for this group said, "They liked what you said, but they LOVED the fact you went to talk to them."

How does this concept work in corporate America? I spoke at an IBM partner conference last January. I was working the crowd before the presentation and told them, "If you like me, write 'bring her back and pay her double' on the evaluation sheets."Afterward the agent for this job said, "What did you do to that crowd, so many wrote . . . (guess what!!!)" I have had substantial spin-off business from that job, including another big job for IBM in San Francisco. The planner said, "We don't usually book anyone we have not seen, but your reviews were so good at the January meeting we made an exception."

Another example is when I meet a big boss, male or female, I drop to my knees and make kissy sounds at their hand and say, "Let me kiss your ring." The secret of my success is I always suck up to the boss!! Could many others do this? Would they want to? No.

I also give out Fripp buttons that say "I have been Frippnotized." I tell them to keep them, they are magic. But the real value is simply to reinforce ideas that are productive and profitable. It helps me make a personal connection with my audience.

Patricia Fripp, CPAE, CSP was the first female president of the National Speakers Association. She received the highest award given by that organization for professionalism and excellence in speaking, an award held by fewer than 100 speakers worldwide. She is the author of numerous books and tape programs on contemporary business topics.

Joyce M. Saltman, Humorist, Professor, Therapist

Women presenters *are* different. Beyond the obvious anatomical distinctions, we sound different. As women, we tend to work to join with our audience, to make contact. Unlike most male comics, for example, who want to *kill*, women want to feel connected to the audience. Highest praise is "They loved me!" Men have a contest, while women have a romance.

As a lecturer on the topic of "Laughter, RX for Survival" for the past twelve and one-half years, I have addressed teachers, medical personnel (including physicians!), corporate trainers, and every manner of volunteer organization. My varied experiences could fill a book, but a few stand out as representative.

Several years ago, I gave a keynote address and an experiential workshop for a school system. The teachers were responsive and laughed heartily through the presentation, with the exception of one male teacher who kept his arms crossed during the entire one and one-half hour "lecture," never cracking a smile. No matter how hard I tried to engage him, he was immovable. During lunch, I dined with four female teachers, all of whom were surprised at this particular gentleman's lack of participation. In that school, he was noted as the comedian, always making funny comments during faculty meetings. Clearly, power, as seen through the role of the presenter of humor, was threatening his position. While this may have been true regardless of the gender of the presenter, when power is perceived by a male as relinquished to a female, it is all the more difficult for him to accept. Interestingly, during the afternoon experiential session he participated fully and was, indeed, "the star."

This particular phenomenon has been noteworthy in several other settings where men appear threatened by a female "in charge" as in a group of vocational high school teachers ("shop" teachers—all male!) and husbands during a session with their wives.

Another fascinating change in the presentation field has been the advent of the Political Correctness movement. Recently I had two calls from large corporations, both interested in hiring me, both of whom had seen my presentation in person or on video, and both requesting specific omissions that would be required for me to be "acceptable" for their present corporate climate. Stories about having been flatchested at 12 or wetting my pants on the way home from the library as a result of a laughing fit at age 14 were considered inappropriate for their PC audience. As a seasoned professional who gives 100 presentations each year, I generally can sense the tone of the audience and edit as I go along, but these companies were taking no chances. As it happened, one of the corporations had me give two workshops prior to the keynote. At dinner preceding the address, the most conservative of the chairpeople came over to me and said, "I've had nothing but positive feedback on your afternoon sessions. Please feel free to give your talk as you see fit. Do not concern yourself about our restrictions!" I have no idea whether I could more easily have been censored as a male, or perhaps not hired at all if I had not been able to convince the chairperson that I could tailor my talk to their needs. It is unfortunate that often those in positions of decision-making for their organizations do not have faith in the professionalism of presenters and perhaps do not have faith in their own colleagues' ability to handle an inadvertent offensive remark, should one be made. The overriding message for those of us who lecture and those for whom we offer presentations should be: "Lighten Up!"

Joyce Saltman is a full-time professor of Special Education at Southern Connecticut State University in New Haven and a Gestalt Therapist with a private practice in Cheshire, Ct. She chose to receive her doctoral degree in Higher and Adult Education from Columbia University because she loved the color of their doctoral gown. She holds four graduate degrees in Special Education and Counseling and has been a stand-up comedienne at nationally known comedy clubs.

Marianna Nunes, Speaker

As a female humorist, I test the waters of all my audiences in four ways:

1. I go early and try to meet as many people as possible. This warms them up to me, eases my nervousness, and I get a sense of how serious or playful they may be as audience members.

2. I go early so I can sit in on other programs. I see how readily they laugh or do not laugh, which lets me know what to expect for my program. If they're playful in one program they will usually be playful in the next program. Also, I can pick out the playful audience members that I may use in my program. If something significant occurs in an earlier program, I can tie it in to my speech in a humorous way.

3. I trust my intuition or gut sense when I walk into my audience. I actually can feel if there is a serious or playful tone in the room.

4. I prepare my introduction (which I insist that they read exactly as written) with a few humorous lines. If the audience does not laugh at those lines, I know I'm probably in for a long hour and not to expect too much laughter from the audience.

As a general rule for female humorists, it is usually easier to get more laughs and interaction from an all-female audience. In a mixed audience, I find that the women are more open to laughter and they keep the audience alive. An all-male audience is usually more reserved and more difficult to warm up. They also prefer more content. With an all-male audience, I act more corporate in my speech, my dress, and my entrance. These are general experiences that I have encountered, and I have had many, many exceptions.

The most critical piece of advice is to match your audience. If they are serious, begin a little more subdued so they can relate to you. I recently saw a great performer with such high energy (not matching her quiet audience) that many people left because they were so uncomfortable. The way to sell yourself to your audience is to make them feel they are like you! Thus, match them as much as possible with the tone of how you begin, your content, and your dress.

Marianna Nunes is a keynote speaker who captivates, motivates, and educates her audiences nationwide. At the lowest point in her life, Marianna was diagnosed as having cancer. Her personal relationship and business fell apart, and she was forced to go into debt. However, through a long process of raising her self-esteem and using laughter as a healing source, Marianna succeeded in rebuilding both her life and her career. She travels extensively, offering programs to business and association clients of all kinds. She is also well known for her popular singles program "The Art of Flirting."

Liz Curtis Higgs, Encouraging Humorist

Ten years and one thousand presentations later, I can state confidently that when it comes to using humor to wake up your audiences, one thing is certain: men and women are different! Women love to laugh at themselves, but men prefer to laugh at "the other guy." One study of male and female comics (reported by J.B. Levine in *Journal of Communication*) revealed that 63% of the funny females included self-disparaging comments in their material, compared to only 12% of the males.

As a "big, beautiful woman in a narrow, nervous world," I know those statistics to be accurate. I always open my program with several gentle stabs at my abundantly-blessed physique, just to communicate to the audience, "Yes, I know I'm a size 24 Tinkerbell and, yes, I'm okay with it!" If the audience is 70% or more female, I may go on for several minutes along this line. Ethel Barrymore said, "You grow up the day you have your first real laugh—at yourself." We grown-up women love to laugh at ourselves; in fact, J.R. Cantor (in *Journal of Communication*) observed that "self-disparagement may play a unique role in the establishment of a female sense of humor."

If, on the other hand, the audience is predominantly male, I will focus on such "self-deprecating" comments for a mere minute or two, then move on to another topic. Men enjoy humor about money, status, sports, or business. They like material that is short and to the point, and laugh harder at one-liners than longer, more detailed stories.

Another observation: men may not choose to put themselves down, but are perfectly comfortable if the speaker "roasts" another attendee. On one occasion, I was on the platform at a corporate meeting for KFC International and was discussing fried chicken (what else?) in Oprah-fashion with a corporate executive who had a reputation for giving people a hard time. He found his opportunity when I shared some research with the audience, stating that "people prefer larger pieces of chicken to small ones." He quickly retorted, "There is such a thing as too big," and stared pointedly at me.

The mostly-male audience gasped audibly, then fell silent, waiting for my comeback. Gulp. Now what? A million thoughts run through a speaker's mind at such a moment. Do I toss a zinger at him and risk offending not only him but the CEO as well? Do I ignore it and just roll my eyes? If I say the wrong thing, is the rest of my presentation down the tubes? It was probably only a few seconds (but seemed like minutes) before the perfect response presented itself. I smiled broadly, looked directly at the audience and said, "Kind of makes you want to compare paychecks for the day, doesn't it?"

The audience—including the CEO—roared with approval. I'd aimed my barb at Mr. Cool's two most vulnerable spots: his ego and his wallet. They'd been waiting for somebody to put this weisenheimer in his place for years, and it took an outsider to pull it off. Humor is always risky, and the best humor requires the greatest risk. The key for using humor successfully with any audience, male or female, is reading their reactions accurately and adjusting your content on the spot, expanding or contracting according to response.

There are certain stories I save for predominantly female audiences—anything to do with childbirth, menopause or other "for women only" subjects—but I don't have any stories that I use exclusively for male audiences, in part because I seldom address them. In fact, I am only willing to stand before a mostly-male audience in a daytime keynote situation, and turn down the offers to do their evening banquets by repeating our corporate motto: "Liz doesn't talk to men after dark!" Even in this enlightened age of equality, the truth is that men and women are still very different when it comes to humor. In an interview with Joel Goodman (in *Laughing Matters*), comedian Jay Leno admitted, "All men laugh at the Three Stooges, and all women think they are dumb. When Moe hits Larry with a shovel, the guy cracks up; the woman will get up, mutter 'Stupid!' and turn the set off. When was the last time you saw two women go, 'Nyuk, Nyuk, Nyuk?'"

Since 1986, Liz Curtis Higgs, CSP, CPAE, has presented more than 1000 humorous, encouraging programs for audiences in nearly all fifty states. She's the author of six books, all published by NelsonWord, including Only Angels Can Wing It, The Rest of Us Have to Practice.

Sue Hershkowitz, Speaker

When I was 24, I was a candidate for the position of trainer for a major New York seminar company. They flew me to NY and then interviewed me for two days. Finally, at the end of the second day, I got to meet the top guy. He didn't stand when I walked in the room. Instead, he put both his feet up on his desk, crossed his arms, and said, "I've been in business as long as you've been alive. What do you think you could teach me?"

Needless to say, I was shocked. Would he have treated a male counterpart that way? You've got to be kidding! What would I do if this happened today? I'd laugh and then suggest that the answer was probably nothing . . . then I would keep quiet, allowing him to realize the stupidity of his chauvinistic comment.

At the time, I learned a good lesson from his response. I realized (after I was offered the position) that as a young woman, I would encounter lots of men who might feel the same way—even though they might have better manners than this man. I realized that before I could introduce humor or fun or an easygoing style into my delivery, I would have to begin by jolting the group with hard, specific facts so, I began each program by asking questions that I knew they couldn't answer. (In all fairness, if they could have answered them, they could have been giving the workshop!) I'd pour on the statistics for anywhere from two to five minutes. Then, I'd relax and smile—and so would they, because they realized I knew my stuff. (By the way, I don't do that now, but I'm no longer 24 either!)

Now, I'm certain I know my stuff. I guess that confidence comes across to the audience in my authenticity. I tell my audiences up front, "Words that come from the heart enter the heart." I think they accept me on a different level now. It's not so important whether I'm male or female, but that we're all human beings.

One other point: I've been told that I'm attractive and I find it's the women in the audience who can be much more critical of me than the men. To combat this problem, I go out of my way to spend more time with the women before the program. I select more women as active participants and, in general, pay much more attention to the women in the audience than the men. It's really important to me that they feel comfortable and not in any way threatened. They turn into my biggest supporters.

Sue Hershkowitz, CSP, is a professional speaker and entrepreneur. She is the author of two books, Power Sales Writing: What Every Sales Person Must Know to Turn Prospects Into Clients! *and* Dog Tales for the Heart. *She has presented to more than one million people in 49 states and 7 countries. Sue is on the Board of Directors of the National Speakers Association.*

Well there you have it. You've heard from the real experts when it comes to women presenters. It's still not easy being a female presenter, but if you incorporate many of the tips you just read that are relevant to your speaking style you should have a much greater chance for success.

Closing Comments

I really hope that by the time you have read this far that you underlined many of the techniques you found in this book. However, underlining will not make you a true NO ZZZZZs presenter. You must implement the ideas and try them out in a variety of situations. If you are still apprehensive, just vow to take one little baby step in trying something new. I wish I could show you the letters I have received that were sent to me by people who took those baby steps. They tell me of the thrill they got when a one-liner or other piece of humor worked and how those early successes spurred them on to use more humor and to create more excitement when they spoke. I know that if you practice the techniques in this book and work with them to fit your style, you will be the one who Wakes 'em Up! Good Luck.

Tom Antion

Landover Hills, Maryland

APPENDICES

A: Action Plan to Improve Your Use of Humor

B: Addresses

C: Tips for Television & Videotape and Videoconferencing

D: Worldwide Video Color Systems

E: Room Setup Checklist

F: Tom's Banquet/Luncheon Tips

G: Selected Bibliography

H: Wake 'em Up Glossary

APPENDIX A
ACTION PLAN TO IMPROVE YOUR USE OF HUMOR

● Decide that no matter how good (or bad) you are now, you can do better.
  Add humor to your presentations gradually.
  Practice bits.
  Pick one joke or story from any source and practice that joke or story 10 times per day for one week. Tape record the first and last time you tell the story and then compare.
  Practice jokes, one-liners, and stories 30-50 times before you use them in a presentation.
  Develop pre-planned ad-libs for problems that may occur in your presentations.
  Read, listen, or watch humorous material daily.
  Start a humor library.
  Start a humor file and cross-reference system.
● IMMEDIATELY write down anything you hear or see that strikes you as funny. If you don't, it will be lost.
● Audio or video tape all your presentations.
  Get feedback from pros and/or get coaching.
  Develop a pre-program questionnaire.
  Write several new introductions for yourself.
  Write a suggestion letter to be given to your introducer.
  Vow to get to your presentations one-half hour earlier than you normally do to control as many variables of the room setup as you can.
  Visit with as many members of your audience as you can before your presentations.

 Most of all—keep smiling!

APPENDIX B
ADDRESSES

Audio and Video Tapes

Anchor Publishing, Box 2630, Landover Hills, MD 20784,
(800) 448-6280, Fax (301) 552-0225, tom@antion.com, tomantion@aol.com,
74117.226@compuserve.com, www.antion.com. *Make 'em Laugh: How to Use
Humor in Business Presentations,* video and audio and *Tom Antion's Humor System.*

Nightingale Conant Corporation, 7300 Leigh Ave. Chicago, IL 60648
(800) 572-2770. Audio and video tapes on various business topics.

Also see Humor Project and Royal Publishing below.

Books

Greenwood Publishing Group, 88 Post Rd. West, Box 5007, Westport, CT
06881 (800) 225-5800. Biggest humor research bibliography I know of: *Humor
Scholarship: A Research Bibliography by Don L.F. Nilsen.*

Humor Project, 110 Spring St., Saratoga Springs, NY 12866
(518) 587-0362, Fax (800) 600-4242. Complete catalog of humor books; audio
and video tapes.

Resources for Organizations, 7620 W. 78th St., Bloomington, Minnesota 55439
(800) 383-9210. Training products.

Also see Royal Publishing below.

Book Search Services

Book Look, 51 Maple Ave., Warwick, NY 10990,
(914) 986-1981.

Wolf's Head Books, Box 3705, St. Augustine, FL 32085,
(800) 521-5061.

Comedy Writing/Stand-up Comedy Workshop

Jeff Justice's Comedy Workshoppe, Box 52404, Atlanta, GA 30355,
(404) 262-7406, Fax (404) 841-9586, Just4Yuks@aol.com.

Greg Dean's Comedy Workshop, Box 2929, Hollywood, CA 90078,
(310) 285-3799, gregdean@primenet.com.

Computer Programs

Comedy Writer™ from Ideascapes,
323 Curacao Cove North, Niceville, FL 32578,
(904) 897-5407, ideascapes@aol.com.

Just Joking: America's Funniest Jokes and Quotes,
WordStar International, 201 Alameda del Prado,
Novato, CA 94948, (800) 523-3520.

Exercises, Brainteasers, Activities, Icebreakers

Make It a Winning Life by Wolf J. Rinke, Ph.D., Rockville, MD, Achievement
Publishers, (800) 828-9653. Brainteasers, mental stretch breaks, and humor
spread throughout the text.

Games Trainers Play series, *Complete Book of Games* and *Big Book of Business
Games,* Ed Scannell and John Newstrom, McGraw-Hill
11 W. 19th St., New York, NY 10011, (800) 262-4729.

International Resources

Culturgram, Kennedy Center Publications, Brigham Young University,
Box 24538, Provo, Utah 84602, (801) 378-6528.

The International Business Communication Desk Reference, Susan Munger,
Amacom, 135 West 50th St., New York, NY 10020, (800) 225-3215.

Mary Murray Bosrock International Education Systems, 26 East Exchange St.,
Suite 313, Saint Paul, MN 55101 (612) 227-2052, Fax (612) 223-8383. *Put Your
Best Foot Forward* Series.

Marie Betts-Johnson International Business Protocol, 7944 Hollow Mesa Ct.,
San Diego, CA 92126, (619) 549-0202, Fax (619) 452-9148. Protocol training.

Joy E. Fox, CMP, 377 Crescent, Oakville, Ontario, Canada L6L 3L6,
(905) 825-8061, (905) 825-4149, 74117.733@compuserve.com.
International, corporate, and diplomatic protocol.

Witty World International Cartoon Magazine, Box 1458, North Wales, PA
19454, (215) 699-2626 , (310) 337-7003.

Music Licensing

Broadcast Music Inc. (BMI), 320 West 57th St., New York, NY 10019, Help line (800) 669-4264.

American Society of Composers, Authors and Publishers (ASCAP), 3350 Cumberland Circle, Atlanta, GA 30339, (800) 505-4052.

Newsletters

Laughter Works Newsletter, Box 1076, Fair Oaks, CA 95628, (916) 863-1592, Humor in business newsletter.

Lighten Up Club, 22 Union St., Brighton, MA 02135, (617) 783-3421. Sells wooden "Cents of Humor" and membership for those who need to lighten up.

Steve Wilson Report, 344 South Merkle Road, Bexley, OH 43209, (800) 669-5233, Fax (614) 237-4055. Humor in business newsletter.

Professional Joke Services

Funny Business Newsletter, Georgetown Publishing, 1101 30th St. N.W., Washington, D.C. 20007, (800) 915-0022.

The Jokesmith, 44 Queensview Rd., Marlborough, MA 01752, (508) 481-0979.

Linda Perret's Humor Files, 30941 W. Agoura Rd., #228, Westlake Village, CA 91361, (818) 865-7833.

Tom Adams Productions, Box 10246 Honolulu, HI 96816, (800) ADAMS 50, (808) 373-9800, Fax (808) 373-9801.

Props

Just for Laughs, Mazza Gallerie, 5300 Wisconsin Ave, N.W., Washington, D.C. 20015, (202) 244-GRIN (4746).

Morris Costume, 3108 Monroe Road, Charlotte, NC 28205, (704) 332-3304. Props, costumes and magic.

Props for Today, 121 W. 19th., 3rd. Floor, New York, NY 10011, (212) 206-0330.

Speaker Services

Royal Publishing & Walters Speakers Services, Box 1120, Glendora, CA 91740, (818) 335-8069, Fax (818) 335-6127. Full line resources for speakers, consulting, international speakers bureau and *Sharing Ideas* news magazine for professional speakers.

Speaking Organizations

International Platform Association (IPA), Box 250, Winnetka, IL 60093, (708) 446-4321.

National Speakers Association (NSA), 1500 South Priest Drive, Tempe AZ 85281, (602) 968-2552, Fax (602) 968-0911.

Toastmasters International, 23182 Arroyo Vista, Rancho Santa Margarita, CA 92688, (714) 858-8255, Fax (714) 858-1207.

Speech Writing and Research Services

Executive Speaker, Box 292437, Dayton, OH 45429, (513) 294-8493. Research services and publications for speechwriters and speakers.

Executive Speechwriter Newsletter/Words Ink, Emmerson Falls Business Park, St. Johnsbury, VT 05819, (802) 748-4472. Research services and publications for speechwriters and speakers.

Speaker's Idea File, Lawrence Ragan Communications, Inc., 212 West Superior St., Suite 200, Chicago, IL 60610, (312) 335-0037, Fax (312) 335-9583.

APPENDIX C
TIPS FOR TELEVISION & VIDEOTAPE AND
VIDEOCONFERENCING

Here are some things you should keep in mind when a television camera is trained on you:

TELEVISION & VIDEOTAPE TIPS

Make gestures smaller.

● Make sure clothing is "broken in" and comfortable when you are sitting and standing.

Prior to your performance, have instant photos or video taken of you while sitting and standing. Make sure your clothes look good in both positions.

● Find out the background color of the set if possible. You don't want your clothing to blend in and make you invisible.

Ask the producer for wardrobe color suggestions.

● Do not wear any clothing with tight patterns or pin stripes. This causes an optical illusion called a moiré pattern which makes you look bad.

● Avoid clothing with large patterns or geometric shapes. The audience will watch your clothes instead of you.

Avoid wearing black, white, or red on television or video. Even the best of cameras have trouble with these colors.

Avoid flashy jewelry. It reflects light.

Avoid jangly jewelry. It reflects light and makes noise that will be picked up by your microphone (this applies whether you are on TV or not).

Wear your eyeglasses if you want, but avoid shiny frames.

Tip the bows of your eyeglasses up slightly off your ears. This angles the lenses down to reduce glare from lights.

● Wear makeup. It has the practical purpose of reducing the glare of TV lights. Apply it to all exposed body parts, like backs of hands, arms, neck, etc.

● Apply cover-up below eyes to mask bags and/or wrinkles.

Dress for the heat, but bring a jacket or extra cover-up to be used while you are waiting to go on. Good studios are kept cool to negate the effect of the hot TV lights. You may freeze for a while until the lights are turned on, then you may burn up.

Bring a handkerchief or tissues to dab perspiration during breaks.

● Don't second guess the camera. Act as if you are always on screen.

● Make sure your makeup, wardrobe, and hair are consistent with your message.

MEN

Wear knee-length socks.

Always keep double breasted jackets buttoned.

Open single-breasted jackets if you wish—but not too wide.

I SAY AGAIN—Wear Makeup. TV lights can penetrate several layers of skin. You can't possibly shave close enough to prevent whiskers from showing without makeup.

Don't forget makeup on receding hairlines or bald heads.

Trick: Run the thin part of your tie through the loop in the back of the main part of your tie then clip the thin part to your shirt below the loop. This will keep your tie perfectly centered without the tie clip showing.

WOMEN

Don't wear vivid red lipstick or lip gloss. Stick to softer tones and dab lips with a little powder.

Consider dress shields if you perspire easily.

Make sure your hair will stay where you want it. You don't want to be fooling with it while on the air.

Make sure a lavaliere or lapel microphone and transmitter can be attached to your clothing.

Lillian Brown has written the best resource I know of on the topic of appearing on television. It's called *Your Public Best: The Complete Guide to Making Successful Public Appearances in the Meeting Room, on the Platform and on TV* (Newmarket Press: New York 1989).

VIDEOCONFERENCING

If possible prior to the videoconference, send remote location participants handouts, copies of agenda, and copies of visuals.

Try to get someone else to operate the camera and other equipment. Have them shoot close up if possible. With more than one presenter, if you leave the camera on wide angle, the viewers will have trouble picking out who is talking.

Periodically ask for feedback from the remote sites. Your chances for misunderstanding multiply when communicating electronically.

Remember—assume you are always on camera. Use the mute button for your microphone if you must converse off the main program.

APPENDIX D
WORLDWIDE VIDEO COLOR SYSTEMS

Remember things change rapidly. Always check before you convert your tapes to these systems.

Algeria	PAL	Hungary	SECAM
Argentina	PAL	Iceland	PAL
Australia	PAL	India	PAL
Austria	PAL	Indonesia	PAL
Barbados	NTSC	Iran	SECAM
Belgium	PAL	Iraq	SECAM
Bermuda	NTSC	Ireland	PAL
Bolivia	NTSC	Israel	PAL
Brazil	PAL	Italy	PAL
Bulgaria	ECAM	Ivory Coast	SECAM
Canada	NTSC	Japan	NTSC
Canary Islands	PAL	Jordan	PAL
Chile	NTSC	Kenya	PAL
China	PAL	Korea	NTSC
Colombia	NTSC	Kuwait	PAL
Congo	SECAM	Lebanon	SECAM
Costa Rica	NTSC	Liberia	PAL
Cuba	NTSC	Libya	SECAM
Czech Rep.	SECAM	Luxembourg	SECAM
Denmark	PAL	Malaysia	PAL
Dominican Rep.	NTSC	Mexico	NTSC
Ecuador	NTSC	Micronesia	NTSC
El Salvador	NTSC	Monaco	SECAM
England	PAL	Netherlands	PAL
Finland	PAL	New Caledonia	SECAM
France	SECAM	New Zealand	PAL
Germany	SECAM/PAL	Nicaragua	NTSC
Ghana	PAL	Niger	SECAM
Greece	SECAM	Nigeria	PAL
Greenland	NTSC	Norway	PAL
Guadeloupe	SECAM	Oman	PAL
Guam	NTSC	Pakistan	PAL
Guatemala	NTSC	Panama	NTSC
Guyana	NTSC	Philippines	NTSC
Haiti	SECAM	Poland	SECAM
Hong Kong	PAL	Portugal	PAL

Puerto Rico	NTSC	Tanzania	PAL
Qatar	PAL	Thailand	PAL
Saudi Arabia	SECAM	Trinidad/Tobago	NTSC
Senegal	SECAM	Tunisia	SECAM
Sierra Leone	PAL	Turkey	PAL
Singapore	PAL	U.S.A.	NTSC
South Africa	PAL	Uganda	PAL
Spain	PAL	United Arab Rep.	PAL
Sudan	PAL	Uruguay	NTSC
Surinam	NTSC	Venezuela	NTSC
Sweden	PAL	Virgin Islands	NTSC
Switzerland	PAL	Western Samoa	NTSC
Syria	SECAM	Zamba	PAL
Tahiti	SECAM	Zaire	SECAM
Taiwan	NTSC		

APPENDIX E
ROOM SETUP CHECKLIST

Your first priority is safety. Know where fire exits and extinguishers are.

Have backup equipment and backup plan in case of failure.

Keep room lights at maximum intensity unless slides and/or video projection are being used.

If room lights are down, put a soft light on presenter.

● Schedule breaks during program.

Tape door latches to prevent them from making loud noises.

Use semicircular seating if possible.

● Provide hardback writing surface if needed.

● Locate your presentation area as close to front row as you can.

If seats can't move—YOU MOVE!

Without screen, set to long side of the room.

With screen, set to short side of the room.

Avoid long, narrow rooms (switch rooms if possible).

Avoid placing chairs next to walls.

Cut aisles behind poles.

Set aisles wider as they get nearer exits.

Seat for least distraction—audience members should not have to cross more than six others to get to a seat.

● Force audience to front with "Reserved" signs or put out fewer chairs than the expected attendance. Stack additional chairs in back corner of room so they are handy if needed.

Arrange for a good sound system. Thoroughly check sound system BEFORE program.

Check climate. Locate climate controls or know who to call.

Make sure water and glasses are available.

Locate restrooms, phones, snackbars, elevators or stairs, and business center.

Make sure signs are posted to direct participants to your room.

Personalize this checklist for your presentations.

Other:

_____

_____

_____

Trick: Ask someone from the hotel maintenance crew or wait staff what are some of the problems with the room. They might point you to a troublesome light switch or some other pesky problem. They know the rooms, and their advance warning will give you a chance to figure out a way to handle the problem. Chances are they won't offer their advice unless you ask.

APPENDIX F
TOM'S BANQUET/LUNCHEON TIPS

I have done many talks in settings where meals are part of the program. You may want to politely remind the program coordinator to consider some of the following points:

ROOM SETUP (Many of these tips work whether food is being served or not)

- Avoid spacing round tables widely apart in an attempt to fill the available space. Distance makes audience involvement and participation much more difficult. A better idea would be to space the tables as close together as practicable (allowing enough room for comfortable waiter and waitress movement). Empty room space could be filled with a decorative divider of some sort.

- Avoid a great distance between the head table/dais/speaker area and the first row of tables. Remember—distance is a great barrier to interaction.

- Try to set the head table/speaker area on the long side of the room. This will allow the back row participants to be closer to the speaker than if you set the head table/speaker area on the short side of the room where participants will feel they are really far from the action.

- Consider allowing the speaker a choice of speaking areas. Many top speakers can do a better job if they are not confined behind a head table and/or lectern. Besides, most audiences like being closer to the speaker. To accomplish this, place extra chairs near the front of the room for the head table participants to use after dinner (of course, this would depend on your overall program). You would not want the head table participants seated behind the speaker during the program. Set head table back from the front of the podium. Speaker can perform in front of the head table.

- Set buffet tables far to the side or on the opposite end from the speaker area. Those who go back for late seconds or arrive late will not be disruptive.

- Discourage use of the doors anywhere near the head table/speaker area.

TIMING

- When on a tight time schedule, have desserts placed on the table midway through the meal.

● Arrange with banquet staff to cease all bussing of tables on a pre-arranged signal. Many functions have less than interesting openings because service personnel are running around for the first 10 minutes of a talk. This gets everything off to a bad start.

● Ten minutes before the program is to start, it is very helpful to announce something like the following: *The program will start in 10 minutes. Please get your drink refills, go to the little boys and little girls room, grab another piece of cake, and then take your seats and get ready for a great program!*

● When planning lighthearted/humorous programs, avoid heavy subjects before the speaker, i.e., don't show tearjerker slides of starving children (actually happened to a speaker friend of mine) in an effort to raise funds. Don't get me wrong, I'm all for raising funds for good causes, but if you do this just before a humorist or comedy show, you may have wasted your money on the talent and actually made it inappropriate for them to do the job for which they were hired (see *"In fun,"* Chapter 2).

APPENDIX G
SELECTED BIBLIOGRAPHY

Anderson, Stewart. *Sparks of Laughter.* 1923.

Arnold, Edward. *Ruthless Rhymes for Heartless Homes.* 1899.

Arnold, Edward. *More Ruthless Rhymes for Heartless Homes.* 1930.

Axtell, Roger. *Gestures: Do's and Taboos of Body Language around the World.* New York: John Wiley & Sons, 1991.

Bandy, Greg. *Multimedia Presentation Design for the Uninitiated.* Aldus/Kodak, 1993.

Bauer, Jill. *From "I Do" to "I'll Sue" An Irreverent Compendium for Survivors of Divorce.* New York: Penguin, 1993.

Bedrosian, Margaret. *Speak Like a Pro.* New York: John Wiley & Sons, 1987.

Blakely, James (Doc), Joe Griffith, Robert Henry, and Jeanne Robertson. *How the Platform Professionals Keep 'em Laughin'.* Houston: Rich, 1987.

Blumenfeld, Dr. Warren. *Pretty Ugly: More Oxymorons & Other Illogical Expressions That Make Absolute Sense.* New York: Perigee, 1989.

Bonham, Tal. *Treasury of Clean Business Jokes.* Nashville: Broadman, 1985.

Bosrock, Mary Murray. *Put Your Best Foot Forward: Asia.* St. Paul: International Education Systems, 1994.

Bosrock, Mary Murray. *Put Your Best Foot Forward: Europe.* St. Paul: International Education Systems, 1995.

Bosrock, Mary Murray. *Put Your Best Foot Forward: Mexico/Canada.* St. Paul: International Education Systems, 1995.

Bosrock, Mary Murray. *Put Your Best Foot Forward: Russia.* St. Paul: International Education Systems, 1995.

Brandt, Richard C. *Flip Charts: How to Draw Them and How to Use Them.* San Diego: Pfeiffer & Company, 1986.

Brown, Lillian. *Your Public Best: The Complete Guide to Making Successful Public Appearances in the Meeting Room, on the Platform, and on TV.* New York: Newmarket Press, 1989.

Collins, Paul. *Today's Chuckle: 2500 Great One-Liners for Every Occasion.* New York: Perigee Books, 1993.

Dickson, Paul. *Toasts: The Complete Book of the Best Toasts, Sentiments, Blessings, Curses and Graces.* New York: Delacorte, 1981.

Droke, Maxwell. *The Speaker's Handbook of Humor.* New York: Harper & Brothers, 1956.

Eisenberg, Helen and Larry. *The Public Speakers Handbook of Humor.* Grand Rapids: Baker Book House, 1992.

Esar, Evan, ed. *Dictionary of Humorous Quotations.* New York: Dorset Press, 1949; 1989.

Fechtner, Leopold. *Encyclopedia of Ad-Libs, Crazy Jokes, Insults and Wisecracks.* New York: Parker, 1977.

Friedman, Edward L. *The Speechmaker's Complete Handbook.* New York: Harper & Row, 1955.

Fuller, Edmund. *2500 Anecdotes for All Occasions.* New York: Avenel Books, 1990.

Fulmer, Dave, ed. **A Gentleman's Guide to Toasting**. Oxmoor House 1990.

Golf Quotations. Lombard, IL: Great Quotations Inc.

Helitzer, Melvin. *Comedy Writing Secrets.* Cincinnati: Writer's Digest Books, 1987.

Hilton, Jack. *How to Meet the Press: A Survival Guide.* New York: Dodd, Mead & Co., 1987.

Hoff, Ron. *I Can See You Naked.* Kansas City, MO: Andrews and McMeel, 1992.

Hood, Kenneth. *Spice for Speakers, Sports & Squares: Effective Use of Humor, Quotes and Anecdotes in Speaking, Writing and Conversation.* Danville, IL: Interstate, 1976.

Iapoce, Michael. *A Funny Thing Happened on the Way to the Boardroom: Using Humor in Business Speaking.* New York: John Wiley & Sons, 1988.

Jeffreys, Michael. *Speaking with Magic.* Los Angeles: Powerful Magic Publishing, 1989.

Johnston, Lynn. *Hi Mom! Hi Dad!.* New York: Simon & Schuster, 1977.

Josefsberg, Milt. *Comedy Writing for Television & Hollywood.* New York: Harper & Row, 1987.

Klein, Allen. *Quotations to Cheer You Up When the World is Getting You Down.* New York: Wings Books/Random House, 1994.

Kushner, Malcolm. *Successful Presentations for Dummies.* Chicago: IDG Books Worldwide, 1996.

Leeds, Dorothy. *PowerSpeak.* New York: Berkley Books, 1988.

Leno, Jay. *Headlines III.* New York: Warner, 1991.

Mason, Eileen. *Witty Words.* New York: Sterling, 1992.

Mincer, Richard and Deanne. *The Talk Show Book: An Engaging Primer on How to Talk Your Way to Success.* New York: Facts on File Publications, 1982.

Mingo, Jack and Javna, John. **Primetime Proverbs: The Book of TV Quotes.** New York: Harmony Books, 1989.

McKenzie, E.C. *14,000 Quips & Quotes For Writers & Speakers.* New York: Random House, 1980.

Mullen, Jim. *Dumb Men Joke Book.* New York: Warner Books, 1992.

Munger, Susan H. *The International Business Communications Desk Reference.* New York: Amacom, 1993.

Murphy, Edward F. *2,715 One-Line Quotations for Speakers, Writers & Raconteurs.* New York: Bonanza Books, 1989.

Nave, Orville. *Nave's Topical Bible.* Chicago: Moody, 1992.

Nilsen, Don L.F. *Humor Scholarship: A Research Bibliography.* Westport, CT: Greenwood Press, 1993.

Paulson, Terry. *Making Humor Work*. Los Altos, CA: Crisp, 1989.

Peoples, David A. *Presentations Plus*. New York: John Wiley & Sons, 1992

Perret, Gene. *Comedy Writing Step by Step*. Hollywood: Samuel French, 1982.

Perret, Gene. *Comedy Writing Workbook.* New York: Sterling, 1990.

Prochnow, Herbert. *Dictionary of Wit, Wisdom and Satire.* New York: Harper and Row, 1962.

Raines, Claire. *Visual Aids in Business.* Menlo Park, CA: Crisp Publications, 1989.

Rinke, Wolf J. Ph.D. *Make It a Winning Life.* Rockville, MD: Achievement Publishers, 1992.

Rogers, James. *The Dictionary of Cliches.* New York: Wings, 1985.

Rosenbloom, Joseph. *The Looniest Limerick Book in the World*. New York: Wings, 1982.

Scannell, Edward and Newstrom, John. *Games Trainers Play.* New York: McGraw-Hill, 1980.

Scannell, Edward and Newstrom, John. *More Games Trainers Play.* New York: McGraw-Hill, 1983.

Scannell, Edward and Newstrom, John. *Still More Games Trainers Play.* New York: McGraw-Hill, 1991.

Scannell, Edward and Newstrom, John. *Complete Book of Games.* New York: McGraw-Hill, 1995.

Scannell, Edward and Newstrom, John. *Big Book of Business Games.* New York: McGraw-Hill, 1996.

Schafer, Kermit. *All Time Great Bloopers.* New York: Avenel, 1973.

Skovgard, Robert, ed. *Openings.* Compiled from *The Executive Speaker.*

Smart Alec's Beastly Jokes For Kids. Ballantine Books, 1987.

Stolzenberg, Mark. *How to be Really Funny.* New York: Sterling, 1988.

Tempel, Earle. *More Press Boners.* New York: Pocket Books, 1968.

Uncle John's Third Bathroom Reader. St. Martins Press, 1990.

Walters, Lilly. *Secrets of Successful Speakers.* New York: McGraw-Hill, 1993.

Walters, Lilly. *What to Say When...You're Dyin' on the Platform.* New York: McGraw-Hill, 1995.

Walters, Dottie and Lilly. *Speak and Grow Rich.* Englewood Cliffs, NJ: Prentice Hall, 1989.

Wilde, Larry. *Library of Laughter*. New York: Ballantine, 1988.

Wilson, Steve. *The Art of Mixing Work and Play*. Advocate Publishing Group, 1992.

APPENDIX H
WAKE 'EM UP GLOSSARY

Acronym: A form of abbreviation where the letters of the abbreviation form a new word as in *HUD* for *The Department of Housing and Urban Development.*

Ad-lib: Unplanned words or phrases spoken during a presentation.

Alliteration: The repetition of the same sound at the beginning of words or in accented syllables as in from "stem to stern."

Anachronism: A person, place, or event placed in a time period in which it does not belong, such as George Washington sitting in front of a computer.

Analogy: A comparison of two things that are alike in some ways and different in others. An example is *your brain is similar to a computer.*

Anecdote: A short interesting or amusing incident.

Aside: In the theater, something said to the audience that is not to be heard by the other actors. In television, the actor would look right at the camera and talk to the viewers. In a presentation, the speaker would make a temporary departure from the main theme or topic.

Attribution: Crediting the source of material used in a presentation.

Audience gag: A joke pulled on the audience, sometimes with some of the audience members used as shills.

Audience participation: The audience doing something other than listening. Some of them could be on-stage with you, carrying on group discussions, playing games, singing, etc.

A/V: Abbreviation for audiovisual equipment, such as overhead projectors, tape recorders, slide projectors, microphones, etc.

Bits: A short section of material so related that it is easy to memorize. Also called **Chunks, Series.**

Black humor: According to *Webster's Dictionary*, "Humor that ignores human suffering and looks for the absurdity in any experience, even the most tragic." Used as a stress reliever in many high pressure occupations (medicine, law enforcement, military, etc.). Also **Sick humor, Gallows humor.** (Note: Please don't use in a professional presentation)

Blocking: Positioning of you and your equipment on the stage. Also your intended movement on the stage.

Blooper: A clumsy mistake, especially one made in public; a faux pas.

Blue humor: Risqué or dirty humor —the kind of humor everyone likes, but won't admit. (OK, I'm kidding—or am I?) Also called **Off-color humor.**

Bomb: In the USA, a GIANT failure; in Great Britain, a smashing success.

Bombproofing: Term coined by your lovable author to signify the steps you take as a presenter to be sure you don't bomb.

Breakout session: Splitting the entire group into smaller groups to hear special interest topics.

Callback: Referring to a word or phrase you mentioned earlier in your presentation.

Canned act: The use of standard material regardless of the makeup of the audience (not customized). Also **Planned spontaneity.**

Canned ad-lib: Pre-planned response to a presentation problem or audience member comment.

Caricature: A picture in which the subject's distinctive features are deliberately exaggerated to produce a comic or grotesque effect.

Cartoon: An illustrated joke. Also **Comic strip.**

Cheap laugh: Simple, sometimes tasteless, laughs that anyone, regardless of skill level, could elicit from the audience (this is my specialty Ha-ha).

Chunks: See **Bits.**

Classroom seating: Seating style where chairs are placed behind tables that are parallel to the front of the room.

Cliché: A worn-out saying such as "It's better to be safe than sorry" (that's a sorry cliché).

Comeback: A humorous or clever retort to an audience comment. Also **Repartee** or **Riposte.**

Comedian: An amusing person whose primary purpose is to entertain. Also **Comic.**

Comedienne: Older, less politically correct, term for a female comedian.

Comic: See **Comedian.**

Comic relief: An amusing element introduced into a serious speech or play to temporarily relieve tension.

Comic strip: Cartoon progressing over a series of scenes.

Concurrent session: A session occurring at the same time as another session.

Content: The usable information in a presentation.

Convulsive laughter: Violent laughter that causes a person to lunge forward, backward, or both.

Cordless microphone: A microphone which works by transmitting radio signals to a receiver which is connected to the public address (PA) system. Also **Wireless microphone.**

Custom humor: Humorous comments, skits, role playing, gags, or costuming devised specifically for a particular audience.

Dais: A raised platform in the front of the room where the speaker stands. Also **Podium, Riser, Stage** or **Platform.**

Deadpan expression: A serious expression contrasted with funny lines.

Demo tape: An audio or video tape used to promote speakers, bands, magicians, etc.

Downstage: The area of the stage closest to the audience.

Dynamic range: Gradation of intensity available for use by a presenter with regard to various speaking parameters.

Easel: A tripod or frame used to support flip chart pads or other visuals.

Emcee (abbrev. "MC"): An informal term for **Master of Ceremonies.** Also **Toastmaster, Roastmaster.**

Exaggeration humor: Expanding or diminishing features or information to outrageous proportions for comic effect.

Extemporaneous: An impromptu or spontaneous presentation.

Extender line: Line added to the end of a humorous comment that evokes additional laughter.

Flip chart: Large pieces of paper either bound or loose that are supported on an easel.

Flop sweat: 1.) Fear of performing, 2.) perspiration while fearful of performing or while bombing.

Fluff: Normally lighthearted information in a presentation used to entertain or motivate (not hard data).

Gag: Wordplay or horseplay with the audience.

Gag order: Meeting planner tells you to shut up (I couldn't resist throwing this one in).

General session: All attendees present at the same presentation.

Gesticulate: To gesture in an animated and excited manner or simply to gesture.

Goldwynism: 1940s term for comical misuse of language. Named after movie mogul Sam Goldwyn. Also **Malaprop.**

Greenroom: A backstage room where speakers and performers can relax when they are not on stage. Also applies to television studios.

Handheld microphone: A corded or cordless microphone that can be held to your mouth or mounted on a lectern or microphone stand.

Handout: Any promotional or educational material given to each audience member.

Handsfree microphone: A corded or cordless microphone that attaches to the presenter's clothing. Also **Lavaliere.**

Head table: A table at the front of the room reserved for the leaders, special guests, and speakers at an event.

Heart story: Touching story that normally brings tears to the eyes of audience members.

Heckler: Audience member who purposely annoys or bothers the presenter usually by verbal abuse (sometimes throws things).

Hey stupid question: Trite question posed to the audience, such as *How many of you want to make more money?*

Honorarium: Payment for speaking or other professional services.

House lights: Lights that illuminate the audience.

Humorist: Speaker who uses humor to make points, convey a message, and entertain.

Humorous acknowledgment: Mildly amusing admission of guilt immediately followed by a serious response.

Idiom: An expression of a given language that cannot be understood from the individual meanings of its words, as in *keep tabs on.*

Impostor guest speaker: Speaker with false credentials employed to pull a gag on the audience for stress reduction, morale boost, and/or entertainment.

In fun: A climate in the presentation area such that the speaker and audience are in the mood for laughter.

Introducer: Person who presents the speaker to the audience and gives a brief account of the speaker's history.

Introduction: An opening to a speech used by the introducer to present the speaker to the audience.

Jokes: Something said or done to create laughter or amusement.

Juxtaposition humor: The placing, side by side, of two ideas or items usually for the purpose of comic comparison or contrast.

Keynote: The main speech at a meeting delivered to all attendees in a general session. Originally the main point of a speech.

Lavaliere: A corded or cordless microphone worn around the neck or attached to a piece of clothing. See **Hands free microphone.**

Lectern: A stand with a sloping top from which a speaker delivers his or her program. Sometimes incorrectly called a *podium.*

Localization and personalization: The process of changing details of a story or joke to suit the intended audience

Malaprop: An absurd misuse of words. See **Goldwynism.**

Master of ceremonies: A person who acts as host of an event, making the welcoming speech and introducing other speakers or entertainers. Also **Toastmaster, Roastmaster, Emcee, MC.**

MC: *n.* Abbreviation for Master of ceremonies. *v.* Acting as Master of ceremonies as in *Joe will MC the event.*

Meeting planner: The person in charge of planning the logistical parameters of a meeting like room setup, hotel arrangements, meals, travel, and sometimes hiring of speakers. Also **Coordinator, Organizer,** or **Planner.**

Metaphor: A figure of speech in which a word or phrase that ordinarily designates one thing is used to designate another, thus making a comparison, as in *She is an angel on the platform.*

Mic: Abbreviation for microphone; pronounced *mike.*

Moderator: Person who presides over a meeting, panel, or debate.

Multimedia: The use of several media, such as movies, slides, music, and lighting in combination, normally for the purpose of education or entertainment.

Off-color humor: See **Blue Humor.**

Off the cuff: In an extemporaneous or informal manner. Old time speakers would make notes on their shirt cuffs instead of preparing for a talk.

One-liner: A general term for a very short piece of humor.

Overhead projector: Device used to project images from transparent film onto a screen or the wall.

Oxymoron: Two concepts {usually two words} that do *not* go together, but are used together like *old news, pretty ugly, direct circumvention* and *random order.*

PA: Abbreviation for public address system.

Panel: A group of presenters, normally seated, that hold a discussion on a particular subject. Audience members are invited to pose questions to individual presenters or to the group as a whole.

Parody: A humorous imitation of a serious piece of literature or song.

Planned spontaneity: See **Canned ad-lib.**

Plant: A person pretending to be a normal audience member, who, in fact, is there to assist the speaker in some way. Also **Shill.**

Platform: Raised area in front of the audience where the speaker stands. Also, **Dais, Riser, Podium,** or **Stage.**

Pleonasm: The bringing together of two concepts or words that are redundant like *frozen ice, sharp point, killed dead, sandy beach, young child, positive praise.*

Plug: An informal advertisement made during a presentation used to promote a product or service.

Podium: See **Platform.** Many people call a *lectern* a *podium.* This is technically incorrect, but very common. Also **Dais, Riser,** or **Stage.**

Practical joke: A playful trick that usually puts the receiver in an embarrassing position. Also **Prank.**

Prank: A practical joke that could be good-natured or malicious. See **Practical joke.**

Pratfall: In comedy, an on-purpose, exaggerated fall to the floor usually accompanied by flailing arms and legs for effect.

Pre-program questionnaire: Information gathering document used to customize a presentation.

Press kit: A package of information used to promote a speaker or performer.

Prompter: A device used to electronically display a magnified version of the script that the speaker can see, but the audience can't. (Commonly called a **TelePrompter,** which is actually a registered trade name.)

Prop: A shortened version of the theatrical term "property;" used to describe any object handled or used by an actor in a performance.

Public address system: Abbrev. **PA.** The equipment used to amplify sound for the audience.

Public domain: Material that anyone can use without the need to give credit.

Public seminar: An educational event which is open to the public.

Pun: The humorous use of words that sound alike or nearly alike but are different in meaning as in, *Isn't this a punny book?*

Punch line: The climactic word or phrase of a humorous statement that provokes laughter.

Q&A: Abbreviation for the question and answer portion of a presentation.

Rapport: A relationship with the audience, especially one of mutual trust or emotional attraction.

Rehearse: To practice for a presentation until all the rough spots are smoothed.

Relevance, Theory of: Belief that the only humor used in a business presentation should be related to the subject of the presentation, the speaker, the audience, or the location.

Repartee: A conversation full of quick, witty replies. Also **Comeback, Riposte.**

Repeat engagement: A second presentation for the same group.

Response to Introduction: After the introduction, comments directed to the introducer or the audience about the introduction or introducer.

Riposte: Sharp, quick action or reply. Also **Comeback.**

Riser: See **Platform**. Also, **Dais, Podium,** or **Stage.**

Roast: An event where the guest of honor is ridiculed and teased in a good-natured, comical manner.

Roastmaster: The Master of Ceremonies at a roast.

Role play: An audience involvement exercise where the audience members and/or the presenter interact while assuming the attitudes and actions of others.

Rule of Three: Structure of humor where two serious items set a pattern then the third unexpectedly switches the pattern which provokes laughter, or three jokes on one topic in a bit.

Running gag: A gag that repeats itself or plays off a gag that occurred earlier.

Saver line: Comment made to recover from a (supposedly) humorous comment that failed.

Sarcasm: A cutting, often ironic, form of wit intended to make its victim the butt of contempt or ridicule.

Segue:. To move smoothly and unhesitatingly from one section or theme of a presentation to another. Pronounced *seg-way*.

Self-effacing humor: A very powerful form of humor that highlights your own weaknesses.

Seminar: An educational session lasting from 30 minutes to several days.

Series: See **Bits.**

Shill: In comedy, a person planted in the audience to assist in a gag.

Shtick: A characteristic attribute, talent, or trait that is helpful in securing recognition or attention. In entertainment, a routine or gimmick attributed to a particular performer, i.e., smashing watermelons is part of Gallagher's (the comedian) shtick.

Sick humor: See **Black humor.**

Signature story: A story that is credited to a particular person. This type of story should never be used without attribution.

Simile: A comparison of two things which, however different in other respects, have some strong point or points in common. The words *like* and *as* will normally be used when making the comparison as in *His brilliance is like a burned out light bulb.*

Site: The location of the meeting. Also **Venue.**

Slapstick: Broad comedy involving boisterous action like throwing pies and fake violence ala the Three Stooges.

Slide: A 35mm transparency. Sometimes used to describe an overhead transparency.

Sound man (person): Person in charge of public address system, sound board, recording, etc., during a presentation.

Sound system: See **Public address system.**

Speakers bureau: A service company that provides speakers for meeting planners.

Spokesperson: A person who speaks for or represents a company, organization, or other person.

Stage: See **Dais.**

Stage fright: Nervousness associated with performing or speaking before an audience.

Stage left: As the performer faces the audience, the side of the stage to his/her left.

Stage lights: Lights illuminating the stage area only.

Stage right: As the performer faces the audience, the side of the stage to his/her right.

Stooge: An entertainer who feeds lines to the main performer and frequently is the butt of the joke. Also, **Straight Man.**

Straight man (Straight person): See above.

Tailoring: Adjusting material to better suit a particular audience. Not quite customizing.

TelePrompter: See **Prompter.**

Test humor: Humor used either in the introduction or early parts of a talk to determine the extent to which the audience is *in fun.*

Testimonial: A statement, usually written, in support of a another's character or worth; a personal recommendation.

Theater style seating: Seating where chairs are set in rows without tables.

Timing: Adjusting one's speaking and pausing for dramatic or comical effect.

Toastmaster: See **Emcee.**

Trainer: A person who conducts workshops and training sessions.

Transcribe: To make a written copy of a voice recording or presentation.

Transparency: A slide that is viewed by light shining through it from behind or by projection. Also **Slide.**

Two-step seminar: A free seminar where attendees are asked to buy a second seminar or purchase products.

Upstage: The area of the stage farthest from the audience. Also to steal the focus of the audience from the intended main performer.

Venue: See **Site.**

View-graph: Alternate name for overhead transparency.

Wings: Extreme sides of the stage normally hidden from the audience by curtains or walls.

Wireless microphone: See **Cordless microphone.**

Whisper: Attention-gaining device where presenter speaks with extremely low volume to one audience member.

Workshop: An educational session lasting from one hour to many days. Usually includes hands-on practice in the particular skills being taught.

INDEX

A

Accent, 24
Acknowledgments to tough
  situations, 111
Action plan, 260
Ad-libs, 57, 102-112, 151, 184, 246
Addresses, 261-264
Adult learning theory, 123
Age, 12, 25, 120, 175, 176, 185
Agendas, 28
Air conditioning, 49
Aisles, 46, 269
Alcmaeon, 61
Alcohol, 35, 83, 86
America Online, 198
American Society of Composers,
  Authors, and Publishers
  (ASCAP), 48
Americans, 25
Anecdote, 58, 68, 193, 247
Animation, 42, 94
Anticipation, building of, 190
Antion, Tom, Every page Hahahahaha
Antoinette, Marie, 156
Aphorism, 58
Appearance, 115, 175, 184
Applause, 21, 26, 71, 73, 184, 230
Atmosphere, 38
Attendee list, 217
Attention gaining devices, 63, 64, 69,
  90, 91, 94, 117, 128, 150, 167,
  183, 207, 228, 239
Audience
    breaking up, 128
    disruptive members, 126
    gags, 126, 150-152, 161, 170
    hostile, 111, 131, 132
    picking your, 92
    size, 16, 89, 121, 208, 209, 211
    superiority, 88, 101, 155, 174,
      175
    technical, 68, 226
Audience Centered Seating™, 41, 46

B

Audio tape, 138-140, 194, 196, 197,
  260, 261
Auditory style, 36
Authority, 117
Axtell, Roger, 19

Background, 50
Backlighting, 50
Bad habits, 118, 119
Balloons, 28
Balls, 126, 167
Bandy, Greg, 221
Banquet, roundtables, 44
Banquet tips, 271, 272
Barnum, P.T., 72
Barriers, 124, 238
Barrymore, Ethel, 254
Bedrosian, Margaret, 78, 128
Believability, 186, 189
Benny, Jack, 89
Betts-Johnson, Marie, 25
Bibliography, 273-277
Bits, Chunks, Series, 65-67, 69, 136,
  168, 260
Blakely, Doc, 77
Blanchard, Captain Ernie, 77
Blockbuster Video, 197
Blumenfield, Dr. Warren S., 160
Board room, 43
Body
    angles, 116
    heat, 49
    language 120, 124, 137-139, 237,
      246
    of speech, 61-69
Bomb, 54, 58, 85, 92, 112, 226
Bombproofing, 99-114
Book search service, 196, 261
Books, 194-196, 199, 235, 261
Bookstores, 154, 195
Boom box, 48, 239
Boredom, 62, 120, 183, 184, 195, 229

Bosrock, Mary Murray, 21
Brag lines, 54
Brainteasers, 128, 262
Brandt, Richard C., 210
Breaks, 39, 229, 269
Breath control, 83
Brevity, 97, 101, 185, 213, 255
    of numbers, 182
Brigham Young University, 21
Broadcast Music Incorporated (BMI),
    48
Buchwald, Art, 124
Bulbs, 91, 102, 106, 205
Bulletin boards, 199
Bullets, 219, 226
Bunker, Archie, 165
Busboys, 45
Bush, George, 110
Business Week, 213
Buttons, 251
Butts, Earl, 77

C

Caffeine, 83
Calero, Henry H., 121
Callbacks, 88
Canned ad-libs, (see Pre-planned
    ad-libs)
Cantor, J.R., 254
Captions, 154, 214
Carson, Johnny, 101
Cartoons, 23, 28, 153, 154, 196, 197,
    199, 201, 214
CD-ROM, 203, 214
CEO, 15, 16, 57, 76, 89, 100, 140,
    211, 213, 245, 246, 255
Chairs, 37, 41, 46, 167, 206, 269, 271
Challenging statement, 55
Chapman, Antony, 40, 87
Character switching, 189
Cheat sheet, 66, 67, 69, 168, 209
Chevron seating pattern, 44
Children, 213, 218
Chunks, (see Bits)
Church marquee, 177

Churchill, Winston, 171
Clarity, of presentation, 203
Classroom, 44, 45
Cleese, John, 213
Climate, 37, 49, 270
Clipart, 30, 154, 211, 214
Clipping service, 215
Closings, 71-73, 91, 170
    humorous, 71,72
    serious, 72
Clothing, 27, 96, 115, 119, 120, 136,
    248, 249, 265
    coat, 120, 266
    glasses, 119, 120, 265
    hats, 119, 168
    jewelry, 119, 265
    ties, 119, 265
Clumsy waiter, (see *Cuss Your Lunch*)
Coaching, 92, 116, 119, 139, 140,
    213, 246, 260
Cocktail hour, 35
Cognitive dissonance, 132
Collins, Paul Harlin, 166
Color, 30, 220, 221
Comedy writing, 179, 261
Comedy club, 38
Comfort, 41
Comic strips, 23, 153, 154
Comic relief, 6, 131, 145, 165
Communication, nonverbal, 115
Competitors, 76, 153, 214
CompuServe, 198, 214
Computer
    filing, 200
    post-program, 217
    pre-program, 214-216
    printers, 154, 214
    research, 214, 215
    software, 154, 215, 217, 262
Confidence, 87, 88, 101, 136, 174,
    175
Connecting with the audience, 36, 52,
    66, 118, 128, 146, 167, 174, 176,
    187, 197, 206
Controversy, 27, 58, 78
Converters, 25

Corel Draw, 154
Cosby, Bill, 182, 247
Costumes, 156, 157, 168
Creators Syndicate, 23
Credibility, 66, 175, 225, 246
Crosby, Norm, 165
Crossword puzzle, 34, 167, 214
Culturgram, 21
Cuss Your Lunch, 152
Customer service, 151, 157, 237

D

Dais, 111
Daley, Mayor, 153
Daly, John Jay, 176, 209
Darrow, Clarence, 172
Databases, 215
Daydream, 62
Deadpan, (see Expression)
Delivery, 79-97, 100
Dhery, Robert, 28
Dictation, 194
Dining, 26
Discomfort, 41
Distance, 41, 66, 124, 246, 269, 271
Distractions, 49, 117-119, 121, 207, 238
    doors, 49, 269, 271
    noise, 91, 269
Drugs, 83
Dynamic Range, 92-96
    quick fixes, 96

E

E-mail, 235
Edison, Thomas, 106, 172
Eisenberg, Helen & Larry, 196
Eisenhower, Dwight D., 159
Eisenstodt, Joan, 6
Eliot, George, 73
Emcee, 27, 57, 86
Emergency, 109, 110, 269
Emerson, Ralph Waldo, 184

Emotions, 128-131, 186, 188
Encyclopedia, 214
Engineers, 225
Enthusiasm, 183, 184
Enunciation, 84
Equipment, 37
    audio/visual, 83, 203-217
    failure, 37, 38, 204, 205, 239, 269
Esar, Evan, 196
Evaluations, 230, 232
Excitement, 68, 156, 203, 233
Executive Speaker Newsletter, 58
Experience level, 101-103
Expression
    deadpan, 89, 217
    facial, 38, 39, 41, 89, 119, 120, 124, 136, 139, 159, 188
Extender line, 67, 146, 157
Eye contact, 25, 26, 38, 67, 84, 89, 115, 120, 139, 206, 207, 211

F

Facts, 97, 130, 159, 186
False guest speaker, (see Impostors)
Fast, Julius, 121
Faxes, 234
Feigelson, Sheila, 28, 248-250
Female, 15, 241-256
Fig leaf position, 121
File cabinet, 200, 201
Filing, 194, 200, 260
Financial presentations, 225, 231-232
Fire, 269
Flip chart, 36, 48, 126, 167, 203, 210-212, 238
Food, 83, 181, 182, 184, 235, 238, 271
Fox, Doug, 230, 231
Fripp, Patricia, 35, 251-252
Frost, Robert, 158
Fulghum, Robert, 247

G

Gag gifts, 235
Genius technique, 97, 149, 171, 190, 201
Gestures, 41, 89, 115, 116, 119, 120, 121, 137, 139, 265
Gifts, 24, 26
Gillebaard, Lola, 250-251
Girard, Joe, 236
Giving credit, 197, 199
Gleason, Jackie, 116
Gliner, Art, 24, 167
Glossary, 278-288
Goldwyn, Sam, 164
Golf, 217
Goodman, Dr. Joel, 150, 249, 255
Gorden, Dave, 96
Graphics, 214
Griffith, Joe, 196
Groans, 78, 88
Guarantees, 35

H

Hair, 266
Hale, Nathan, 106
Hall, Edward T., 115
Hall, Monte, 84
Handouts, 30-35, 68, 146-148, 167, 205, 212, 214, 227, 266
Hardwicke, Cedric, 115
Hay, Peter, 196
Home Box Office (HBO), 197
Heckler lines, 35
Hecklers, 151
Henry, Patrick, 106
Herford, Oliver, 158
Hershkowitz, Sue, 256
Higgs, Liz Curtis, 254-255
Highlighter, 107, 211
Hilton, Hermine, 20
Hoff, Ron, 4
Honesty, 121
Hope, Bob, 173
Hoven, Vern, 231, 232

Howe, Ed, 145
Hubbard, Elbert, 157, 158
Humility, 188
Humor writing, 179, 181
Humor, risk, 100, 101, 243
Humor,
    amount to use, 64, 69, 90, 102
    benefits of, 4-7
    placement of, 90, 185
    rating of, 67
Humor, types of,
    abbreviations, 145
    acronyms, 145
    ad-libs, 57, 102-112, 151, 184, 246
    advertisements, 147, 148, 196, 197
    alliteration, 148
    anachronism, 148, 149
    anecdote, 58, 68, 193, 247
    aphorism, 58
    aside, 58, 149, 150
    audience gags, 126, 150-152, 161, 170
    bloopers, 148, 152, 239
    callbacks, 88
    canned ad-libs, (see Pre-planned ad-libs)
    captions, 154, 214
    caricature, 153, 158, 196
    cartoons, 23, 28, 153, 154, 196, 197, 199, 201, 214
    comic strips, 23, 153, 154
    comic verse, 154-156, 196
    costumes, 156, 157, 168
    definitions, 157
    dialect, 77
    ethnic, 77, 247
    exaggeration, 153, 158, 159, 172, 179, 182, 189
    faxes, 234
    food, 181, 182
    general, 76
    heckler, 35
    impostors, 151
    industry specific, 199

insulting, 101, 172-174, 255
joke, 47, 48, 62, 77, 84, 85, 88, 90, 100, 101, 159, 186, 196, 197, 198, 199, 211, 246, 247, 260
juxtaposition, 160, 179
letters, 161, 162
limericks, 156
magic, 23, 96, 163
malaprops, 164, 165
maps, 181, 182
names, 182
nametags, 28
news, 127, 195, 197
newsletter, 194, 199, 263
newspaper, 58, 193, 194, 197, 199
numbers, 181, 182
off-color, 76, 77, 78
old, 198
one-liner, 58, 64, 68, 85, 88, 93, 149, 166, 178, 179, 193, 197, 198, 236, 260
oxymoron, 91, 160
parody, 166
people, 76, 186
places, 76, 181, 182
pleonasm, 160
poems, 154-156, 196
pointers, 217
political, 198, 199
pre-planned ad-lib, 50, 57, 102-112, 194, 204, 220, 235, 239, 260
props, 28, 36, 68, 96, 167-169, 246, 263
proverbs, 169, 196
puns, 76, 78
questions, (see Questions, Question & Answer below)
quotations, (see Quotation, Quotation books below)
racist, 76
religious, 76, 77, 177, 194
roast, 132, 133, 172-174, 255
role-play, 133
running gag, 150

sarcasm, 22,
saver, 101, 102, 114
self-effacing, 15, 22, 25, 58, 131, 165, 173-176, 185, 188, 199, 213, 218, 254
sexist, 76, 78
signs, 49, 176, 177, 194, 209, 239, 270
simile, 178, 179
singing, 109, 167
skits, 133
sounds, 107,168, 181
sports, 130, 255
surveys, 162, 163, 171
telegrams, 161, 162
test, 53, 59, 137, 236, 244, 253
toasts, 20, 26, 179, 180
tombstone, 176, 177
two-liner, 65, 197
words, 24, 181,
Humor Project, 150, 213, 249
Humorists, 196
Humphrey, George, 135

I

Icebreakers, 167
Ideas, 194
Idioms, 24
Image, corporate, 100
Impact, 72, 154, 170, 176, 195, 210, 214, 218, 246
Impostors, 151
In Fun, 27, 30, 34, 78, 86, 115, 217, 272
Information Superhighway, 194, 198
Ink color, 212
Integrity, 197
Intensity curve, 63, 66, 67, 90, 91
Interaction, 39, 42, 43, 118, 205, 213, 228
Interest level, 62-64, 117, 118, 138, 167, 183, 228, 231
International issues, 17-27, 116, 153, 154, 156, 262
Internet, 171, 198, 199, 215, 226

Interplay, 132
Interpreters, 24
Introducer, 44, 45, 51, 57, 84
Introductions, 51, 59, 62, 253, 260
    participant, 228
    response to, 54-56
    self, 54
    video, 213
Involvement, 123-126, 178, 188, 211,
    228

J

Jarvis, Dr. Charles, 27, 77, 135
Jefferson, Thomas, 176
Jeffreys, Michael, 23
Joel, Billy, 130
Johnson, Eric W., 196
Joke, 47, 48, 62, 77, 84, 85, 88, 90,
    100, 101, 159, 186, 196, 197, 198,
    199, 211, 246, 247, 260
    books, 131, 159, 178, 197, 199
    computer programs, 215
    punch line, 85-87, 89, 90, 96, 97,
        185, 198, 215
    services, 198, 199, 263
    setup, 86
    writers, 199
Jones, Dewitt, 96
Juggling, 23, 96, 231, 232
Justice, Jeff, 179

K

Kennedy, John F., 19
Kennedy, David M. Center for
    International Studies, 21
Keystone
    effect, 206
    eliminator, 206
Kinesthetic style, 36
Kipling, Rudyard, 172
Kiwanis, 141
Knapp, Jack, 196
Knight, Bobby, 135
Koepke, Denise, 244-245

Koppel, Ted, 213
Krugman, Carol, 20

L

Language
    diction, 96, 138
    fancy, 78
    sexist, 78
    vocabulary, 96
Laser pointer, 137, 207
Laughter, 39, 40, 66, 67, 72, 85, 87-
    89, 102, 120, 137, 154, 171, 181,
    184, 185, 187, 194, 230, 234
Lectern, 38, 66, 84, 85, 108, 115, 118,
    124, 150, 167
Leeds, Dorothy, 116
Length of presentation, 90, 112-114,
    187, 227, 228, 230
Leno, Jay, 127, 148, 255
Letter to introducer, 52, 260
Letterman, David, 127
Levine, J.B., 254
Library, 196, 214, 260
Life incidents, 194, 195, 199
Lighting, 37-39, 41, 105, 205-207,
    210, 214, 269
Likeability, 174
Lincoln, Abe, 88, 135, 172, 183
Lindbergh, Anne Morrow, 86
Line of sight, 41, 49, 206
Lipstick, 266
Listening
    pattern, 61-63, 90, 185
    speed of, 62
Localization, 56
Longfellow, Henry Wadsworth, 71,
    172
Lucas, Bob, 120

M

Magazines, 148, 154, 193, 194, 214
Magic, 23, 96, 163
Mail, 194
Mailing labels, 217

Makeup, 265, 266
Making a point, 65, 69, 101, 145, 154, 165, 168, 184, 194, 195, 198
Male, 15
Maps, 181, 182
Martin, Steve, 116
Marx, Groucho, 35, 59, 180, 184
Masking tape, 206
Mason, Eileen, 196
Material
    logging of, 201
    organization of, 200, 201
    selection of, 75, 99, 204
    sources of, 193-200
McGuire, Frank, 213
McKenney, Mac, 164
McKinley, Mike, 99
McMahon, Ed, 233
Measurement units, 24
Meeting planner, 49, 112, 151, 162, 201
Mehrabian, Albert, 115
Meirers, Mildred, 196
Memorability, 156, 167, 183, 198, 212, 232
Memorization, 65, 97, 154, 168, 186, 201
Microphone, 47, 59, 83, 84, 86, 91, 102, 105, 120, 132, 137, 151, 209, 232, 239, 266
Mihalip, Hope, 247-248
Misspelling, 88, 108
Mistakes, 102, 103, 108, 165
Modem, 214
Mondale, Walter, 112
Money, 255
Monotone, 138
Monteith, Kelly, 72
Montesquieu, 113
Morley, John, 75
Morris Costumes, 23, 157, 163
Move to action, 71
MTV Generation, 213
Multimedia, 203, 216, 217
Munger, Susan H., 23
Murphy, Edward, 196
Music, 47, 48, 83, 166, 197, 239, 263

N

Names, 182
Nametags, 28
National Storytelling Association, 189
National Speakers Association, 141, 197
Nervousness, (see Stage fright)
News, 127, 195, 197
Newsgroups, 198
Newsletters, 194, 199, 263
Newspaper, 58, 193, 194, 197, 199
Newstrom, John, 128
Newsweek, 154, 194
Nierenberg, Gerard I., 121
Nightingale Conant Corporation, 197
Nixon, Dick, 145
Noisemakers, 168
Notes, 34, 65-67, 83, 97, 118, 136, 167, 168, 212, 221
Numbers, 181, 182
Nunes, Marianna, 253-254

O

Ogden, Tom, 23, 96
One-liner, 58, 64, 68, 85, 88, 93, 149, 166, 178, 179, 193, 197, 198, 236, 260
Openings, 54-59, 91
Orben, Bob, 4
Organization, 184, 193, 200
Ott, Rick, 96
Outdoor presentations, 16
Overhead
    alignment of, 206
    orientation of, 206
    projection benefits, 204, 205, 209
    projector, 137, 167, 204, 205-209
    transparency, 36, 146-148, 154, 160, 201, 203-209, 211, 214, 216-218
Overlays, 208

P

Pager, 114
Patter, 163
Pauses, 68, 86, 89, 90, 102, 126
Pei, Mario, 116
People, 76, 186
Periodicals, 148
Permission, 23, 154
Perret, Gene, 159
Personal space, 19, 20
Personalization, 52, 56, 196, 197, 199
Philip, P.J., 40
Photography, 176, 196, 209
Places, 76, 181, 182, 186
Planned spontaneity, 91
Plotter, 211
Pointers, 167, 207, 217
Political correctness, 77, 252
Popularity, 183
Post cards, 235
Poster machine, 211
Practice, 66, 67, 71, 85, 97, 135-141,
    168, 186, 204, 260
    dumbbells, 119
    mirror, 119, 136
Pre-planned ad-lib, 50, 57, 102-112,
    194, 204, 220, 235, 239, 260
Pre-program questionnaire, 9-14, 75,
    95, 260
Privacy, 22
Prizes, 125
Program coordinator, 44, 45, 86, 271
Props, 28, 36, 68, 96, 167-169, 246, 263
Public domain, 197
Punch line, (see Joke)

Q

Questions, 58, 68, 91, 126, 127, 129,
    132, 230, 246
    hostile, 111
    stupid, 127
Question & Answer, 24, 121, 139,
    151, 170, 171, 229, 232

Quotations, 48, 59, 72, 114, 165, 171,
    172, 187, 196, 197, 200
Quotation books, 171

R

Radde, Dr. Paul O., 41
Radio, 193, 198
Rankin, A.M., 40
Rapport, 57, 124, 231, 236
Rate of speech, 62
Reader's Digest, 199
Reagan, Ronald, 112, 131, 173, 175
Recaps, 68
Record albums, 196
Recording, 137, 138, 194, 200, 260
Reference material, 195, 214
Rejection, 235, 239
Relevance, 85, 91, 99, 100, 114, 157,
    185
Resistance, 52, 53, 187, 188
Resources for Organizations, 48
Reveal technique, 146, 208
Rich, David, 236
Rickles, Don, 174
Rinke, Dr. Wolf J., 128
Riser, 42, 50
Rituals, 26
Roast, 132, 133, 172-174, 255
Role-play, 133
Rolfe, Katherine, 174
Room size, 46, 214
Roosevelt, Franklin Delano, 157, 172
Rosen, Nance, 242-244
Rotary, 141
Rounds, Mike, 226-230
Royal Publishing, 23
Rule of Three, 87, 88, 163

S

Safety, 39, 269
Sales
    follow up, 237
    presentations, 233-239
    resistance, 236, 237
    tools, 201, 213

Saltman, Dr. Joyce, 6, 235, 252-253
Sanfillippo, Barbara, 245-246
Santa, 179
Sarcasm, 22,
Saver lines, 101, 102, 114
Scannell, Edward, 128
Schafer, Kermit, 152
Screen, 41, 118, 184, 204-206, 269
Seasons, 24
Seating, 39-41, 46, 205, 239, 269
    fixed, 42, 44
    semi-circular, 40-42, 44, 46, 269
    standard arrangement, 43
Segue, 68 (also see Transitions)
Self-effacing, 15, 22, 25, 58, 131,
    165, 173-176, 185, 188, 199, 213,
    218, 254
Series, (see Bits)
Service bureau, 214
Sexual harassment, 77
Shakespeare, 6
Shaw, George Bernard, 79
Showmanship, 236
Signs, 49, 176, 177, 194, 209, 239,
    270
Silence, (see Pause)
Simmons, Sylvia, 72, 196
Simon, Neil, 181
Sincerity, 121
Singing, 109, 167
Skits, 133
Skovard, Robert, 58
Slang, 24
Slanting a story, 187
Slide projector, 91, 210, 216
Slides, 38, 106, 107, 160, 176, 203,
    209, 214, 216-218
Smile, 83, 115, 238, 260
Snacks, 28, 167
Sound system, 37, 47, 84, 239, 270
Sounds, 168, 181
    "k," 107, 181
Speaker services, 264
Speaking organizations, 264
Speech writers, 199, 264
Speed of delivery, 24, 62, 113, 188

Sports, 130, 255
Stage fright, 79, 115
    reduction strategies, 81-84
    symptoms of, 80, 81, 207
Stage, 50
    movement, 115, 117, 118, 138,
        139, 269
    persona, 88, 89
    position, 68, 117, 118
Stand-up comic, 47, 68, 85, 93, 101,
    247, 261
Standing Ovation, 25, 73, 124, 125,
    230
Standing-up, 117, 210, 238
Status, 100, 236
Stengel, Casey, 164
Stevenson, Adlai, 59
Stooges, The Three, 255
Stooges, 170, 171
Stories, product related, 237-239
Story, 58, 62, 85, 90, 96, 114, 128,
    136, 149, 168, 183-190, 193, 194,
    196, 197, 198-200, 226, 247, 260
Strength, 174
Stress, 194
Stress reducer, 32
Stuffed shirt, 174
Surprise, 217
Syndicates, 24
Synergy effect, 66, 67

T

Tablets, 43
Talkshows, 197
Targets, 57, 75, 76, 173, 199
    celebrities as, 76
    inappropriate, 76, 77, 173
Team presentations, 231, 232
Technical presentations, 225-231
Telephone, 150
Television, 121, 140, 152, 193, 197,
    198, 199, 213, 265
    comedy channel, 197, 235
    sitcoms, 197, 235
Tempel, Earle, 152

Temperature, 49
Tennyson, Alfred Lord, 204
Terminology, 24
Test humor, 53, 59, 137, 236, 244, 253
Testimonials, 239
   celebrity, 213
The New Yorker, 154
Theater style seating, 40, 44
Things, 76, 186
Thoreau, Henry David, 157
Throwing things, 150, 211
Time of day, 16
Timer, 114
Timing, 89, 139, 204, 271
Toastmasters, 81, 141
Toasts, 20, 26, 179, 180
   birthday, 179
   Christmas, 179
   friendship, 180
   health, 20, 180
   luck, 180
   marriage, 180
   meals, 179
   New Year, 180
Tombstone inscription, 176, 177
Touch, 133
Tracy, Larry, 131
Trade journals, 194, 197
Transcription, 138
Transitions, 68, 69 (also see Segue)
Translators, 24
Trembling, 83
Tripping, 108, 109
Truman, Harry S., 159
Twain, Mark, 59, 73, 108, 164, 165, 172, 193
Two-liner, 65, 197

U

U-shape seating, 44, 45
Unique humorous opening, 55
University of Minnesota, 117, 238
Updating humor, 196-199
USA Today, 242

V

Variety, 167, 229, 231
Ventriloquist, 28
Versatility, 92
Video
   color systems, 267, 268
   conferencing, 121, 265, 266
   projection, 214, 269
   tape, 94, 96, 116, 118, 119, 138-140, 194, 196, 197, 203, 213, 235, 239, 260, 261, 265
Visual style, 36, 167, 168
Visual design, 218-221
Visualization, 81, 137
Visuals, 48, 68, 107, 117, 118, 167, 176, 193, 203, 206, 210, 238, 239, 266
Voice inflection, 90, 186, 188, 189, 246
Voltaire, 113
Volume, 26, 136
Volunteers, 125, 126, 150, 161, 211

W

Waitresses, 45
Wall sconces, 50
Walls, 46
Walters, Lilly, 112, 246, 247
Walters, Dottie, 9
Walton, Sally, 156
Washington Post, 77
Washington, George, 149
Water, 83, 270
Watt, James, 77
Wave effect, 16, 89
Web sites, 198, 215, 216
Weinstein, Matt, 124
Wells, Thelma, 128
Wharton School of Business, 117, 204, 239
Wheeler, Elmer, 3
Wilde, Larry, 84, 85
Wilson, Woodrow, 157, 172
Winget, Larry, 96, 201

Witty World International Cartoon Magazine, 23
Women, presentation tips for, 241-256
Woollcott, Alexander, 172
Words, 24, 129, 136, 181, 187
    adjectives, 186
    placement, 138
    verbs, 186
Worldwide Standards, 25
WOW factor, 96, 149, 163
Wright, D.S., 87

Y

Yard sales, 195
Yelling, 126, 245

Z

Ziglar, Zig, 64

Would you like to see your name in this book?

Do you know any advanced speaking techniques that were not mentioned here?

If so, send your technique along with all your contact information (name, address, phone, fax, e-mail) to Tom. If you are the first to present a new idea, and if Tom uses it, you will be credited for submitting the idea and you will receive an autographed copy of the book for *FREE*.

Tom looks forward to hearing from you.

Send your one page idea to:

Tom Antion
Box 2630
Landover Hills, MD 20784
Fax (301) 552-0225

(If he needs clarification he will contact you)

They laughed
when I got up to speak:
And that's exactly what I wanted them to do.

Make 'em Laugh and be the hit of your next meeting or convention.

The <u>only</u> video program that teaches this invaluable skill!

Make 'em Laugh:
How to Use Humor in Presentations

- 4½ Hour Video Seminar in a Box
- (3) VHS Tapes, Video Log to keep track of over 87 segments, Handy Workbook covering additional Specialty Humor Topics like Roasts, Toasts and Emcee duties.

You will learn:

USING HUMOR WILL HELP YOU TO:
- Make more money
- Break down sales resistance
- Appear confident and visionary
- Enhance your leadership skills
- Make your message more memorable
- Make technical information more interesting
- Motivate your staff, clients and audiences to action

ROOM SET-UP:
- How to seat your audience for "Maximum Mirth"
- Lighting for Laughter
- Microphone handling

AUDIENCES:
- How to know your audiences so you really connect
- The differences between all-male and all-female audiences
- How to handle differences between large and small audiences
- How to interact with the audience
- How to be successful with international audiences

SPEECH CONSTRUCTION:
- How to control your introductions

- Openings and closings
- When & how much humor to use

STORYTELLING:
- The importance of timing
- How to tell funny stories
- Three things you should NEVER say when telling a story

HANDLING DISASTER:
- What to say if your humor fails
- Pre-planned ad-libs
- How to make mistakes funny
- How to be sure you NEVER bomb

PROPS:
- Making points with props
- How to make overheads and slides funny

ORGANIZATION & SOURCES:
- Where to find instantly usable humor
- Filing your humor for quick access
- How to quickly build a cheap humor library

PLUS:
- Audience involvement secrets
- Overcoming stage fright
- How to get started and much, much more . . .

Price: $149.95 (Individual) • $595.00 (unlimited use business license)

**To Order Call 1-(800) 448-6280 or
Fax to (301) 552-0225**

Two Ways to *Wake Up* Your Next Meeting or Convention

You've read the sure-fire tips and techniques in this book for creating your own memorable presentations. Now, imagine what would happen if you . . .

1. Invite Tom Antion to Speak at Your Group's Next Gathering

Tom Antion travels world-wide constantly making audiences laugh and learn. As you can guess, he's a great speaker. Make him part of your next meeting when you need . . .

- **An Electrifying Speaker to open or close your convention.**
- **An Experienced Banquet Entertainer.**
- **A High-Content Business Seminar Leader.**

To arrange a fully customized event, call
Tom directly at the number below
(or contact your favorite speakers bureau).

2. Give Everyone in Your Organization a Copy of This Book

Quantity discounts make this book a valuable business tool you can afford to give you attendees, your staff, and your leadership . . . to help them learn how to create impact. They'll appreciate your effort to enhance their professional development.

To book Tom Antion for your next gathering, and/or to order *Wake 'em Up* in quantity, call (800) 448-6280

Rave Reviews!!!

"You made your speech unique to our group. Your humor was great and every attendee could identify with something you mentioned."
—Christine King, GEICO Corporation

"Your endless enthusiasm, perfect choice of words, and obvious compassion made the night an event." —Mary Blankemeier, Home of the Brave Foundation

"Your program was fun and entertaining, but also carried a serious and useful message. You indeed made points with our group."
—Rick Slusher, Virginia Employment Commission

ORDER FORM

Fax orders: (301) 552-0225

☎ Telephone orders: Call Toll Free: 1 (800) 448-6280. Have your VISA, MasterCard or American Express card ready.

🖥 On-line orders: Tom@antion.com, tomantion@aol.com

✉ Postal orders: Anchor Publishing, P.O. Box 2630, Landover Hills, MD 20784, USA, Telephone: (301) 459-0738

Please send the following books and tapes:
I understand that I may return any books or tapes in saleable condition for a full refund—for any reason, no questions asked.

Qty. _____ *Make 'em Laugh* Video Seminar(s) @ $149.95
($595.00 unlimited use business license)

Qty. _____ *Wake 'em Up Business Presentations* @$24.95

Other: _____

Company name: _____

Address: _____

City: _____ State: _____ Zip: _____

Telephone: _____ Fax: _____

E-Mail: _____

Sales Tax: Please add 5% for items shipped to Maryland addresses.
Shipping: $4.00 for first book, $2.00 for each additional book.
$2.00 for single audio tapes, $6.50 for *Make 'em Laugh* Video.
Payment: ❏ Check ❏ Credit card: ❏ Visa ❏ MasterCard ❏ Amex

Total including shipping and sales tax: _____

Card Number: _____ Exp. Date: _____

Name as it appears on card: _____

Signature: _____

Call toll free and order now!

ORDER FORM

📋 Fax orders: (301) 552-0225

☎ Telephone orders: Call Toll Free: 1 (800) 448-6280. Have your VISA, MasterCard or American Express card ready.

💻 On-line orders: Tom@antion.com, tomantion@aol.com

✉ Postal orders: Anchor Publishing, P.O. Box 2630, Landover Hills, MD 20784, USA, Telephone: (301) 459-0738

Please send the following books and tapes:
I understand that I may return any books or tapes in saleable condition for a full refund—for any reason, no questions asked.

Qty. _____ *Make 'em Laugh* Video Seminar(s) @ $149.95
          ($595.00 unlimited use business license)

Qty. _____ *Wake 'em Up Business Presentations* @$24.95

Other: _____

Company name: _____

Address: _____

City: _____ State: _____ Zip: _____

Telephone: _____ Fax: _____

E-Mail: _____

Sales Tax: Please add 5% for items shipped to Maryland addresses.
Shipping: $4.00 for first book, $2.00 for each additional book.
          $2.00 for single audio tapes, $6.50 for *Make 'em Laugh* Video.

Payment: ☐ Check ☐ Credit card: ☐ Visa ☐ MasterCard ☐ Amex

Total including shipping and sales tax: _____

Card Number: _____ Exp. Date: _____

Name as it appears on card: _____

Signature: _____

Call toll free and order now!